GCSE WJEC Eduqas
English Literature

Studying for WJEC Eduqas GCSE English Literature? You've come to the right place — this brilliant CGP book will make your exams feel like *Much Ado About Nothing*.

It's packed with clear study notes for poetry, drama and prose — plus plenty of realistic exam-style questions for all the set texts on the WJEC Eduqas course.

We've also included worked answers, brilliant advice on how to approach the exam, and a full set of practice papers to make sure you're prepared for the real thing.

How to access your free Online Edition

This book includes a free Online Edition to read on your PC, Mac or tablet.
You'll just need to go to **cgpbooks.co.uk/extras** and enter this code:

1741 3967 1394 5969

By the way, this code only works for one person. If somebody else has used this book before you, they might have already claimed the Online Edition.

Complete
Revision & Practice
Everything you need to pass the exams!

Contents

Section One — Exam Basics

Exam Structure 1
Planning Answers 2
P.E.E.D. 3
Using Examples 4
Writing Well 5
Reading with Insight 6
Spelling, Punctuation and Grammar 7
    Revision Summary 11

Section Two — Prose and Drama

Writing About Prose and Drama 12
Writing About Characters 14
Themes and the Writer's Message 16
Audience Response 17
The Writer's Techniques 18
Using Quotations 21
    Warm-Up Questions 22
    Exam-Style Questions 24
    Revision Summary 25

Section Three — Drama

Reading Plays 26
Writing About Plays 28
Writing About Modern Plays 30
Writing About Shakespeare 32
Shakespeare's Language 34
The Structure of Shakespeare's Plays 36
    Warm-Up Questions 37
    Worked Exam-Style Question — Paper 1 (Shakespeare) 38
    Worked Exam-Style Question — Paper 2 (Post-1914 Drama) 40
    Exam-Style Questions 42

Section Four — Prose

Writing About Prose 43
Analysing Narrators 45
19th-Century Context 46
    Warm-Up Questions 49
    Worked Exam-Style Question — Paper 2 (19th-Century Novel) ... 50
    Worked Exam-Style Question — Paper 2 (Post-1914 Prose) 52
    Exam-Style Questions 54

Section Five — Poetry

Poetry — What You Have To Do 55
Form and Structure 56
Poetic Techniques 57
Comparing Poems 62
    Warm-Up Questions 63
    Revision Summary 64

Section Six — Poetry Anthology

The Poetry Anthology 65
How to Structure Your Answer 66
How to Answer the Question 67
How to Write a Top Grade Answer 70
    Warm-Up Questions 71
    Worked Exam-Style Questions 72
    Exam-Style Questions 76

Section Seven — Unseen Poetry

Five Steps to Analysing a Poem 77
    Worked Exam-Style Question 78
Comparing Two Poems 81
    Worked Exam-Style Question 82
    Warm-Up Questions 85
    Exam-Style Questions 86

Practice Papers

Paper 1: Shakespeare and Poetry 88
Paper 2: Post-1914 Prose/Drama, 19th-Century Prose and Unseen Poetry 96

Answers 109
Glossary 135
Index 139

Published by CGP

Editors:
Andy Cashmore, Emma Crighton, Kelsey Hammond, Katharine Howell,
Louise McEvoy, Gabrielle Richardson and James Summersgill.

With thanks to Tom Carney for the proofreading
and Ana Pungartnik for the copyright research.

Acknowledgements:
Page 82: Ghosts by Robert W. Service used by courtesy of Mrs Anne Longepe.

Page 86: At Sea by Jennifer Copley.

Page 107: Fleur Adcock, Poems 1960-2000 (Bloodaxe Books, 2000).
Reproduced with permission of Bloodaxe Books. www.bloodaxebooks.com

Page 108: The Beautiful Lie by Sheenagh Pugh (Seren, 2002)

Every effort has been made to locate copyright holders and obtain permission to reproduce sources.
For those sources where it has been difficult to trace the copyright holder of the work, we would be grateful
for information. If any copyright holder would like us to make an amendment to the acknowledgements,
please notify us and we will gladly update the book at the next reprint. Thank you.

ISBN: 978 1 78908 266 1

Clipart from Corel®
Printed by Elanders Ltd, Newcastle upon Tyne.

Based on the classic CGP style created by Richard Parsons.

Text, design, layout and original illustrations © Coordination Group Publications Ltd. (CGP) 2019
All rights reserved.

Photocopying more than one section of this book is not permitted, even if you have a CLA licence.
Extra copies are available from CGP with next day delivery • 0800 1712 712 • www.cgpbooks.co.uk

Section One — Exam Basics

Exam Structure

It's time to get to grips with English Literature — here's what to expect...

There are Two Exams for WJEC Eduqas English Literature

1) For your English Literature GCSE, you'll have to sit two exams — Paper 1 and Paper 2 (or 'Component 1' and 'Component 2').

2) Paper 1 lasts 2 hours. It's worth 80 marks (40% of the GCSE).

3) Paper 1 is split into two sections:

> - Section A: two questions about a Shakespeare play (see p.32-36) — e.g. 'Macbeth', 'The Merchant of Venice'.
> - Section B: two questions about two poems from the WJEC Eduqas poetry anthology (see p.65-76).

4) Paper 2 lasts 2 hours 30 minutes. It's worth 120 marks (60% of the GCSE).

5) Paper 2 is split into three sections:

> - Section A: an essay question asking you about a modern text, written after 1914 — e.g. 'Blood Brothers', 'Lord of the Flies'. This could be a play (see p.30-31) or a novel (see p.43-45).
> - Section B: an essay question about a novel from the 19th century (see p.46-48) — e.g. 'A Christmas Carol', 'Jane Eyre'.
> - In Section C, there'll be two unseen poems — you'll have to answer two questions, in which you analyse and compare them (see p.77-87).

Assessment Objectives are the Skills you need for the Exam

The assessment objectives cover all the things you need to do to get a good grade in the exams. They are:

AO1
- Give your own thoughts and opinions on the text.
- Back up your interpretations using evidence from the text (e.g. quotes).

AO2
- Explain how writers use language, structure and form, and what effect this has on the reader.
- Use technical terms to support your analysis.

AO3
- Show that you understand how the text relates to the context in which it was written or set.

AO3 is only tested in Section B of each paper.

AO4
- Use a range of sentence structures and vocabulary, so that your writing is clear and effective.
- Write accurately, paying particular attention to spelling, punctuation and grammar.

AO4 is only tested in Section A of each paper. It counts for 5% of your overall mark.

You don't need to remember the assessment objectives word for word...
There's no need to memorise these assessment objectives — they're just here to give you an idea of the things you need to think about when you're revising, and when you're writing your answers in the exam.

Planning Answers

We've all been there — you turn over your exam paper, read the question, notice that time's slipping away and start scribbling your answer. But I promise, if you take a few minutes to plan, you won't regret it.

Read the question Carefully and Calmly

1) Before you start writing an answer, give yourself time to read through the question properly. If you're given an extract from a text you've studied or any poems to go with the question, read those too.

2) Always read the question before any extracts or poems that go with the question — that way, you'll know what to look out for.

3) Make sure you're clear about what the question is asking you to do by underlining the key words.

> Write about the relationship between Antonio and Bassanio throughout the play.
> In your response, you should focus on how Shakespeare presents this relationship.

PAPER 1

4) Once you've read the question, carefully read through any extracts or poems that are part of the question. It's a good idea to highlight key words or phrases that will help you to answer the questions — but don't spend ages doing this.

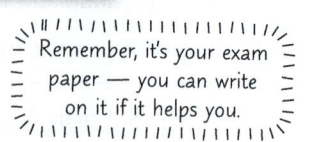

Remember, it's your exam paper — you can write on it if it helps you.

Jot down your Main Ideas before you start writing

1) You'll need to spend a few minutes planning most of your answers.

2) Don't go into too much detail — just get your main ideas down and outline the structure of your answer.

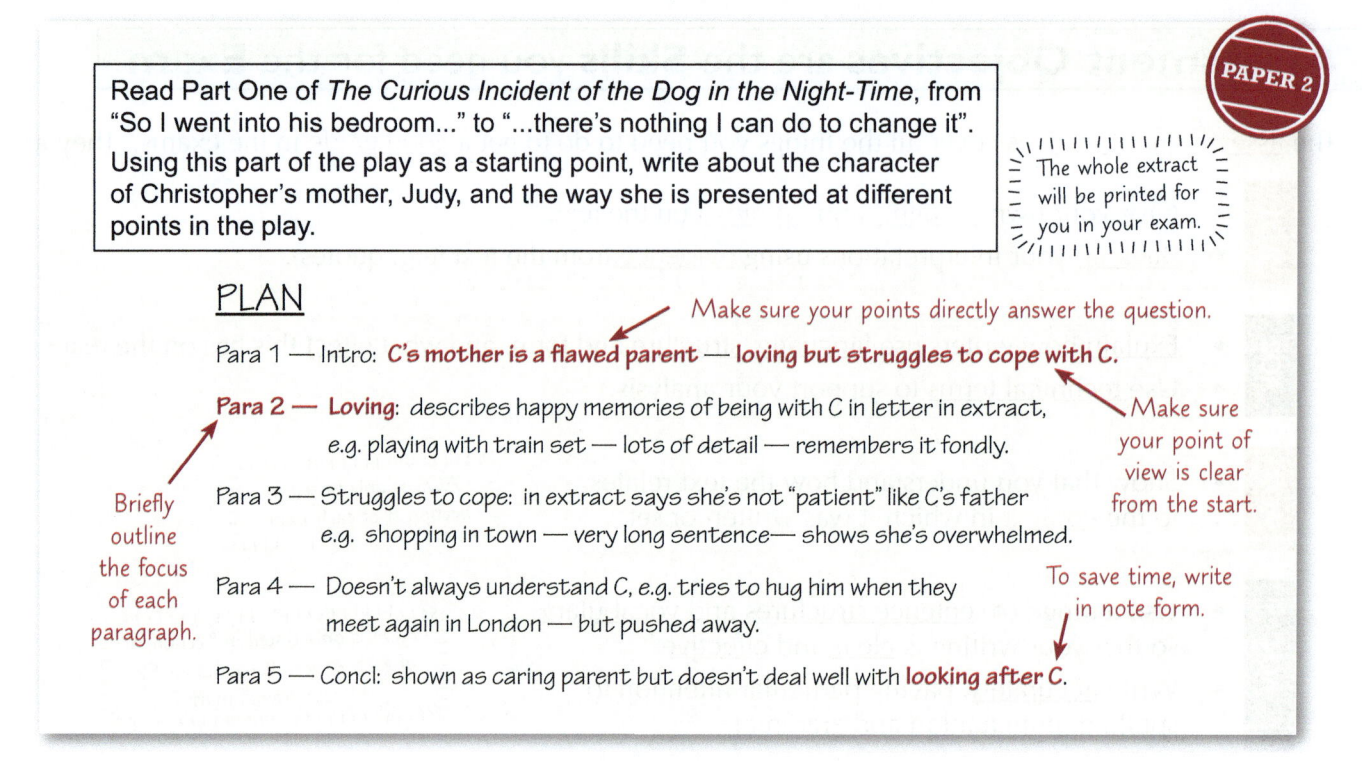

> Read Part One of *The Curious Incident of the Dog in the Night-Time*, from "So I went into his bedroom..." to "...there's nothing I can do to change it".
> Using this part of the play as a starting point, write about the character of Christopher's mother, Judy, and the way she is presented at different points in the play.

PAPER 2

The whole extract will be printed for you in your exam.

PLAN

Make sure your points directly answer the question.

Para 1 — Intro: **C's mother is a flawed parent — loving but struggles to cope with C.**

Para 2 — **Loving**: describes happy memories of being with C in letter in extract, e.g. playing with train set — lots of detail — remembers it fondly.

Para 3 — Struggles to cope: in extract says she's not "patient" like C's father e.g. shopping in town — very long sentence — shows she's overwhelmed.

Para 4 — Doesn't always understand C, e.g. tries to hug him when they meet again in London — but pushed away.

Para 5 — Concl: shown as caring parent but doesn't deal well with **looking after C**.

Briefly outline the focus of each paragraph.

Make sure your point of view is clear from the start.

To save time, write in note form.

Planning will keep your writing focused...

You need to stick to the question you've been asked in the exam, or you won't get the marks. Planning will help keep you on track when you're writing your answer. Don't forget to check your work at the end, too.

P.E.E.D.

To get good marks, you need to explain and develop your ideas properly. That's why P.E.E.D. is useful.

P.E.E.D. stands for **Point, Example, Explain, Develop**

To write good English essays about texts you've read, you must do four things:

1) Make a point to answer the question you've been given.
2) Then give an example from the text (see page 4 for more on this).
3) After that, explain how your example backs up your point.
4) Finally, develop your point — this might involve saying what the effect on the reader is, saying what the writer's intention is, linking your point to another part of the text or giving your own opinion.

The explanation and development parts are very important. They're your chance to show that you really understand and have thought about the text. Here are a couple of examples:

PAPER 1

Read Act 1, Scene 7, from "Was the hope drunk..." to "...As you have done to this."
Paying close attention to Lady Macbeth's actions and dialogue, write about how an audience could react to this extract.

This introduces the main point of the paragraph. → **Shakespeare presents Lady Macbeth as even more obsessed with power than Macbeth himself.** She calls Macbeth a **"coward"** and says that he **"dare not"** murder Duncan in order to become king. Manipulating him to commit a terrible crime **shows how desperate she is for Macbeth to attain power so that she can rule alongside him. The audience is left feeling shocked by her manipulative personality and obsession with gaining power.** ← *Quotes are used as the example here.*

This explains the effect of the example.

This develops the point further by explaining the effect on the audience.

PAPER 1

In 'Hawk Roosting', Hughes writes about the theme of animals.
Select one other poem from the anthology and compare how the two poems present animals.

Start with a point that mentions both poems. → Both 'Hawk Roosting' and 'Death of a Naturalist' **present animals as threatening and violent.** Hughes uses the oxymoron **"My manners are tearing off heads"** to describe the hawk killing its prey. **This juxtaposition of politeness with the verb "tearing" emphasises the brutality of the hawk.** Similarly, Heaney uses violent language, describing the frogs as **"cocked"** and **"mud grenades"**, **which suggests that they are like weapons that are poised to fire or explode, making them seem dangerous.** In both poems, **using language associated with violence to describe animals makes the reader feel threatened.**

Give examples from both poems.

Explain how the examples relate to your opening point.

Sometimes you can develop your point for both poems at the same time.

P.E.E.D. should help you to explain and develop your points...

Other versions of P.E.E.D. also focus on explaining and developing — P.E.E.R. (Point, Example, Explain, Relate), P.E.E.C.E. (Point, Example, Explain, Compare, Explore) and so on. Use the one you've been taught.

Section One — Exam Basics

Using Examples

However fabulous the point you make in your answer is, it won't get you top marks unless you can back it up with examples from the text. Cue a page that shows you how it's done...

Use **Details** from the text to **Back Up** your points

Whenever you make a point about a text, you need to use short pieces of evidence to back it up.

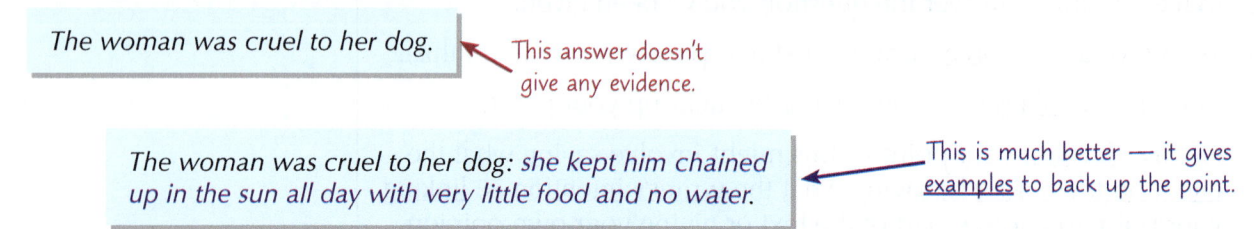

> *The woman was cruel to her dog.*

← This answer doesn't give any evidence.

> *The woman was cruel to her dog: she kept him chained up in the sun all day with very little food and no water.*

← This is much better — it gives examples to back up the point.

Your evidence can be **Quotes** or **Examples**

1) Your evidence could be a quote from the text. If you use a quote, keep it short. It'll really impress the examiner if you embed it in a sentence, like this:

   > *The writer refers to the situation as "indefensible", suggesting that he is extremely critical of the way it has been handled.*

   Using short embedded quotes like this lets you combine the 'example' and 'explain' parts of P.E.E.D. (see p.3) in one sentence.

2) Paraphrased details from the text also work well as examples. You just need to describe one of the writer's techniques, or one of the text's features, in your own words, like this:

   > *Sheers uses enjambment between stanzas to emphasise the fragmented nature of the soldiers' bodies.*

3) Here's an example to show you how to work your evidence into your answer:

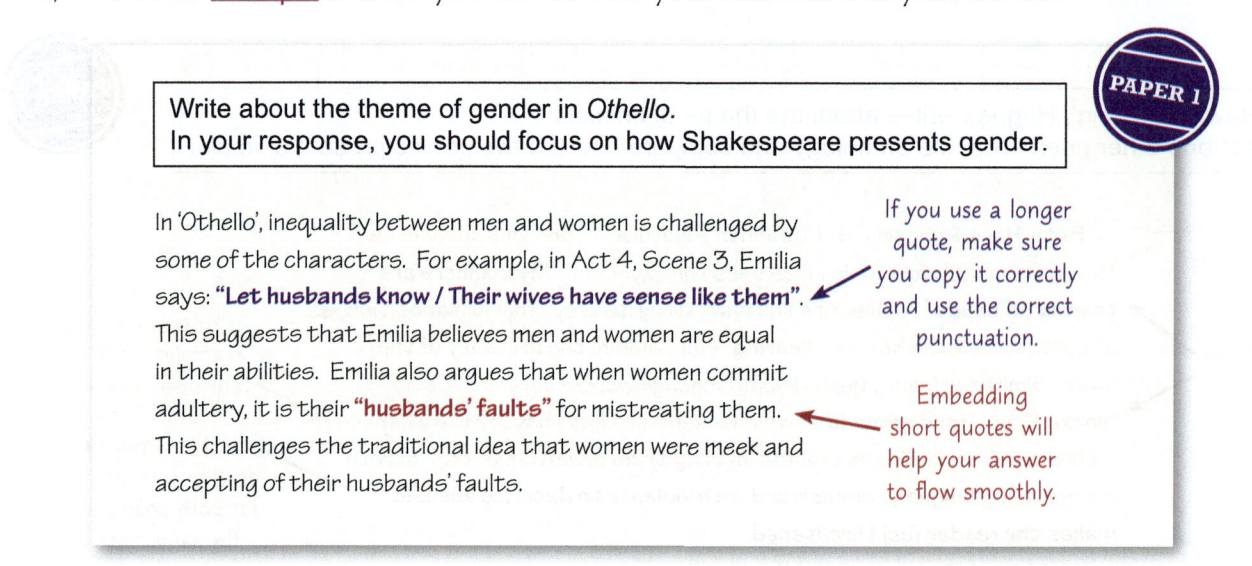

   PAPER 1

   > Write about the theme of gender in *Othello*.
   > In your response, you should focus on how Shakespeare presents gender.

   > *In 'Othello', inequality between men and women is challenged by some of the characters. For example, in Act 4, Scene 3, Emilia says:* **"Let husbands know / Their wives have sense like them"**. *This suggests that Emilia believes men and women are equal in their abilities. Emilia also argues that when women commit adultery, it is their* **"husbands' faults"** *for mistreating them. This challenges the traditional idea that women were meek and accepting of their husbands' faults.*

   If you use a longer quote, make sure you copy it correctly and use the correct punctuation.

   Embedding short quotes will help your answer to flow smoothly.

Use examples to support your ideas...

Whether you paraphrase or use a quote, backing up your points with evidence from the text is really crucial in your English Literature exams. Just make sure that you then explain how the evidence supports your point.

Section One — Exam Basics

Writing Well

In these exams, it's not just what you write that's important — it's how you write as well.

Keep your writing Formal but Interesting

1) For these exams, it's important that you write in Standard English.
2) Standard English is the version of English that most people think is 'correct'. There are a few simple rules that you can follow to make sure you're writing in Standard English:

- Avoid using informal words and phrases (e.g. putting 'like' after sentences).
- Avoid using slang or local dialect words that some people might not understand.
- Use correct spelling, punctuation and grammar (have a look at pages 7-10).

Use clear Explaining Words and Phrases

1) You should use explaining words and phrases to make your answers easy to follow.

- This signifies that...
- This is reminiscent of...
- This highlights the fact that...
- Furthermore...
- This imagery reflects...
- This continues the idea of...

2) Using words and phrases like these makes your writing sound more professional.
3) They're also really useful when it comes to P.E.E.D. (see page 3). They help you to link the explanation and development parts of your answer to your main point.

Use Paragraphs to structure your answer

1) Your points need to be clearly organised and linked together. To do that you need to write in paragraphs.
2) You can use different paragraph structures to organise your points in different ways. For example:

- You could write a paragraph for every point you want to make, and each paragraph could have a P.E.E.D. structure (see page 3).
- You could make two points that contrast or agree with each other within a paragraph — this can be useful when comparing two texts.
- You could make one point and link together lots of examples with different explanations within a paragraph.

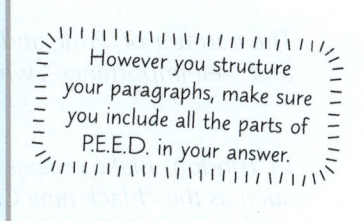

However you structure your paragraphs, make sure you include all the parts of P.E.E.D. in your answer.

3) Linking your paragraphs together smoothly makes your writing sound confident and considered. You could use linking words like these to help you do this:

- However...
- In the same way...
- In contrast...
- In addition...
- On the other hand...
- Alternatively...
- Equally...
- Conversely...

Your answer needs to have a clear structure...

Organise your ideas into paragraphs, and use the phrases on this page to link them together smoothly.
A clear structure will show the examiner that you've thought about your answer, and make it easier to read.

Section One — Exam Basics

Reading with Insight

To get the top grades, you need to show that you can 'read with insight' — you've got to make it clear that you understand more than just the obvious things. You can think of it as 'reading between the lines'.

You need to look Beyond what's Obvious

1) You may understand what happens in a text, or what it's about, but you'll need to write about more than just that in your answers.

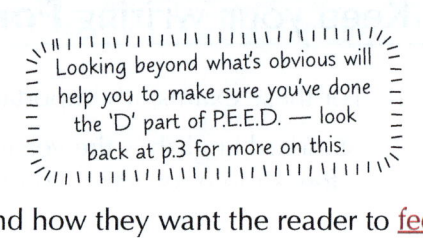

Looking beyond what's obvious will help you to make sure you've done the 'D' part of P.E.E.D. — look back at p.3 for more on this.

2) You can show insight if you work out what the writer's intentions are and how they want the reader to feel.

3) Here's an example of the kind of thing you could write:

> *In 'Dulce et Decorum Est', Owen uses grotesque similes like "Obscene as cancer" to show the trauma of war, which suggests he wants the reader to feel ashamed about glorifying it.*

Think about the reasons why the writer has included certain features — show you've understood their intended effect on the reader.

4) Remember to include examples from the text to support your interpretation:

> *Darcy is portrayed as an unlikeable character in this extract. He is described as "above being pleased", hinting at his arrogance and haughtiness. However, the swiftness with which the ball-goers change their opinion of him shows their fickleness and hints that their judgement is not to be trusted.*

Try to explain how the writer creates a particular impression of a character or event. Examiners love it if you can give alternative interpretations that go beyond the obvious.

Inference means working things out from Clues

1) Writers don't usually make things obvious — but you can use evidence from the text to make an inference about what the writer really wants us to think.

2) You need to analyse details from the text to show what they reveal about the writer's intentions:

> *The narrator of 'Pride and Prejudice' uses the words "self-conceit" and "self-importance", which imply disdain for Mr. Collins.*

The writer's language indicates their emotions and attitude.

> *In 'London', Blake creates a bitter tone using powerful imagery such as the "black'ning Church" and the "blood" on the "Palace walls". This shows his anger at these institutions.*

The writer will often use a particular tone to emphasise their message.

3) You could use phrases like these to show that you've made an inference:

| The writer gives a sense of... | The writer appears to be... | This suggests that... |

Think about the effect the writer wants to create...

Everything in a text has been carefully crafted by the writer, so look for clues that reveal their intentions. Demonstrate that you understand what the writer is showing you, not just what they're telling you.

Section One — Exam Basics

Spelling, Punctuation and Grammar

There are lots of marks available in these exams for correct use of spelling, punctuation and grammar, or SPaG for short. These pages should help you to avoid the most common SPaG errors...

You can Gain Marks for SPaG

1) It's important that you use correct spelling, punctuation and grammar in all of your answers.
2) However, it's particularly important in Section A of each paper, where some of the marks will be for your ability to write accurately and clearly — which includes good SPaG.
3) Read the next few pages for some tips to help keep your writing as accurate as possible.

Check over your Work when you've finished

1) Try to leave a few minutes at the end of the exams to check your work.

2) There might not be time to check everything thoroughly. Look for the most obvious spelling, punctuation and grammar mistakes.

3) Start by checking your answers to Section A in each paper, as there are marks for accuracy available in these sections.

This is how you should Correct any Mistakes

1) If you find a spelling mistake, put brackets around the word, cross it out neatly with two lines through it and write the correction above.

> *Curious*
> In 'The (~~Curius~~) Incident of the Dog in the Night-Time', Stephens explores ideas about family.

2) If you've written something which isn't clear, put an asterisk (*) at the end of the sentence. Put another asterisk at the end of your work, and write what you mean beside it.

> By using a cliché to describe her partner*, Dove brings a playful tone into 'Cozy Apologia'.
> *, describing him as a knight in shining armour

3) If you realise you should have started a new paragraph, put // to show where it starts and write "(para)" in the margin.

> In this way, Hill uses the setting of 'The Woman in Black' to create fear in the reader. // Hill's descriptions of fog and mist also build suspense.   *(para)*

4) If you find you've missed out a word or two, put a "∧" where the words should go, then write them in above the line.

> *more*
> In Act 3, Scene 5, Juliet feels more and isolated.
>   ∧

Section One — Exam Basics

Spelling, Punctuation and Grammar

Here are some common traps to try to avoid when you're writing your answers...

Avoid these Common Mistakes

Follow these rules in the exam — otherwise it could really affect your grade.

Don't put the word 'them' in front of names of objects — always use 'those'.	✗ Do you really want them problems? ✓ Do you really want those problems?
Don't write 'like' when you mean 'as'.	✗ Macbeth did like Lady Macbeth told him. ✓ Macbeth did as Lady Macbeth told him.
'Who' is used to talk about people. 'That' or 'which' is used for everything else.	✓ I stared at the man, who turned away. ✓ It was his expression that made me curious.

Don't confuse Different Words that Sound the Same

Words that sound similar can mean completely different things. Here are some common examples:

effect/affect

1) Effect is a noun — it is the result of an action. ⟶ The emotive language has a powerful effect on the reader.
2) Affect is a verb meaning to act on or influence something. ⟶ Dim lighting affects the mood of the scene.

where/were/wear

1) Where is used to talk about place and position. ⟶ Where had she seen that symbol before?
2) Were is a past tense form of the verb 'to be'. ⟶ The boys were hiding behind a statue.
3) Wear is a verb used with clothes, hair, jewellery etc. ⟶ He wears armour of burnished gold.

there/their/they're

1) There is used for place and position. ⟶ Jo dived behind the sofa and waited there, listening hard.
2) Their shows possession. ⟶ Both poets use metaphors to emphasise their message.
3) They're is the short form of 'they are'. ⟶ They're the most dramatic lines in the play.

Here are some more Spelling hints

1) Make sure any technical terms, like 'metaphor' or 'onomatopoeia', are spelt correctly.
2) Make sure any information taken from the extract is spelt correctly, including the names of characters.
3) Learn how to spell the author's name for each of your set texts.

Section One — Exam Basics

Spelling, Punctuation and Grammar

You need to punctuate your writing correctly — the more accurate you are, the clearer your answers will be.

Use **Full Stops**, **Colons** and **Semi-colons** correctly

1) Make sure you've used full stops at the end of sentences and question marks at the end of questions.
2) Don't confuse colons and semi-colons:

- Colons can be used to introduce a list or if you want to add a piece of information that explains your sentence.

| *The mood of the poem changes towards the end: it becomes much more solemn.* | ⟶ | You should only use a colon if the first part leads on to the second part. |

- Semi-colons can separate longer phrases in a list, or they can be used to join two sentences together — as long as both sentences are about the same thing and make sense on their own.

| *Immigration was a source of tension in the 1970s; the novel's language reflects this.* | ⟶ | The parts on either side of the semicolon are connected and equally important. |

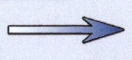

Use **Commas** to put **Pauses** in sentences

1) Commas are used to separate the parts of long sentences so that the meaning is clear. For example:

| *In the valley below, the villages seemed very small.* | ⟶ | Without the comma, the sentence would begin 'In the valley below the villages'. |

2) Commas are also used to break up items in a list:

| *The waves reared, twisted, leapt and raged around the stricken boat.* | ⟶ | The commas separate the different verbs listed in the sentence. |

In a list, the last two items are always separated by a conjunction instead of a comma.

3) Pairs of commas work like brackets to add extra information to the middle of sentences:

| *The novel, despite its melancholy start, finishes on an optimistic note.* | ⟶ | The sentence would still work without the bit in the middle. |

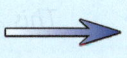

Add an **Apostrophe** to show who **Owns** Something

1) Apostrophes show when something belongs to someone or something.

| *The writer's tone is aggressive.* | ⟶ | The tone belonging to the writer is aggressive. |

2) There's one exception to this rule: 'it's' with an apostrophe is short for 'it is' or 'it has' — 'its' never has an apostrophe to show belonging.

| *The elephant lifted its gnarled trunk and lumbered slowly away.* | ⟶ | The trunk belongs to the elephant, so 'its' doesn't have an apostrophe. |

3) If you're writing a plural word, just add the correct letters to the end — never use an apostrophe to show something is plural.

Section One — Exam Basics

Spelling, Punctuation and Grammar

Try not to get your grammar mixed up — here are a few useful rules to remember...

Verbs **Change** according to **Who** did the action and **When**

When you're writing, make sure your verbs are in the correct form and the correct tense.

A verb has to match its subject — the person or thing that's 'doing' or 'being' in the sentence.
→ ✗ The writer use imagery in the play.
✓ The writer uses imagery in the play.

A verb's subject can be singular (only one person or thing) or plural (more than one person or thing).
→ The poem has an upbeat tone.
Both poems have an upbeat tone.

Verbs change according to whether the action is happening in the past, present or future.
→ The sun glared down upon the pitiful figures.
The sun glares down upon the pitiful figures.
The sun will glare down upon the pitiful figures.

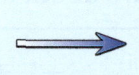

Don't change verb tenses in your writing by mistake.
→ ✗ The writer uses rhetorical questions, which made the text persuasive.
✓ The article uses rhetorical questions, which make the text persuasive.

'No' isn't the **Only** negative word

1) The easiest way to make a phrase negative is to add 'no' or 'not'.

   There is a logical solution to the situation. ⟹ There is no logical solution to the situation.
   The poem is written in free verse. ⟹ The poem is not written in free verse.

2) Words ending in -n't are also negative.

   This argument has got a lot of credibility. ⟹ This argument hasn't got a lot of credibility.

Don't use a **Double Negative**

Words ending in '-n't' are negative, so you don't need to add 'no' or 'not'.

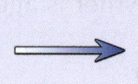

I don't agree with no politicians. → This really means 'I do agree with politicians'. Two negative words in the same phrase make it positive. You should only use one negative at a time.

Check your work to avoid common mistakes...

Remember — leave plenty of time to check through your exam answers and correct any mistakes.
You'll miss out on some easy marks if you've used double negatives or misspelled words like 'Shakespeare'.

Section One — Exam Basics

Revision Summary

Most of the sections in this book finish with a page like this one. It'll help you check you really know your stuff from the section. But don't worry — everything you need to know is covered on the previous pages.

- Try the questions below and <u>tick off each one</u> when you <u>get it right</u>.
- When you've done <u>all the questions</u> under a heading and are <u>completely happy</u> with it, tick it off.

Planning Answers (p.2) ☐

1) Is the following statement true or false?
    "If the question comes with an extract from a text, you should read the extract before reading the question."
2) What are the two main things that you should include in a plan?
    a) your main ideas   b) lots of detailed evidence from the text
    c) the exact wording of your answer   d) the structure of your answer
3) Give one way that you can save time when writing a plan.

P.E.E.D. and Using Examples (p.3-4) ☐

4) What does P.E.E.D. stand for?
5) Give three ways that you could develop a point.
6) In your answers, how many of your points should be backed up with evidence from the text?
    a) a few of them b) about half of them c) some of them d) all of them
7) Quotes from the text should usually be: a) short   b) long
8) Choose two answers. When using a longer quote, make sure that you:
    a) copy it correctly   b) include a capital letter
    c) don't include quotation marks   d) use the correct punctuation

Writing Well and Reading with Insight (p.5-6) ☐

9) Which of these words and phrases could you use to link paragraphs in an exam answer?
    a) secondly b) safe to say c) in addition to this d) conversely
10) Give two examples of things you could comment on to show that you are reading with insight.
11) What does 'inference' mean?
12) Give an example of a phrase you could use to show that you've made an inference.

Spelling, Punctuation and Grammar (p.7-10) ☐

13) Write down the correction symbols for the following situations:
    a) when a new paragraph should start   b) when a word or two is missing
    c) when something isn't clear
14) Which of the following sentences is correct?
    a) I think the writer's use of metaphors in this extract is very effective.
    b) I think the writer's use of metaphors in this extract is very affective.
15) Does the following sentence use a semi-colon correctly?
    Gazing out of the open window; Tomek dreamt of the day when he would be free from revision.
16) Give three uses of commas.
17) Write these sentences out, correcting the mistakes:
    a) The hamster has looked very happy since I brushed it's coat.
    b) Its nice to see a smile on its little face.
18) What is a double negative?

Section One — Exam Basics

Section Two — Prose and Drama

Writing About Prose and Drama

Prose and drama are similar in lots of ways, so this section covers some of the common features found in the two types of text. Sections Three (Drama) and Four (Prose) deal with issues specific to each type of writing.

Think about what the Question is Asking

1) Read the question carefully to make sure you're clear on what it is asking you to focus on. This could be:

- the presentation of a character
- a specific mood or atmosphere
- a specific theme or message
- how an audience responds to the text
- relationships between characters

2) Here's an example of the type of question that might come up in the exam:

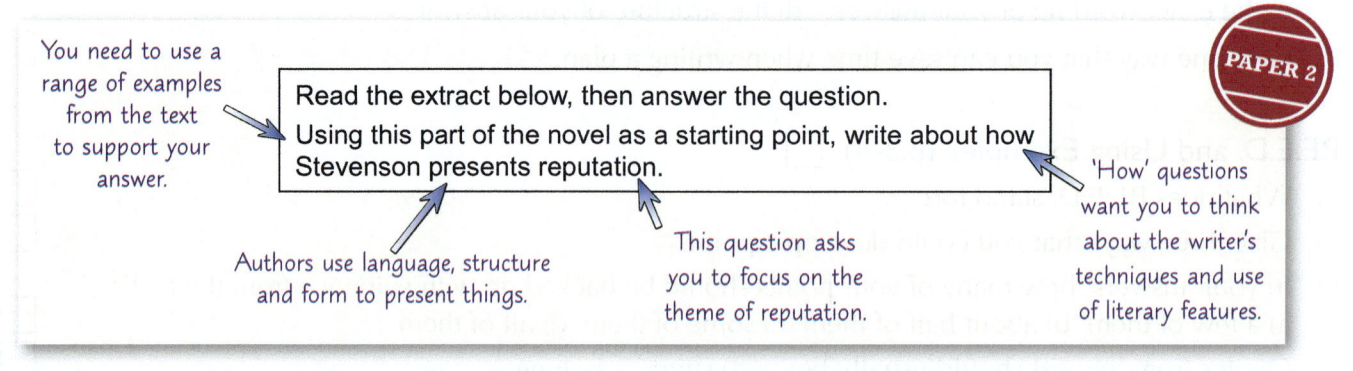

You need to use a range of examples from the text to support your answer.

> Read the extract below, then answer the question.
> Using this part of the novel as a starting point, write about how Stevenson presents reputation.

PAPER 2

Authors use language, structure and form to present things.

This question asks you to focus on the theme of reputation.

'How' questions want you to think about the writer's techniques and use of literary features.

Some questions ask about an Extract from the Text

1) The exam question might ask you to focus on the whole text, an extract from the text, or both.
2) If you're asked to write about an extract, it's doubly important to focus on things like language, structure and form. The examiner knows that you've got the text in front of you, so they're expecting you to pick out and explain some of the features in it.
3) Here are some examples of the types of question that might come up:

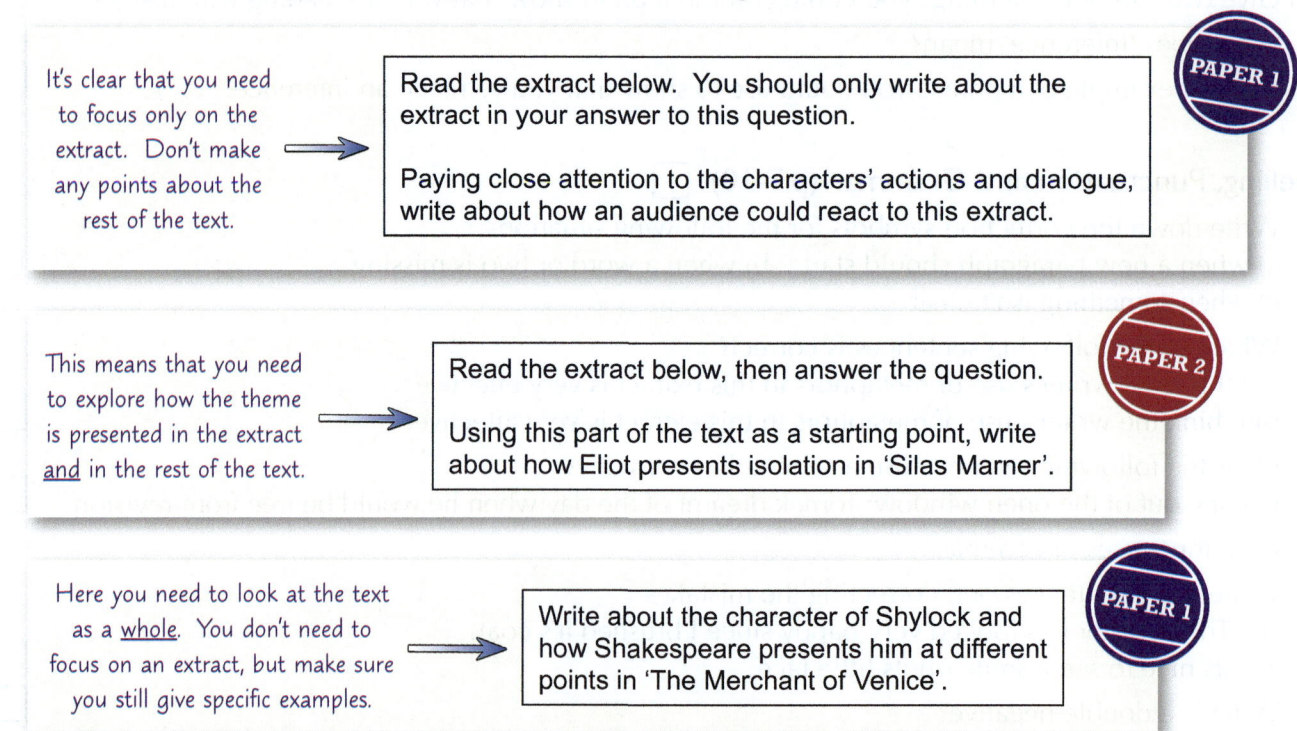

It's clear that you need to focus only on the extract. Don't make any points about the rest of the text.

> Read the extract below. You should only write about the extract in your answer to this question.
> Paying close attention to the characters' actions and dialogue, write about how an audience could react to this extract.

PAPER 1

This means that you need to explore how the theme is presented in the extract and in the rest of the text.

> Read the extract below, then answer the question.
> Using this part of the text as a starting point, write about how Eliot presents isolation in 'Silas Marner'.

PAPER 2

Here you need to look at the text as a whole. You don't need to focus on an extract, but make sure you still give specific examples.

> Write about the character of Shylock and how Shakespeare presents him at different points in 'The Merchant of Venice'.

PAPER 1

Section Two — Prose and Drama

Writing About Prose and Drama

Make sure you Answer the Question you're given

1) It's important to focus on the question — read it carefully a couple of times before planning your answer.
2) Some questions might give you bullet points of things to consider when writing your essay.

> Using this part of the novel as a starting point, explore how Brontë portrays the relationship between Mrs Reed and Jane.
>
> In your answer, make sure you:
> - write about both the extract and the text as a whole;
> - show that you understand the events and characters in the text;
> - write about the novel's contexts.

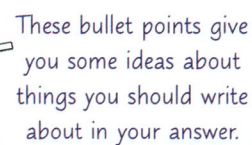

PAPER 2

These bullet points give you some ideas about things you should write about in your answer.

3) Make sure everything you write in your essay answers the question — irrelevant points won't get you any marks.

Mrs Reed is Jane's aunt. She lives at Gateshead Hall with her children: John, Eliza and Georgiana. → This is too general — it doesn't tell you anything about how Brontë presents the relationship between Mrs Reed and Jane.

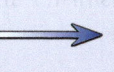

Brontë presents Mrs Reed as a stern, bitter character, who treats the young Jane with "miserable cruelty". → This is much better — it comments on the presentation of the relationship between Mrs Reed and Jane, including a quote from the text to support the point.

4) If there aren't any bullet points, then it might be useful to write some of your own, for example:

> Explore how Shakespeare presents the character of Fluellen in 'Henry V'.
> - What does Fluellen say and do in the play?
> - How does he treat other characters?
> - How does Shakespeare want the reader to feel about Fluellen? How does he achieve this?

PAPER 1

Make sure you Know the text in Detail

1) You need to show the examiner that you know the text really well, and that you understand what happens and the order it happens in.
2) Make sure you're familiar with all the characters in the text — the examiner will be impressed if you make references to the minor characters as well as the major ones.
3) Learn some key quotes from the text that you can use in your essay to support your points
4) To get a top grade, you need to find something original to say about the text. You can make whatever point you like, as long as you can back it up with evidence from the text.

See pages 14-15 for more on writing about characters.

The best way to keep focused on the question is to write a plan...
Take a couple of minutes at the start of each question to plan how you're going to write your answer. It will help you get all of your ideas down before you begin and keep you focused on the question.

Section Two — Prose and Drama

Writing About Characters

You need to know about something called 'characterisation' — this means the methods that an author uses to convey information about, or make the reader feel a certain way about, a character in the text.

Characters are always there for a Reason

1) When you're answering a question about a character, bear in mind that characters always have a purpose.
2) This means that you can't talk about them as if they're real people — make it clear that the author has created them to help get a message across.
3) A character's appearance, actions and language all help to get this message across.

Find bits where the writer Describes the characters

Find descriptions of how the characters look, and then think about what this might say about them.

> In 'Lord of the Flies,' Golding's description of Jack's face as "crumpled" and "ugly without silliness" implies that he might have a sinister and unpleasant personality.

Look at the way characters Act and Speak

1) Look at what characters do, and then consider what that says about them.
2) Try to work out why a character does something. Most characters are motivated by a variety of things, but there's usually one main driving force behind what they do.

> In 'Romeo and Juliet', Tybalt's confrontational and violent actions (e.g. stabbing Mercutio) are ultimately driven by his fierce loyalty to the Capulets.

3) The way characters, including the narrator, speak tells you a lot about them.
4) Remember to think about why the author is making their characters speak the way they do. Think about how the author wants you, the reader, to perceive the character.

> In 'An Inspector Calls', Birling repeatedly shouts "Rubbish!" to dismiss what other people have said. But he finishes his own sentences with "of course", to make his own claims seem obvious and matter-of-fact. This means that the audience perceives him to be arrogant and opinionated.

Look at how the characters treat Other People

The writer can tell you a lot about their characters by showing you how they get on with others.

> "I scorn your idea of love," I could not help saying, as I rose up and stood before him...

> In 'Jane Eyre', Jane tries to be self-controlled, but she is also passionate, and shocks St John with her outspokenness.

Looking at how characters treat other people can reveal sides to their character that they keep hidden from the other main characters.

Section Two — Prose and Drama

Writing About Characters

Make sure you're Prepared for Character Questions

Characters are key elements of any text, so it's not really a surprise that examiners enjoy asking about them in exams. Here are some important questions to think about when you're studying or revising characters:

Why is the character important?

- How do they affect the plot?
- Do they represent a particular point of view?
- What would happen if they weren't there?

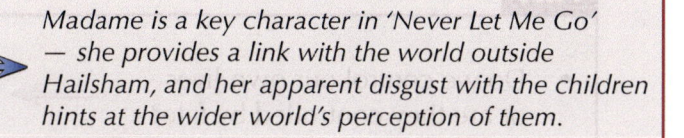

Madame is a key character in 'Never Let Me Go' — she provides a link with the world outside Hailsham, and her apparent disgust with the children hints at the wider world's perception of them.

Does the character change over the course of the story?

- Does the character learn anything?
- Does their personality or behaviour change?
- Are the changes positive or negative?
- How do these changes affect the character?

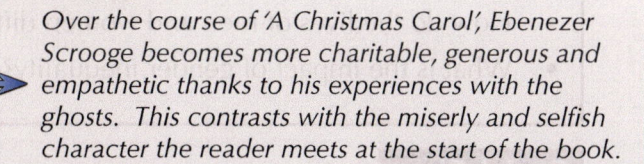

Over the course of 'A Christmas Carol', Ebenezer Scrooge becomes more charitable, generous and empathetic thanks to his experiences with the ghosts. This contrasts with the miserly and selfish character the reader meets at the start of the book.

How does the writer reveal the character's personality?

- How are the character's actions and experiences presented to the reader?
- Is the reader's view of the character the same as other characters' view of them?

In 'Pride and Prejudice', Wickham's and Darcy's true characters are revealed to the reader and Elizabeth at the same time, in Darcy's letter (Chapter 35). This lets the reader share Elizabeth's surprise, and later her frustration with characters who do not realise her views have changed.

How is the character similar or different to other characters?

- How does the character relate to other characters?
- Do differences between characters impact on the plot?
- What is the writer showing us through these differences?

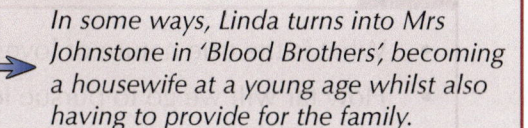

In some ways, Linda turns into Mrs Johnstone in 'Blood Brothers', becoming a housewife at a young age whilst also having to provide for the family.

Does the reader like or sympathise with the character?

- Why does the reader feel that way about the character?
- How does the writer shape the reader's feelings about the character?
- How does the reader's opinion of the character affect their opinion of the text as a whole?

The reader sympathises with Meena in 'Anita and Me' because her loyalty and trust is betrayed by Anita. Having the narrative in Meena's voice helps create empathy, as it means that Meena's viewpoint is heard throughout.

REVISION TASK

Get to know the main characters in your texts...

Draw a mind map for each key character in your texts. Add branches for each main aspect of their character — you can use this page to start off. Don't forget to add quotes to back up your ideas.

Section Two — Prose and Drama

Themes and the Writer's Message

Texts don't just tell a story — they explore significant issues and questions.

Think about the Themes of the text

1) Texts usually have something to say about the society in which they were written or set.
2) Think carefully about the themes of the text, and what the writer might have been saying about them.

Fate

- Do we control our own lives or are they controlled by fate?

→ Characters in 'Romeo and Juliet' blame fate for their problems. This makes the audience question whether what is happening is indeed down to fate or whether the characters should take responsibility for their actions.

Gender

- How do the lives of men and women differ?
- What is the impact of gender inequality?

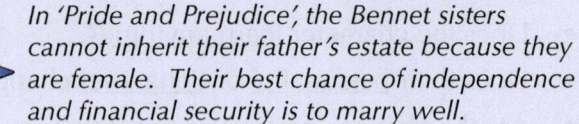

→ In 'Pride and Prejudice', the Bennet sisters cannot inherit their father's estate because they are female. Their best chance of independence and financial security is to marry well.

Social Class

- What is the impact of social class on characters' lives?
- Is it right that social class is so important?

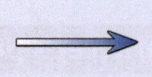

→ In 'An Inspector Calls', Priestley contrasts the actions and qualities of the working-class characters with those of the middle classes to highlight the unfairness of the class system.

Ambition

- Is ambition healthy or destructive?
- How can we control our ambition?

→ By showing Macbeth's downfall, Shakespeare gives the audience a warning about the destructive nature of ambition.

Love

- What is the true nature of love?
- How far will we go to pursue love?

→ In 'Much Ado About Nothing', Shakespeare contrasts Claudio's shallow, fickle feelings for Hero with the deep love that develops between Beatrice and Benedick.

Work out the writer's Overall Message

1) Think about why the writer might have written the book or play.
2) Look at the issues and questions the text raises.

> *Dickens' message in 'A Christmas Carol' is that the rich have a duty to help those less fortunate than themselves.*

> *The central message of 'Lord of the Flies' is that all humans have evil inside them and are capable of committing terrible deeds.*

You need to study the text carefully to work out the message...

It might take a while to work out the writer's overall message, so make sure you read the text carefully. The fates of characters, significant passages of speech and the ending of the text are all worth examining.

Section Two — Prose and Drama

Audience Response

A text isn't just about the writer's message — you need to think about how a text would be received.

Some exam questions ask about Audience Response

1) You should always think about the effect a text has on the audience.
2) Some questions could ask you about it specifically:

> Read the extract below. You should only write about the extract in your answer to this question.
> Paying close attention to the Beatrice's actions and dialogue, write about how an audience could react to this extract.

PAPER 1

3) The question might give you something to focus on, such as how certain characters speak and behave — make sure you write about these things in terms of how they affect the audience.
4) If you're writing about an older text, you can write about how an audience at the time might have responded, or a modern-day audience — or both.

Think about the Effect of the Writer's Techniques

1) Look at the techniques the writer uses in the extract, and think about what kind of effect they might have on the audience, e.g. exciting, frightening or emotional.
2) The writer might use language to influence the audience's response to a scene:

> Lady Macbeth's reference to the "owl that shriek'd, the fatal bellman" adds to the eerie atmosphere. The word "fatal" foreshadows Duncan's murder and increases the audience's feeling of suspense.

3) The writer might also use structure to shape the audience's feelings about a scene or character:

> Shakespeare structures the play to make the audience feel sympathetic towards Desdemona — it is established early in the play that she is innocent and being set up by Iago. This dramatic irony makes her murder by Othello even more emotional and shocking.

Write about your Own Response

1) You should consider your personal response to the text — this should give you a good idea of how an audience might respond. Think about what emotions the text evokes and whether you like or empathise with certain characters.

> The audience feels sympathetic towards Hero when Claudio rejects her.

Don't use "I" when you're talking about your personal response — use "the audience" instead.

If you're writing about prose, use "the reader" instead of "the audience".

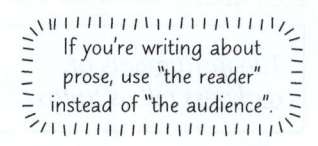

2) If you're writing about an extract, go through and annotate it to show how the text makes you feel at different points. Use these notes to help plan your answer.

Think about how the text makes you feel...

Remember to write about the effect of a text on the audience or the reader — including the effect it has on you. Just make sure you talk about the effect of specific techniques, and avoid using "I" in your answers.

Section Two — Prose and Drama

The Writer's Techniques

There are lots of marks available in English Literature for commenting on the way writers use language.

Analysing the writer's use of Language is key

1) Writers select the language they use carefully — it's up to you to work out why they've chosen a particular word or phrase, and to explain the effect that it has.

2) Look out for any interesting, unusual or specialist vocabulary — think about why it's been used. Take note of any repeated words and phrases too — they will have been repeated for a reason.

> *Anita Rutter laughs "in reverberated echo as the heavens slowly crumbled and fell".* → In 'Anita and Me', Syal uses mythological language to show how powerful Anita is in relation to Meena — she is described as if she were a god.

3) Examining the language used by characters is really important — think about the way characters speak, why they speak in that way and whether the way they speak is different to other characters.

> *"D' they call y' Eddie?"*
> *"Gis a sweet"* → In 'Blood Brothers', Russell uses informal, colloquial language for the Johnstone family — they omit letters off the end of words and use non-standard pronouns. This language is used to reflect their social class.

> *Hyde speaks "with a flush of anger" and makes inhuman noises, e.g. he screams in "animal terror".* → In 'Dr Jekyll and Mr Hyde', Stevenson uses language to reinforce Hyde's incivility — Hyde does not speak as gentlemen were expected to, suggesting to other characters that something is not right.

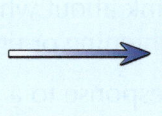

Look out for Imagery

Imagery is particularly common in prose texts, but it does crop up in plays too — Shakespeare uses lots of it.

1) Imagery is when an author uses language to create a picture in the reader's mind, or to describe something more vividly. It can add to the reader's or the audience's understanding of the story.

2) Similes describe something by saying that it's like something else:

> *He seemed to weave, like the spider, from pure impulse, without reflection.* → In 'Silas Marner', Eliot uses the simile "like the spider" to emphasise that Silas weaves instinctively — like a spider, he doesn't have to think about what he's doing.

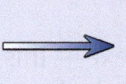

3) Metaphors describe something by saying it is something else:

> *The instruments of darkness tell us truths.* → In 'Macbeth', Banquo's suspicion of the three Witches is shown by his use of the metaphor "instruments of darkness" to describe them.

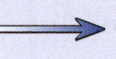

4) Personification describes something (e.g. an animal, object or aspect of nature) as if it were human:

> *It was a wild, cold, seasonable night of March, with a pale moon, lying on her back...* → In 'Dr Jekyll and Mr Hyde', the personification of the moon makes it seem that the whole world has been turned upside down by Jekyll's secret.

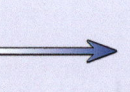

Section Two — Prose and Drama

The Writer's Techniques

Comment on **Sentence Structure**

1) It's not just particular words and phrases that you can comment on — you should also look at how writers use sentences and paragraphs to reinforce their points.

"Life is real again, and the useless and cumbersome and mischievous have to die. They ought to die." →	In 'The War of the Worlds', the artilleryman uses a mix of long and short sentences to persuade the narrator to agree with him.

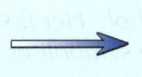

2) Different sentence lengths create different effects, e.g. a succession of short sentences could build tension or excitement, whereas long sentences might show a character getting carried away with their emotions.

"Seen him?" repeated Mr Utterson. "Well?" *"That's it!" said Poole. "It was this way."* →	At the climax of 'Dr Jekyll and Mr Hyde', the characters talk in short bursts. This creates suspense by suggesting that events are happening at a fast pace.

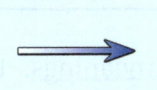

There were great round, pot-bellied baskets of chestnuts, shaped like the waistcoats of jolly old gentlemen, lolling at the doors, and tumbling out into the street in their apoplectic opulence. →	In 'A Christmas Carol', Dickens uses long sentences to describe the activity on the streets when Scrooge walks through London. This gives the Christmas scenes a sense of endless cheer, emphasising the joy Scrooge has excluded himself from.

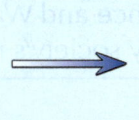

Pay attention to **Descriptions** and **Settings**

1) Writers use settings to influence the way you feel about what's happening and create atmosphere.
2) You need to look at the writer's descriptions and think about why they have been included and what effect they have.

Alleys and archways, like so many cesspools, disgorged their offences of smell, and dirt, and life, upon the straggling streets. →	In 'A Christmas Carol', Dickens uses descriptive language to present his reader with a realistic, harsh vision of poverty in London.

Raw and chill was the winter morning: my teeth chattered as I hastened down the drive. →	In 'Jane Eyre', this cold and bleak setting reflects the lack of emotional warmth Jane has received at Gateshead and suggests that her experiences at Lowood will also be unpleasant.

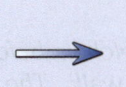

When shall we three meet again? *In thunder, lightning, or in rain?* *Hover through the fog and filthy air.* →	In 'Macbeth', the Witches repeatedly describe the bad weather. This reflects the sinister atmosphere created by the Witches' arrival.

Section Two — Prose and Drama

The Writer's Techniques

Writers can present their ideas using Symbolism

1) Symbols can be used to reinforce the themes that run through a text. Look out for things that could be a symbol for something else, e.g. a thunderstorm could be a symbol for destruction.

> In 'An Inspector Calls', Priestley uses Eva Smith as a symbol. Her first name sounds like 'Eve', the first woman (in the Biblical account of creation), which suggests she symbolises all women. Her surname is very common and it's also the word for a tradesman, which implies that she represents all ordinary, working-class women.

> In 'Silas Marner', the hearth is a symbol of family and community. Eliot emphasises the loneliness of Godfrey's childhood home by describing it as a place "where the hearth had no smiles", whereas Eppie's appearance on Silas's hearth marks the start of a much happier period in Silas's life.

2) Symbols are often used to create additional meanings. If the literal meaning of a sentence sounds strange, try to work out whether there's another layer of meaning.

> *This boy is Ignorance. This girl is Want. Beware them both...* → In 'A Christmas Carol', Dickens uses the characters of Ignorance and Want to symbolise the problems caused by society's neglect of the poor.

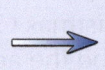

Structure is always important

There's more information about the structure of plays on p.28 and prose texts on p.43.

1) Structure is the order that events happen in. Make sure you think about how a writer has put a text together, and what the effect of this is.

2) Structural devices can be used to make a text more interesting. For example:

- Foreshadowing gives hints about what will happen later on in the story.

> In 'Never Let Me Go', Kathy frequently hints at how significant the character of Madame is to the students' lives, but her exact role in the system is not revealed until near the end of the novel. This creates suspense, as the reader waits for the mystery of the students' existence and Madame's role in their lives to be resolved.

- Flashbacks temporarily shift the story back in time, often showing something from the past that is significant in the present.

> The opening of 'The History Boys' shows Irwin in a wheelchair, before Bennett moves time backwards twenty years and Irwin is able to walk. The audience is therefore left wondering what happens to Irwin and expects that something is going to occur during the course of the play to explain his disability.

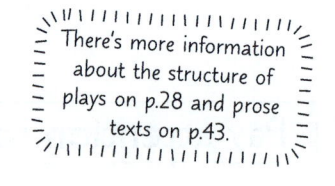

EXAM TIP — Remember to write about the effect on the reader...
It's important to refer to the techniques that the writer uses, but if you want the top marks you'll also need to mention how those techniques affect the reader (or the audience if it's a play).

Section Two — Prose and Drama

Using Quotations

You're not allowed to take any of your texts into the exam, so you're going to need to learn some quotations...

Learn Key Quotations that are relevant to Characters and Themes

1) When you're reading a text, make a note of some good quotes to learn. Examiners aren't expecting you to memorise big chunks of text, so the quotes you pick out should be short and snappy.

2) You need to use the quotes to back up the points in your essay, so make sure the quotes you choose are relevant to things you're likely to write about in the exam, e.g. a key character or theme.

3) When you're revising, it's a good idea to make lists of key quotes for each theme or character.

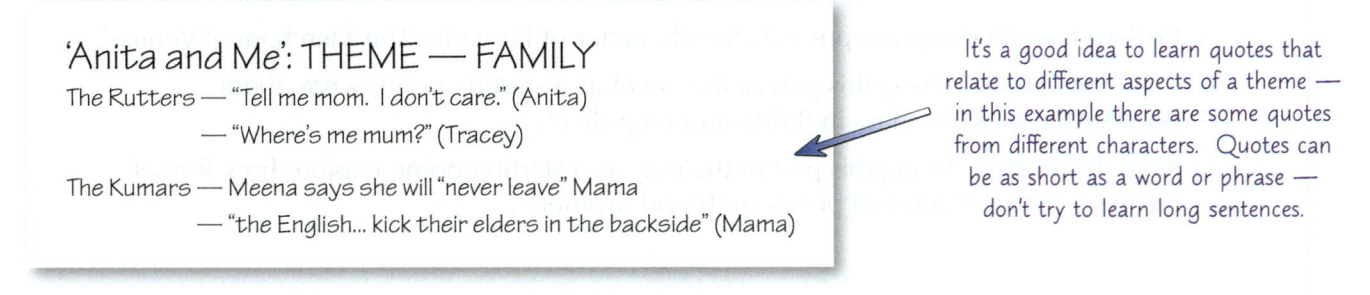

> 'Anita and Me': THEME — FAMILY
> The Rutters — "Tell me mom. I don't care." (Anita)
> — "Where's me mum?" (Tracey)
>
> The Kumars — Meena says she will "never leave" Mama
> — "the English... kick their elders in the backside" (Mama)

It's a good idea to learn quotes that relate to different aspects of a theme — in this example there are some quotes from different characters. Quotes can be as short as a word or phrase — don't try to learn long sentences.

Embed Short Quotations into your sentences

Quoting from Shakespeare is covered on page 35.

1) The best way to use quotes is to embed (insert) them into your sentences. This just means that they should be a natural part of a sentence, allowing you to go on to explain how the quote supports your point.

> *In 'An Inspector Calls', the Inspector describes Eva positively, calling her "pretty" and "lively", which makes the audience feel more sympathetic towards her.*

2) Using shorter quotations allows you to explain the same point in fewer words.

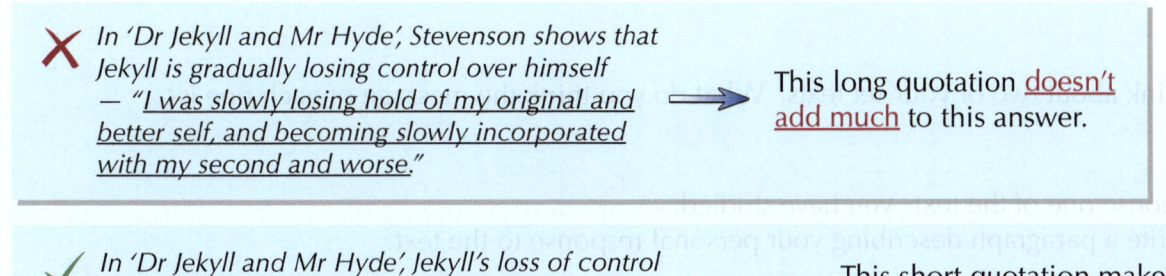

> ✗ *In 'Dr Jekyll and Mr Hyde', Stevenson shows that Jekyll is gradually losing control over himself — "I was slowly losing hold of my original and better self, and becoming slowly incorporated with my second and worse."*

This long quotation doesn't add much to this answer.

> ✓ *In 'Dr Jekyll and Mr Hyde', Jekyll's loss of control is demonstrated when he explains that he is "becoming slowly incorporated" with his evil side.*

This short quotation makes this answer much snappier.

3) For extract questions (see page 12) make sure you quote accurately from the text you're given. But don't be tempted to quote huge chunks of text — always be selective with the quotes you use and make sure you explain their significance or effect.

Don't try to learn very long quotes...

REVISION TIP: When you're revising quotes, don't memorise long chunks of text — short phrases or single words are easier to learn. They'll also help keep your answers concise, which will please the examiners.

Warm-Up Questions

You'll need your set texts to hand when you're answering these questions, but don't worry — you don't need to write any long answers (yet). If you don't know what texts you're studying, now would be a good time to find out from your teacher.

Warm-Up Questions

1) Look at the different types of question in the box and read the sample questions below. For each sample question, write down what type of question you think it is.

   - theme
   - characterisation
   - mood/atmosphere

   a) Explore how Shakespeare presents the character of Portia in 'The Merchant of Venice'.

   b) Read the extract. Using this part of the novel as a starting point, write about how Austen presents class in 'Pride and Prejudice'.

   c) Read the extract. Using this part of the play as a starting point, explore how Russell creates tension at different points in 'Blood Brothers'.

2) Choose a character from one of the texts you have studied.
   Find five key quotations which illustrate something about their personality.
   Write a sentence explaining what each quotation tells you about them.

3) For the character you chose in question 2, explain how you feel about that character and how the author has made you feel that way.
   Use evidence from the text to back up your argument.

4) Choose a text you have studied in class. Write down three of the text's key themes (e.g. social class, gender, power). For each theme, write down an example from the text and explain how it relates to the theme.

5) Think about two of your set texts. What do you think the message of each one is?

6) Choose one of the texts you have studied.
   Write a paragraph describing your personal response to the text.

7) Using one of your set texts, find one example of:
   a) simile
   b) metaphor
   c) personification

Section Two — Prose and Drama

Warm-Up Questions

8) Choose an extract from a text you have studied in class, in which the writer builds a particular atmosphere (e.g. frightening, gloomy, joyful). Explain how the writer creates that atmosphere, and what effect it has on the reader. Remember to use evidence from the text to back up your argument.

9) Read the passages below. For each one, write a sentence or two stating what you think each object or action in bold is a symbol for, and explaining your view.

   a) *In 'Lord of the Flies', the boys use the **conch shell** to bring order to their meetings — whoever is holding it is allowed to speak, while everyone else has to keep quiet and listen.*

   b) *In 'Jane Eyre', Mr Rochester proposes to Jane underneath the old **chestnut tree** in the grounds of Thornfield. That night, the tree is struck by lightning and split down the middle. Later, Jane discovers that Mr Rochester is already married, so she refuses to marry him and runs away.*

   c) *In 'Never Let Me Go', the students are forced into a particular way of life over which they have very little control. When they discuss their futures, many of them claim that they would like to have jobs that involve **driving**.*

10) Using a text you have studied in class, identify an unusual structural feature (e.g. an instance of foreshadowing, a flashback or a jump in time). Write a short paragraph describing the feature and explaining its effect.

11) Which of the following paragraphs shows a better use of quotations? Explain your answer.

   a) *In 'Anita and Me', Meena has unrealistic, childish dreams of what her future holds. She describes winning a talent show and becoming a "major personality" as her "most realistic escape route" from her current life.*

   b) *In 'Anita and Me', Meena has unrealistic, childish dreams of what her future holds. She watches a talent show and says "I knew that this could be my most realistic escape route from Tollington, from ordinary girl to major personality in one easy step."*

Section Two — Prose and Drama

Exam-Style Questions

Writing about texts is an acquired skill — you can only get better at it by practising. The next two sections go into more detail about drama and prose, and you'll find some practice exam questions at the end of each section. To get you into the swing of it, have a go at answering these.

Q1 Choose a character from a Shakespeare play you have studied. Focusing on one scene in the play, explain how Shakespeare uses language to show the character's personality.

Q2 Choose a passage from a prose text you have read which you find particularly tense **or** exciting. Using this part of the text as a starting point, explore how the writer creates tension **or** excitement.

Q3 Choose a character from a modern (post-1914) text you have studied. Starting with one extract, write about your chosen character and the way they are presented in the text.

Q4 Choose a key theme from a 19th-century text that you have studied. Starting with a short extract from the text, write about how the author explores the theme in that extract and in the text as a whole.

Revision Summary

Congratulations — you've reached the end of the section. All in the brain? Have a go at these to check...
- Try these questions and <u>tick off each one</u> when you <u>get it right</u>.
- When you've done <u>all the questions</u> under a heading and are <u>completely happy</u> with it, tick it off.

Writing About Prose and Drama (p.12-13) ☐
1) Is the following statement true or false?
   "You should only look at a single extract for every question you answer."
2) What should you always do when making a point in an answer?
   a) Make sure it answers the question you've been given.
   b) Add as many extra details about the text as you can.

Writing About Characters (p.14-15) ☐
3) What is characterisation?
4) Give three examples of things you could write about when answering a question about a particular character.

Themes and the Writer's Message (p.16) ☐
5) Give three examples of themes that are often addressed in texts.
6) Is the following statement true or false?
   "To work out the overall message, you should consider why the writer may have written the text."

Audience Response (p.17) ☐
7) Which types of audience can you write about when answering a question?
   a) An audience from the time the text was written.
   b) A modern-day audience.
   c) Both of the above.
8) Which of the following sentences is better to include in an essay?
   a) The foreshadowing in 'Never Let Me Go' meant I was intrigued about the story — I wanted to keep reading.
   b) The use of foreshadowing in 'Never Let Me Go' creates intrigue, and makes the reader want to find out more.

The Writer's Techniques (p.18-20) ☐
9) What is the difference between a simile and a metaphor?
10) What is the word given to the type of imagery where something (like an animal or object) is described as if it were human?
11) Why might a writer choose to use a shorter sentence instead of a longer sentence?
12) Write a brief explanation of what authors can use settings for.
13) Explain what symbolism is. Give an example of a symbol from a text you have studied.
14) What is foreshadowing?

Using Quotations (p.21) ☐
15) When quoting from a text, why should you try to include short rather than long quotations?
16) Give two examples of things you need to be especially careful of when quoting from the text to answer an extract question.

Section Two — Prose and Drama

Section Three — Drama

Reading Plays

Writers use stage directions to show what's happening on stage. Different types of speech give clues about a character's personality, their relationships with other characters and their innermost thoughts.

Stage Directions describe the action on stage

Stage directions are usually written in italics or put in brackets to distinguish them from things that are said.

1) When you're reading a play, look out for the stage directions. These are instructions from the playwright to the director and the actors — they can tell you a lot about how the playwright wants the play to be performed.

2) There are lots of things to look out for in the stage directions. For example, music and sound effects might be used to create a specific mood, or the set may be designed to create a certain atmosphere.

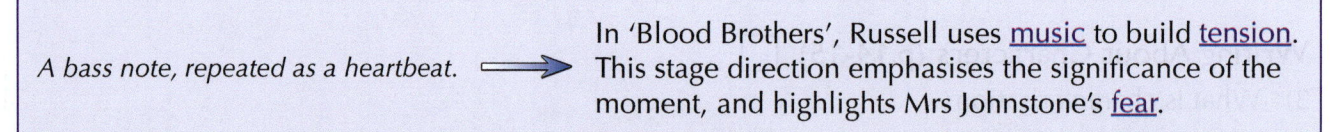

A bass note, repeated as a heartbeat. →	In 'Blood Brothers', Russell uses music to build tension. This stage direction emphasises the significance of the moment, and highlights Mrs Johnstone's fear.

3) Stage directions can also describe the characters' actions and the use of props.

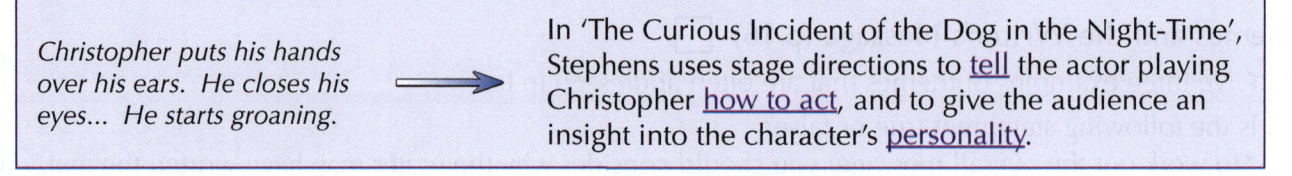

Christopher puts his hands over his ears. He closes his eyes... He starts groaning. →	In 'The Curious Incident of the Dog in the Night-Time', Stephens uses stage directions to tell the actor playing Christopher how to act, and to give the audience an insight into the character's personality.

Stage directions reveal what the writer Wants

You should write about how the stage directions reveal the playwright's intentions.

Action
We see Mickey comb the town, breaking through groups of people, looking, searching, desperate... ('Blood Brothers' — Willy Russell) →	These stage directions describe what's happening on stage — Mickey's desperate search makes this scene dramatic.

Staging
The dining-room of a fairly large suburban house... It has good solid furniture... ('An Inspector Calls' — J. B. Priestley) →	In these opening stage directions, Priestley establishes how he would like the set to look. The set reflects the class and status of the Birlings.

Characterisation
Jo dances on dreamily. ('A Taste of Honey' — Shelagh Delaney) →	This stage direction occurs after Jo has agreed to marry her boyfriend. It hints at her longing to escape and her dreams of a better life.

Dialogue
Irwin *(thoughtfully)* That's very true. ('The History Boys' — Alan Bennett) →	The stage direction here tells the actor playing Irwin how he should deliver his line.

Reading Plays

Plays contain Different types of Speech

1) Dialogue is when two or more characters are speaking.
   It shows how characters interact with each other.

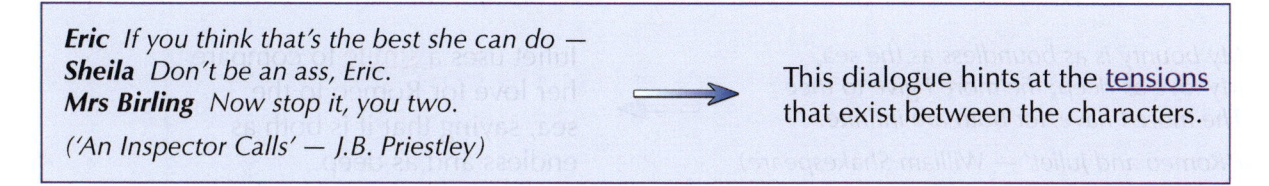

   > **Eric** *If you think that's the best she can do —*
   > **Sheila** *Don't be an ass, Eric.*
   > **Mrs Birling** *Now stop it, you two.*
   > ('An Inspector Calls' — J.B. Priestley)

   → This dialogue hints at the tensions that exist between the characters.

2) A monologue is when one character speaks for a long time and the other characters on stage listen to them.

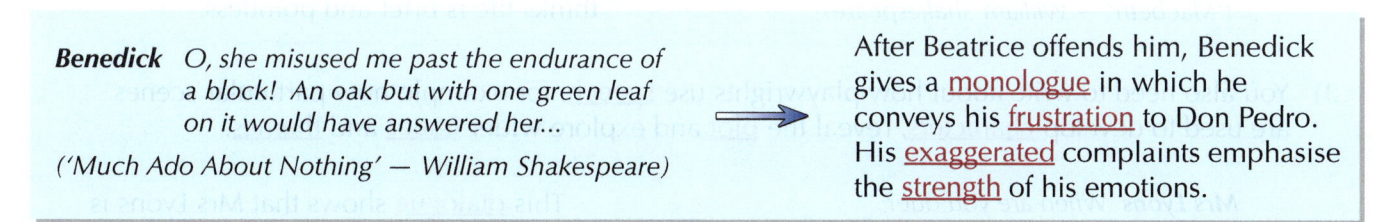

   > **Benedick** *O, she misused me past the endurance of a block! An oak but with one green leaf on it would have answered her...*
   > ('Much Ado About Nothing' — William Shakespeare)

   → After Beatrice offends him, Benedick gives a monologue in which he conveys his frustration to Don Pedro. His exaggerated complaints emphasise the strength of his emotions.

3) In a soliloquy, a single character speaks their thoughts out loud — other characters can't hear them. This reveals to the audience something of the character's inner thoughts and feelings.

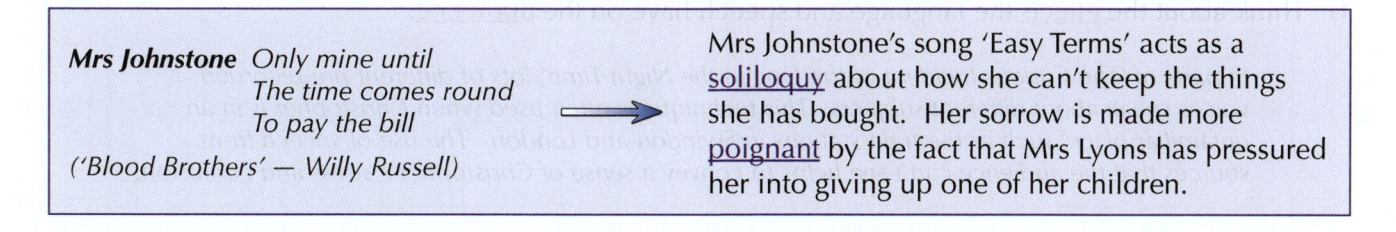

   > **Mrs Johnstone** *Only mine until*
   > *The time comes round*
   > *To pay the bill*
   > ('Blood Brothers' — Willy Russell)

   → Mrs Johnstone's song 'Easy Terms' acts as a soliloquy about how she can't keep the things she has bought. Her sorrow is made more poignant by the fact that Mrs Lyons has pressured her into giving up one of her children.

4) An aside is like a soliloquy, but it is usually a shorter comment which is only heard by the audience — other characters don't hear it.

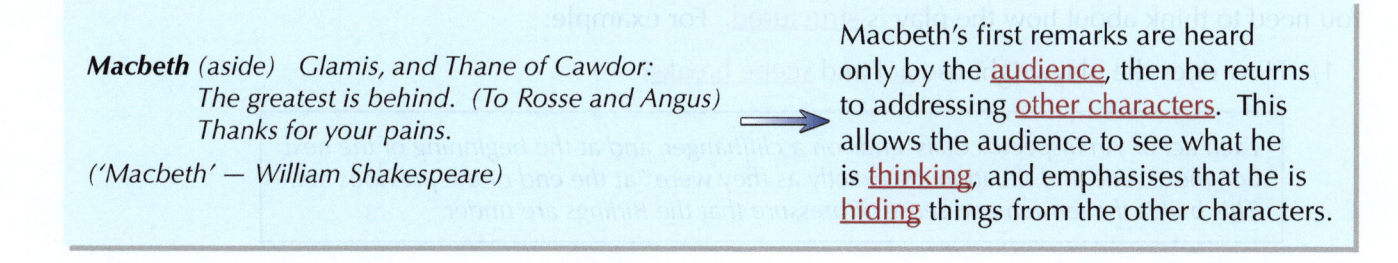

   > **Macbeth** *(aside) Glamis, and Thane of Cawdor:*
   > *The greatest is behind. (To Rosse and Angus)*
   > *Thanks for your pains.*
   > ('Macbeth' — William Shakespeare)

   → Macbeth's first remarks are heard only by the audience, then he returns to addressing other characters. This allows the audience to see what he is thinking, and emphasises that he is hiding things from the other characters.

Some playwrights use stage directions more than others...

Different writers use different methods. Shakespeare didn't use many stage directions — he relied instead on characters' speech to tell the story. Modern writers tend to use more stage directions than Shakespeare.

Section Three — Drama

Writing About Plays

When you're writing about a play, keep in mind the fact that it's intended to be watched by an audience.

Write about the Language of the play

1) You need to write in detail about the language used in the play.
2) Writers often use imagery, like similes, metaphors and personification.

> *My bounty is as boundless as the sea,*
> *My love as deep; the more I give to thee*
> *The more I have, for both are infinite.*
> ('Romeo and Juliet' — William Shakespeare)

→ Juliet uses a simile to compare her love for Romeo to the sea, saying that it is both as endless and as deep.

> *Life's but a walking shadow, a poor player*
> *That struts and frets his hour upon the stage*
> *And then is heard no more.*
> ('Macbeth' — William Shakespeare)

→ Macbeth personifies life, comparing it to an actor whose influence is limited to his time on stage. This shows that Macbeth thinks life is brief and pointless.

3) You also need to write about how playwrights use speech, for example how particular scenes are used to develop characters, reveal the plot and explore wider issues and themes.

> **Mrs Lyons** When are you due?
> **Mrs Johnstone** Erm, well, about... Oh, but Mrs...
> **Mrs Lyons** Quickly, quickly, tell me...
> ('Blood Brothers' — Willy Russell)

→ This dialogue shows that Mrs Lyons is more powerful than Mrs Johnstone — her interruption and use of imperatives like "tell me" show that she controls the conversation.

4) Think about the effects the language and speech have on the audience.

> In parts of 'The Curious Incident of the Dog in the Night-Time', lots of different pre-recorded voices speak about different subjects. This technique is often used when Christopher is in an unfamiliar place, such as the train stations in Swindon and London. The use of speech from sources that the audience can't see helps to convey a sense of Christopher's stress and confusion.

A play's Structure is important too

You need to think about how the play is structured. For example:

1) How does the playwright use act and scene breaks?

> Each act of 'An Inspector Calls' ends on a cliffhanger, and at the beginning of the next act, the "scene and situation are exactly as they were" at the end of the previous act. This builds the tension and sense of pressure that the Birlings are under.

2) How does the playwright show changes in time?

> In 'Blood Brothers', Russell uses a montage (a series of short scenes) to move time forwards four years. The speed at which time passes on stage symbolises the fleetingness of youth, and gives the audience the sense that the play is moving rapidly towards its tragic ending.

Section Three — Drama

Writing About Plays

Show you know that plays are intended to be **Watched** not **Read**

Plays are written to be acted on stage, not read silently from a book. This means that you shouldn't refer to the 'reader' — talk about the 'audience' instead.

> *Siobhan acts as a kind of narrator in 'The Curious Incident of the Dog in the Night-Time' — she reads segments of Christopher's work, which helps the audience make sense of what's happening, and gives them an insight into Christopher's mind.*

→ You should comment on how the play works on stage and how this impacts on the audience.

Show you appreciate **Stagecraft**

1) You also need to show that you appreciate the writer's stagecraft — their skill at writing for the stage. Playwrights use features like silences, actions and sound effects to create a mood, reveal something in a certain way or add drama to a situation — these things are usually mentioned in stage directions (see p.26).

2) Appreciating the stagecraft means asking yourself a few key questions:

   - How would this scene look on stage?
   - How would the audience react?
   - Is it effective?

3) Writers might use stagecraft to vary the pace of the play to keep it interesting for the audience. For example, in Act Two of 'Blood Brothers', Russell uses simultaneous conversations to create a fast-paced scene:

   > *Mickey and Sammy are speaking on one side of the stage whilst Edward and Linda are speaking on the other side. Both conversations have life-changing consequences, and the combination of the two dialogues emphasises the fact that both twins are at a crossroads in their lives.*

4) Writers can also use stagecraft to increase the tension, particularly at a climactic moment in the play. In the final act of 'Romeo and Juliet', Shakespeare uses dramatic irony to build up the suspense:

   > *Romeo fights Paris in the tomb while the audience, knowing that Friar Lawrence is on his way, hope he'll arrive and avert the tragedy. He arrives too late: Romeo has already killed Paris and committed suicide. These events happen in a very short space of time, and the tension is incredible. Even though the audience knows from the start of the play that Romeo and Juliet will both die, we still hope that they won't.*

   Dramatic irony is where the audience knows something that a character on stage doesn't know.

REVISION TIP — **Reading the play aloud will help you understand it...**
Try reading bits of the play out loud. Some lines have a particular rhythm to them that is more obvious when they're spoken. Reading aloud can also help you remember quotes from the play.

Section Three — Drama

Writing About Modern Plays

If you're studying a modern play (that's one written after 1914), read on — this is important stuff...

You might have to write about a Modern Play

1) For Paper 2, you'll have to study either a modern play or a modern prose text. Your teacher will be able to tell you which you're doing.

2) The modern plays you might study are:

- An Inspector Calls by J.B. Priestley
- Blood Brothers by Willy Russell
- The Curious Incident of the Dog in the Night-Time by Simon Stephens
- A Taste of Honey by Shelagh Delaney
- The History Boys by Alan Bennett

See p.43-45 for information on writing about modern prose texts.

Modern plays are often Realistic

1) Many modern plays try to be realistic, featuring characters who lead ordinary lives. They often include:

- Everyday settings. The setting could be real, e.g. Liverpool in 'Blood Brothers', or made-up but realistic, e.g. Brumley in 'An Inspector Calls'.
- Characters who are ordinary people, rather than kings or heroes.
- Characters who speak in a realistic way — for example, they might use slang or a regional accent.

2) Realistic plays tend to feature issues that affect ordinary people in society, e.g. living in poverty in 'A Taste of Honey'.

3) The writer might use their play to encourage the audience to think about these issues in their own lives — and even change their behaviour as a result.

Modern playwrights often criticise Social Divides

1) Modern British plays often focus on social class divides in Britain.

2) They might write about situations when middle and upper-class people have more opportunities than working-class people. This might be reflected in things like education, job prospects and wealth.

In 'Blood Brothers', one twin is raised in a middle-class family, while the other is raised in a working-class family. The play shows how social class affects the boys' lives. Edward goes to university and becomes a councillor, while Mickey struggles with a low-paid, insecure job from which he is eventually laid off.

3) Some modern writers have used their plays to encourage people to treat everyone equally, regardless of their social class or background.

In 'An Inspector Calls', the working-class character Eva Smith/Daisy Renton is mistreated by all the members of the middle-class Birling family. Priestley uses the play to criticise prejudiced attitudes towards poor or working-class people, and to encourage people to take responsibility for one another in society.

Section Three — Drama

Writing About Modern Plays

Being a **Young Person** is explored in many modern plays

1) Modern plays often present the lives of young people or teenagers, showing them growing up and trying to understand the world.

   > One of the themes of 'The Curious Incident of the Dog in the Night-Time' is Christopher coming to terms with the changes in his family, after discovering that his father killed a neighbour's dog. Christopher's journey into London on his own represents him gaining independence and dealing with the changes in his life.

2) Some writers explore ideas about how young people can be different from their parents or disagree with them. E.g. In 'An Inspector Calls', Sheila challenges her parents' authority and, unlike them, takes responsibility for her actions.

Some modern plays explore **Gender** and **Sexuality**

1) Modern plays often explore the experiences of different groups in society.

2) Some plays focus on issues that women face, e.g. the expectation that a woman would get married and have children instead of working.

   > In 'A Taste of Honey', Jo becomes pregnant without being married and wants to work to support the baby. The play shows some of her efforts to become independent.

3) Other plays might explore how people with different sexualities face prejudice or discrimination by others in society.

   > In 'The History Boys', Bennett explores how Posner comes to understand his sexuality, as well as some of his fears about how he will be treated in society because he is gay.

Think about how the play might be **Staged**

1) Modern writers often use stage directions (see p.26) to show how they want a scene to be performed.

   > At the end of Act 1 in 'An Inspector Calls', Priestley writes that the Inspector "appears, looking steadily and searchingly" at Gerald and Sheila. This action emphasises the Inspector's role as a moral judge of the other characters.

2) The use of lighting, music and special effects can affect the way the play is interpreted.

   > At the end of 'The Curious Incident of the Dog in the Night-Time', Christopher demonstrates a maths problem. Stephens gives stage directions for this scene that include the use of lights and projections. By using technology to make Christopher's demonstration more visually impressive, Stephens emphasises Christopher's achievement in his maths A-level and in overcoming adversity.

Modern plays often address social issues...

Modern plays deal with some pretty tricky themes. Finding out a bit about when and where a play is set can really help to understand the problems the writer is addressing and the messages they want to give out.

Section Three — Drama

Writing About Shakespeare

You'll need to know a bit about Shakespeare for your exam. The next few pages will give you a hand.

Shakespeare's plays can be Serious or Funny

1) You'll have to study a Shakespeare play as part of your course. The plays you might study are:
   - Macbeth
   - Romeo and Juliet
   - Othello
   - The Merchant of Venice
   - Much Ado About Nothing
   - Henry V

2) Shakespeare's plays are often split into different genres based on the features they have in common.

Tragedy
- Tragedies (e.g. 'Macbeth', 'Othello', 'Romeo and Juliet') often focus on big topics — e.g. love, death, war, religion. They can be emotionally powerful and often have a moral message.
- Some of Shakespeare's tragedies are set in an imaginary or historical world. The characters are often kings, queens or other rulers.

Comedy
- Comedies (e.g. 'Much Ado About Nothing' and 'The Merchant of Venice') are written to be funny.
- They feature events and characters that are often exaggerated for humorous effect.
- They can still have a moral message though, and often include serious or emotional elements.

History
- Histories are based on real historical events.
- 'Henry V' is a history play — it's about a real king and covers real historical events (e.g. the Battle of Agincourt).

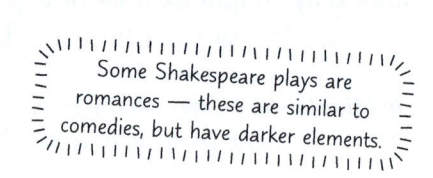

Some Shakespeare plays are romances — these are similar to comedies, but have darker elements.

Shakespeare's plays share Similar Themes

Shakespeare's plays tend to have similar themes. Some of the most common ones are:

Power & Ambition
'Macbeth' explores the title character's ambition to be king. The play shows his downfall after this desire leads to murder, suggesting that too much ambition can be a bad thing.

Fate & Free Will
The events of 'Romeo and Juliet' suggest that a person's fate is unavoidable. The couple's love is described as "death-marked" in the Prologue, and they are unable to escape their families' conflict.

Love & Relationships
In 'Much Ado about Nothing', Shakespeare contrasts the relationship between Hero and Claudio (shallow and immature) with that between Beatrice and Benedick (deeper and more mature) to explore the real meaning of love.

Justice & Revenge
In 'The Merchant of Venice', two different ideas of justice are shown. Portia believes it would be just for Shylock to show mercy to Antonio, while Shylock thinks he deserves revenge. The play debates whether revenge is ever justified.

Section Three — Drama

Writing About Shakespeare

Show you're aware that Shakespeare was writing **400 Years Ago**

1) Shakespeare (1564-1616) wrote his plays about 400 years ago, so it's not surprising that some of the language, themes and ideas can seem a bit strange to us.

2) He lived at the end of a period of European history known as the Renaissance — a time when there were lots of developments in the arts, politics, religion and science. The theatre was very popular at this time.

3) Shakespeare was aware of his audience when writing his plays. A wide range of people went to watch his plays, from the very rich to servants and labourers. Shakespeare tended to include complex imagery and puns for the educated nobles, and slapstick for the uneducated poor.

4) Many people in Shakespeare's Britain believed in the supernatural — people were executed for witchcraft, and superstitious behaviour was common. Several of Shakespeare's plays have supernatural elements, e.g. the Witches in 'Macbeth'. The audience would usually have taken these supernatural characters seriously.

5) Shakespeare was keen to keep the British king or queen of the day happy. His plays often had a royal audience — both Elizabeth I and James I enjoyed performances of his plays.

> *There are many features in 'Macbeth' which could have been included to please King James I. For example, the events following Duncan's murder show the negative consequences for those who try to seize power from the reigning king. James was also obsessed with stamping out witchcraft — Shakespeare's portrayal of the Witches as wholly evil would have pleased the king.*

Learn about **Theatrical Performances** in Shakespeare's time

Knowing a bit about theatrical performances in Shakespeare's time will help you to write top answers about his plays. Here are some of the key features:

1) Only men were allowed to act on stage — all the female roles were played by boys. Shakespeare's comedies include lots of jokes about girls dressing up as boys.

2) Most of the actors wore elaborate costumes that were based on the fashions of when the play was written, and that reflected the status of the character.

3) Musicians helped to create atmosphere in the theatre. They also made sound effects, such as the thunder at the beginning of 'Macbeth'.

4) Plays didn't use much scenery — sets were simple so that they could show different locations in a play, and could be adapted easily to be used for several different plays.

EXAM TIP — **Think about how Shakespeare kept his audience entertained...**
When writing about Shakespeare's plays, remember that he meant them to be performed on stage. Mentioning how a particular method could affect the audience is a great way to pick up marks.

Section Three — Drama

Shakespeare's Language

When you're writing about a Shakespeare play, you need to take a close look at the language, and think about the effect it would have on someone watching the play.

Shakespeare uses lots of Imagery

Shakespeare's imagery includes similes, metaphors and personification.

> *Now does he feel his title*
> *Hang loose about him, like a giant's robe*
> *Upon a dwarfish thief.*
>   'Macbeth' Act 5, Scene 2

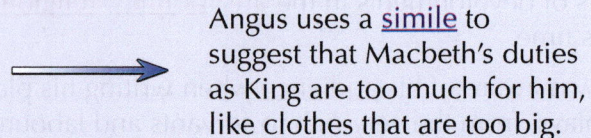

→ Angus uses a simile to suggest that Macbeth's duties as King are too much for him, like clothes that are too big.

> *With as little a web as this will I*
> *ensnare as great a fly as Cassio.*
>   'Othello' Act 2, Scene 1

→ Iago uses a metaphor to compare himself to a spider and Cassio to a fly. This shows how easily he believes he will be able to trap Cassio.

Look out for Striking Words and Phrases

When you read through the text, make a note of any words that jump out at you. Think about why they're important, and what effect they have.

> *If you tickle us, do we not laugh? If you poison us, do*
> *we not die? And if you wrong us, shall we not revenge?*
>   'The Merchant of Venice' Act 3, Scene 1

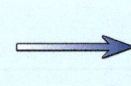

→ Shylock's emotive speech uses rhetorical questions to show that as a Jew he's no different to Christians. The mention of revenge hints at his anger.

> *When the battle's lost and won.*
>   'Macbeth' Act 1, Scene 1

→ The Witches use paradox — this hides their motives from the other characters and the audience, and emphasises that nothing is as it seems.

Humour is also important in Shakespeare's plays

Shakespeare uses lots of puns and jokes. They can help to relieve tension, lighten the mood and highlight key themes.

> *Ask for me tomorrow, and you shall*
> *find me a grave man.*
>   'Romeo and Juliet' Act 3, Scene 1

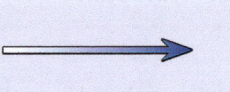

→ Mercutio makes a joke about his own death, playing on the double meaning of "grave" ('serious' and 'a place to put dead bodies').

> **Messenger** *I see, lady, the gentleman*
>   *is not in your books.*
> **Beatrice** *No — an he were, I would*
>   *burn my study.*
>   'Much Ado about Nothing' Act 1, Scene 1

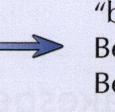

→ Beatrice plays on the meaning of the word "books" — the Messenger means that Benedick is not in Beatrice's favour, but Beatrice deliberately misinterprets him, replying as if he had meant actual books.

Section Three — Drama

Shakespeare's Language

Look at Shakespeare's Verse Forms

1) Shakespeare wrote his plays in a mixture of poetry and prose. You can tell a lot about a character by looking at the way they speak.

2) The majority of Shakespeare's lines are written in blank verse (unrhymed iambic pentameter). Blank verse sounds grander than prose and can be used by almost any characters, but lower-class, comic and mad characters generally don't use it.

A line written using iambic pentameter usually has 10 syllables (five unstressed and five stressed).

> *She loved me for the dangers I had pass'd*
> *And I loved her that she did pity them.*
>   *'Othello' Act 1, Scene 3*

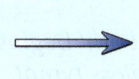

→ Othello is a high-ranking soldier, so it is suitable that he speaks in blank verse. It also sounds formal, which is fitting for making a speech to the Duke.

3) Sometimes Shakespeare uses rhymed iambic pentameter to make speech sound dramatic and impressive, e.g. at the beginning and end of a scene, or when a posh character is speaking.

> *From forth the fatal loins of these two foes*
> *A pair of star-cross'd lovers take their life,*
> *Whose misadventur'd piteous overthrows*
> *Doth with their death bury their parents' strife.*
>   *'Romeo and Juliet' Prologue*

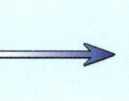

→ The Prologue acts as an introduction to the play, when the audience are told that Romeo and Juliet are doomed to die. The importance of this message is emphasised by the fact that it is in rhymed iambic pentameter.

4) The rest of Shakespeare's writing is in normal prose. Funny bits and dialogue between more minor or lower-class characters are usually written in prose.

> *Come hither, neighbour Seacole. God hath blest you with a good name: to be a well-favoured man is the gift of fortune, but to write and read comes by nature.*
>   *'Much Ado About Nothing' Act 3, Scene 3*

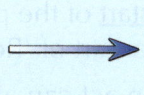

→ Dogberry is a lower-class and comical character. He therefore speaks in prose rather than verse. This makes his speech sound natural and informal.

Look out for switches between Poetry and Prose

1) Check for when characters change between verse and prose. You can tell from the lines — if each new line starts with a capital letter, it's verse, but if it carries on from the last line without a capital, it's prose.

2) The switch can give you clues about a character's state of mind, e.g. Lady Macbeth speaks in prose when she is sleep-walking, which shows her loss of control.

3) You need to quote your play correctly. For prose quotes, just quote as you would from a novel. But if it's verse, and the quote goes over more than one line in the original text, show this using a slash — '/'.

> *The prologue to 'Henry V' is written in blank verse, for example, "A kingdom for a stage, princes to act / And monarchs to behold the swelling scene!".*

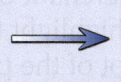

→ This answer uses a quote that's in verse and goes over two lines, so it uses a '/' to show where the line break is in the original text.

Get to grips with the Shakespeare play you're studying...

It's important that you know your Shakespeare text really well. If there are any bits of the play that you don't understand, take the time to reread them carefully and work out what they mean before the exam.

Section Three — Drama

The Structure of Shakespeare's Plays

A text's structure has a big impact on how it's understood. Shakespeare's plays are no different...

Shakespeare **Structured** his plays in **Different Ways**

1) You need to think about the overall structure of your Shakespeare play.

2) Most of Shakespeare's tragedies have a tragic structure. In these plays, the first part builds up to a turning point and the second part deals with the consequences of this.

   → *Mercutio's death in 'Romeo and Juliet' is the play's main turning point. The rest of the play shows the aftermath of this event.*

3) Some of Shakespeare's plays have a cyclical structure. This means they start and end with the same situation or setting.

   → *'Macbeth' begins and finishes with a battle to defeat a merciless tyrant. This shows that the events have come full circle and order is restored at the end of the play.*

4) Some plays feature repetition, with similar images or ideas appearing at different points in the play. This is can create suspense or emphasise important themes.

   → *In 'Othello', the handkerchief is mentioned at several points in the play. It is first used as a symbol of the love between Desdemona and Othello, but later in the play Iago uses it to destroy their relationship, and it becomes a symbol of Othello's jealousy.*

Look at the **Order** of **Scenes** in a play

1) Shakespeare often uses the order of scenes within a play to create particular effects.

   - Some scenes are put near the start of the play to emphasise a key theme — e.g. the fight between the two families at the start of 'Romeo and Juliet' shows how violent the feud is.
   - Putting a scene at the start of an act can also set the mood for the rest the act — e.g. Act 2 of 'Macbeth' has a dark atmosphere after Macbeth goes to murder Duncan at the start of the act.

2) Shakespeare's plays have key scenes and minor scenes. Key scenes are usually about the main plot or characters of the play, whereas minor scenes typically feature less important characters or develop a sub-plot of the play.

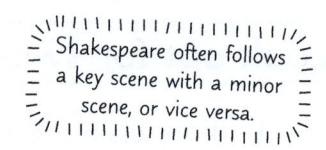

   Shakespeare often follows a key scene with a minor scene, or vice versa.

3) Minor scenes are used to:

   - change the pace — for example, a humorous minor scene coming before or after an emotional key scene can provide light relief for the audience.
   - reflect or contrast different characters, relationships or ideas — e.g. in 'Henry V', Bardolph, Nym and Pistol's petty quarrels and reluctance to fight in the war act as a contrast to Henry's heroism. This highlights Henry's principles and bravery.
   - develop important themes — e.g. in 'The Merchant of Venice', Launcelot's jokes about Jews converting to Christianity highlight the split between Jews and Christians, which is part of the main plot of the play.

REVISION TASK

Work out the structure of your Shakespeare play...

Make a graph of your play's structure. Draw a line that goes up as the tension increases and down as it lessens. Mark any turning points, key and minor scenes and anything else important.

Section Three — Drama

Warm-Up Questions

Plays come in different shapes and sizes, but the way you study them should be pretty much the same — pay close attention to the play's language, structure and stagecraft and you'll be scoring marks all over the place. These questions should get you in the mood for the exam.
Take a look at the suggested answers on page 111 when you're done.

Warm-Up Questions

1) In one of the plays you have studied, find an example of how the writer uses stage directions to create a specific mood or atmosphere.

2) Write a brief definition of each of the terms below.
   Then, using a set play you have studied, find an example of each term.

   | Monologue | Aside | Soliloquy |

3) Find one example of each of the following dramatic techniques in a play you have studied:
   a) imagery
   b) repetition
   c) the rhythm of a character's words having a powerful effect.

4) Find an example of humour in a Shakespeare play you have studied.
   What effect does it have on the scene?

5) Choose a Shakespeare play you have studied in class. Pick a passage you find particularly effective (e.g. frightening, funny or tense) and write two or three paragraphs explaining how Shakespeare makes it so effective. Hint: think about form, structure and language.

6) Read the following extracts, and then complete the tasks below.

   Don Pedro: My love is thine to teach. Teach it but how,
   And thou shalt see how apt it is to learn
   Any hard lesson that may do thee good.
   Much Ado About Nothing Act 1, Scene 1

   Iago: As I am an honest man I thought you had received some bodily wound; there is more of sense in that than in reputation. Reputation is an idle and most false imposition, oft got without merit and lost without deserving.
   Othello Act 2, Scene 3.

   Prince: A glooming peace this morning with it brings,
   The sun, for sorrow, will not show his head.
   Go hence, to have more talk of these sad things;
   Some shall be pardoned, and some punishèd.
   Romeo and Juliet Act 5, Scene 3

   a) For each extract, write down whether it is in verse, blank verse or prose.
      Write a sentence explaining how you can tell.
   b) What effect do the form and rhyme scheme of the Prince's speech have?

Section Three — Drama

Worked Exam-Style Question

Here's an example of how to write a top-notch essay about a play. Give it a read through, even if you aren't studying 'Macbeth' — it shows you the kind of thing you'll need to include in any exam answer.

1 2 Write about the character of Macbeth and how Shakespeare presents him at different points in 'Macbeth'.

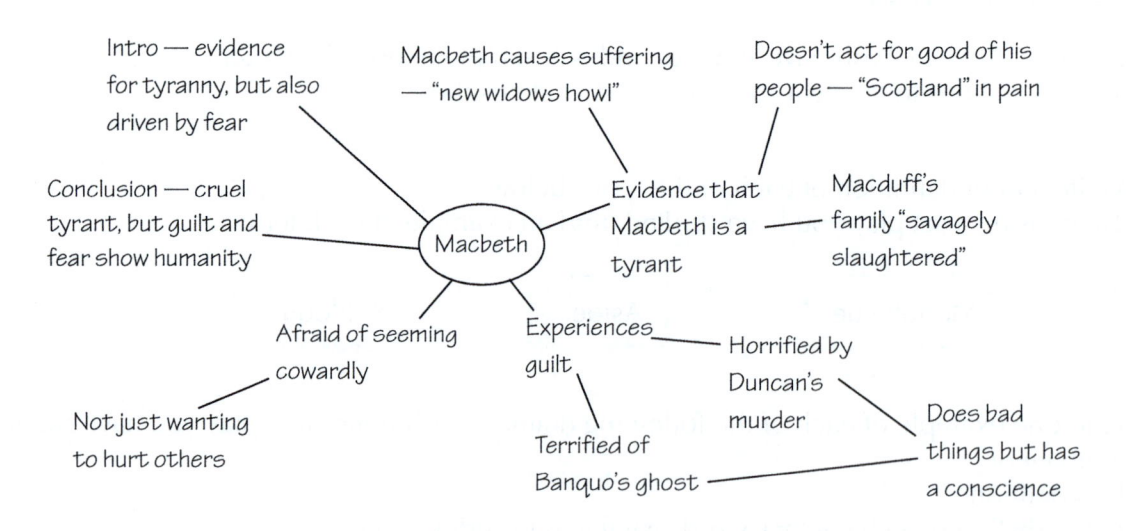

Mind map around central bubble "Macbeth":
- Intro — evidence for tyranny, but also driven by fear
- Macbeth causes suffering — "new widows howl"
- Doesn't act for good of his people — "Scotland" in pain
- Evidence that Macbeth is a tyrant
- Macduff's family "savagely slaughtered"
- Conclusion — cruel tyrant, but guilt and fear show humanity
- Afraid of seeming cowardly
- Not just wanting to hurt others
- Experiences guilt
- Terrified of Banquo's ghost
- Horrified by Duncan's murder
- Does bad things but has a conscience

In 'Macbeth', the character of Macbeth is presented to some extent as a tyrant, killing innocent people to keep his position as king. However, he is also presented as feeling guilty about his bad deeds, and he often acts through fear, suggesting he is not wholly selfish or cruel. He is not simply a cruel tyrant, therefore, but also a flawed character who is easily controlled by his fears.

Outline your argument in the introduction.

In Act Four, Scene Three, Malcolm and Macduff describe Macbeth as a "tyrant" and discuss his cruelty, saying that "Each new morn, / New widows howl, new orphans cry". This shows that Macbeth is causing misery and suffering to his subjects. The repetition of "new" emphasises that the murders are happening regularly. Macbeth seems prepared to go to any length to hold power and is willing to cause suffering to do so. At this point in the play he is therefore presented as a cruel tyrant.

Remember to include quotes, and explain how they support your points.

Shakespeare uses the character of Macduff to show how Scotland as a whole is suffering under Macbeth's rule. Macduff uses personification when describing how heaven "yelled" in pain "As if it felt with Scotland". The word "with" implies that Scotland is also able to feel pain and sadness. This emphasises how the whole country is being oppressed by Macbeth. Macbeth is clearly causing distress rather than acting for the good of the country he rules, reinforcing the reader's impression of him as a tyrannical ruler.

Naming the technique the writer uses will impress the examiner.

Section Three — Drama

Worked Exam-Style Question

Try to pick out the examples that illustrate your point best, rather than just listing the events of the play.

The most clear-cut example of Macbeth's tyranny is when he hires two murderers to ensure that Macduff's wife and children are "Savagely slaughtered", because the witches' apparition warns him to "beware Macduff". The alliteration of "Savagely slaughtered" gives the phrase a harsh tone that makes the murders seem especially aggressive and cruel, suggesting that Macbeth's decision to have them killed was inhumane. This shows how far he is driven by his selfish desire to be king and by his need to destroy any threat to his power.

However, although some of the acts that Macbeth commits are undoubtedly tyrannical, Shakespeare also presents Macbeth as being deeply troubled by what he has done. After murdering Duncan, it is clear that Macbeth feels very guilty. He says "Methought I heard a voice cry, 'Sleep no more! / Macbeth does murder sleep,' the innocent sleep". His rambling speech, with its repetition of "sleep", shows that he is confused, upset and plagued by guilt. The theme of hallucination and imagination, shown here in the voice Macbeth hears, recurs throughout the play, usually as a sign of his troubled conscience. For example, after having Banquo murdered, Macbeth sees his ghost at the banquet, showing that he is horrified at what he has done. Macbeth's regret suggests that he is not entirely a cruel tyrant.

Think carefully about why characters act they way they do.

Furthermore, as a brave man, unused to feeling fear, Macbeth is frightened of being thought weak, cowardly or unmanly. It is this fear, at least in part, that drives him to acts of tyranny, rather than just a desire to hurt others. At first, this is because Lady Macbeth questions his bravery and manliness, and later because he questions it himself, and feels the need to prove himself. When Macbeth is killed, the audience feels a mixture of relief, pity and regret. If he was purely a tyrant, his death would come as a relief, so the audience's reaction at this point demonstrates that his character is more complex than this.

In summary, Macbeth is presented as behaving in a cruel and tyrannical way. However, his guilt about his acts of tyranny and the fact that he is driven to some of these acts through fear show that he is not a straightforward cruel tyrant. Instead, he is presented as a complicated character, driven by a mixture of motives that are not always cruel or oppressive in their nature. These things together show that, ultimately, Macbeth is merely very human.

Good analysis of how the writer uses language to achieve an effect.

Keep referring back to the question to make sure you stay focused.

It's great to show that you've thought about the broader themes of the play.

This is a good personal response to the play.

Write a strong, memorable conclusion to sum up your argument.

Section Three — Drama

Worked Exam-Style Question

This is an example answer to a question on a modern play — it's got some good tips on writing about modern drama, even if you're not studying 'An Inspector Calls', so give it a good read.

---

0 1   Read Act Three, from "Inspector [*taking charge, masterfully*]: Stop!" to "...in fire and blood and anguish. Good night."

Using this part of the play as a starting point, write about the presentation of the Inspector and the ways in which he is important to the play as a whole.

In your answer, make sure you:

- write about both the extract below and the play as a whole;
- show that you understand the events and characters in the play.

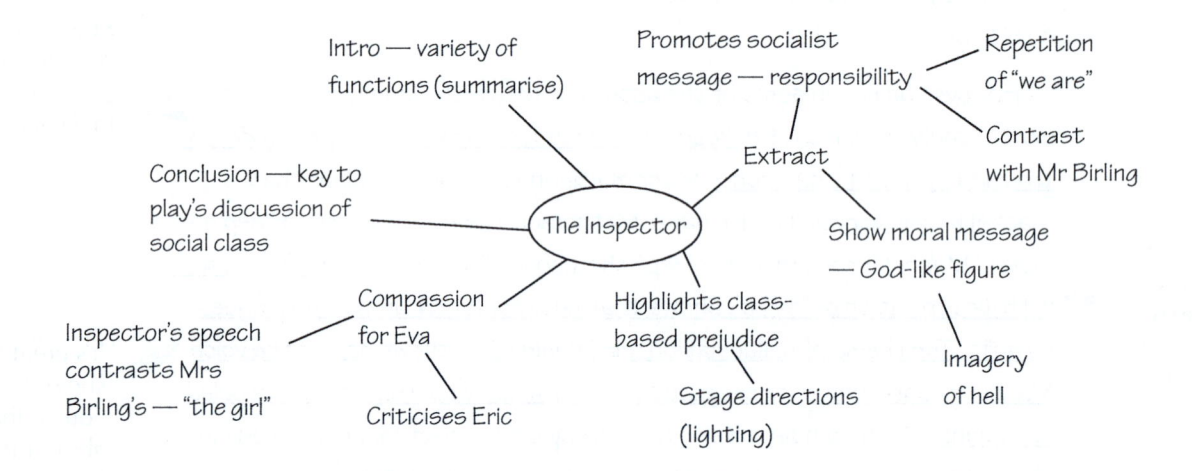

Mind map — The Inspector

- Intro — variety of functions (summarise)
- Promotes socialist message — responsibility
- Repetition of "we are"
- Contrast with Mr Birling
- Show moral message — God-like figure
- Imagery of hell
- Stage directions (lighting)
- Highlights class-based prejudice
- Criticises Eric
- Compassion for Eva
- Inspector's speech contrasts Mrs Birling's — "the girl"
- Conclusion — key to play's discussion of social class

<u>The Inspector in 'An Inspector Calls' serves a variety of important functions within the play.</u> He highlights the importance of people taking responsibility for one another, and serves as an all seeing, God-like figure, giving the impression that those who do not take responsibility for their crimes will be punished. He also makes the Birlings recognise their faults and the consequences of their actions. <u>Priestley presents these aspects of the Inspector's role through the use of repetition, contrasts, imagery and stage directions, especially lighting.</u>

> *Makes sure you address the question in your introduction.*

One important function of the Inspector is to promote Priestley's <u>socialist message: that we should all take responsibility for one another</u>. This is shown in the extract when the Inspector says "We are members of one body. We are responsible for each other". <u>The repetition of "We are" includes both the other characters and the audience, making it clear that this is how everyone should behave.</u> This contrasts directly with Birling's belief earlier in the play that a man has to "look after himself and his own". The difference in the two characters' views highlights the selfishness and cruelty of some middle class attitudes at the time.

> *It's impressive if you can show you understand the play's overall message.*

> *This is a good analysis of the writer's technique.*

Section Three — Drama

Worked Exam-Style Question

In the extract, the Inspector's language also has an almost God-like quality, suggesting that his main role is as a dramatic device to promote a moral message. He states that if people do not take responsibility for others, then they will learn to do so in "fire and blood and anguish". <u>This imagery is reminiscent of Hell, implying that the suffering experienced will be particularly painful, and portraying the Inspector as a God-like figure who can judge others. As the Inspector's language in this speech is out of keeping with the rest of his language in the play</u>, it is implied that the audience is supposed to view him as a dramatic device, rather than a convincing character. In this way Priestley uses the Inspector as a vessel for his own views, and as an important tool to represent the main moral of the play.

<u>Another important function of the Inspector</u> is to highlight problems within the Birling family and, by extension, within the class-obsessed social system of the early twentieth century. <u>This is illustrated by the stage directions when the Inspector arrives at the start of the play</u>, when the lighting changes from "pink and intimate" to "brighter and harder". This suggests that the Inspector will shine a light on the true nature of the Birling family, shattering their illusion of the 'perfect' family and forcing them to 'see' things more clearly. This includes the reality of how their actions have affected other, less fortunate people.

Priestley also uses the Inspector as a contrasting figure to the Birlings, which helps him to show how wrong class-based prejudice is. The Inspector shows compassion for Eva Smith, criticising Eric for treating her "as if she was an animal, a thing, not a person". <u>In contrast, most of the other characters do not show any kindness towards Eva because she is of a lower class.</u> For instance, Mrs Birling repeatedly refers to her as "the girl", as if she cannot bear to mention her name or as if she does not matter as a person. The contrast in the way Mrs Birling and the Inspector talk about Eva, and the Inspector's insistence on treating Eva as a person, makes Mrs Birling appear narrow minded and shows the audience that it is wrong to look down on the working classes.

In conclusion, the character of the Inspector is used by Priestley to show the class-based prejudice of other characters. <u>His primary function as a dramatic device allows him to present Priestley's socialist viewpoint, and the God-like language in his final speech shows that he is used by Priestley to express the play's key messages. Priestley's use of stage directions also shows the Inspector's pivotal role in highlighting the Birling family's flaws, and his compassion contrasts with their unkindness.</u> This gives him a very important role in terms of the play's discussion of social class.

Side notes:

- Comparing different parts of the play shows you understand it as a whole.
- This shows an awareness of the effects of different techniques.
- Make sure you keep linking back to the question.
- Don't forget to consider the writer's stagecraft.
- This uses other characters in the play to make a point about the Inspector's character.
- Summarise your main points in your conclusion.

Section Three — Drama

Exam-Style Questions

Now that you've revised drama, have a go at these practice exam questions. You don't have to answer them all, but you'll find it useful to at least write a plan for any that are relevant to your set plays.

Q1 Read **one** of the following extracts, then answer the question below:

- The prologue of 'Romeo and Juliet'
- Act 1 Scene 3 of 'Macbeth', from "Glamis, and Thane of Cawdor..." to "...Commencing in a truth?"
- Act 5 Scene 2 of 'Othello', from "Behold, I have a weapon..." to "[*Wounds Iago*]"

Write about how an audience would respond to this extract, referring to examples from the extract in your response.

Q2 Using evidence from the text, write about Shakespeare's use of comedy in **either** 'The Merchant of Venice' **or** 'Much Ado About Nothing'.

Q3 Choose an extract from a modern (post-1914) play you have studied.

Using this part of the play as a starting point, explore how **either** gender **or** growing up is presented in the play as a whole.

Q4 Write about the theme of conflict in **either** 'Macbeth' **or** 'Henry V'.
In your response, you should focus on how Shakespeare presents characters and events.

Q5 Choose an extract from a modern (post-1914) play you have studied in which the writer presents the relationship between two central characters.

Using this part of the play as a starting point, write about how the relationship between these characters changes during the course of the play.

Section Three — Drama

Section Four — Prose

Writing About Prose

You'll have to study a 19th-century prose text for your course, and you might study a modern prose text too.

You might have to write about two different types of Prose

1) For Paper 2, Section A, you might have to study some modern prose — the texts you might study are:

   - Lord of the Flies by William Golding
   - The Woman in Black by Susan Hill
   - Anita and Me by Meera Syal
   - Never Let Me Go by Kazuo Ishiguro
   - Oranges are not the Only Fruit by Jeanette Winterson

   If you're not studying a modern prose text, you'll study a modern play instead — see Section Three (p.26-42) for more on writing about drama.

2) For Paper 2, Section B, you'll have to study one of these prose texts from the 19th century:

   - The Strange Case of Dr Jekyll and Mr Hyde by Robert Louis Stevenson
   - A Christmas Carol by Charles Dickens
   - Silas Marner by George Eliot
   - Jane Eyre by Charlotte Brontë
   - War of the Worlds by H.G. Wells
   - Pride and Prejudice by Jane Austen

Structure has an impact on a text

1) Writers work hard to present and communicate their ideas effectively. Your challenge is to work out why they've structured their novel in a certain way and what the effect of their decisions is.

2) Different structures can have different effects on the reader.

   - Texts can be split into chapters or sections. This can create cliffhangers or switch the focus of the plot.

     'Jane Eyre' is divided into three separate volumes — original readers of the book had to buy each volume separately. Brontë used cliffhangers at the end of the first two volumes, which would have encouraged readers to buy the next volume.

   - Think about how the novel starts and ends, and what the impact of this may be on the reader.

     'Never Let Me Go' opens with the narrator, Kathy, talking about her present-day situation. Kathy assumes the reader already knows about "donors" and "Hailsham", but these haven't yet been explained. This has a jarring effect for the reader, encouraging them to keep reading to find out what's going on.

   - Some plots move forwards chronologically (in time order). Others are non-chronological.

     'A Christmas Carol' includes three episodes set in different time periods, each of which jumps between different times and places. This gives them a dreamlike quality.

   - The novel may have one main plot, or several plots that link together.

     'Pride and Prejudice' has several different stories which interlink. The revelations about Wickham, the romance between Bingley and Jane, and Mr Collins' search for a wife all make the novel more interesting. They also allow Austen to further explore themes such as social class and gender.

Writing About Prose

Writers sometimes use Structural Devices

For more on flashbacks and foreshadowing, see page 20.

1) The author may use structural devices such as flashbacks, foreshadowing and different narrative structures.
2) A frame narrative is an overarching story that contains other stories within it.

> 'The Woman in Black' has a frame narrative — the first chapter is set after the events in the main body of the novel, and shows us Arthur looking back on the past. His behaviour in this scene is not fully explained until the last chapter of the novel. This structure allows Hill to build and maintain suspense until the very end.

3) An embedded narrative is a story that is within a frame narrative.

> 'Dr Jekyll and Mr Hyde' has several embedded narratives in the form of written documents (Lanyon's letter, Jekyll's statement) and testimonies from characters. These make the story appear more authentic and make the reader curious — each narrative adds more evidence as the reader starts to form a picture of who Mr Hyde is.

Comment on the writer's choice of Language

1) Authors love using descriptive language, including similes, metaphors and personification.

> "bloodthirsty snarling"
> "the tearing of teeth and claws"
> → In 'Lord of the Flies', Golding uses animal imagery to describe the boys, showing that they are becoming more savage.

2) Particularly keep an eye out for any language or imagery that's repeated — there's usually a reason for this.

> "he locked the note into his safe"
> "he turned to examine the door in the by-street. It was locked"
> → In 'Dr Jekyll and Mr Hyde', there are numerous images of locked doors. These are used to symbolise secrecy, and the way that humans try to hide their dual nature.

3) The language used by characters is also really important. For example:

> "Yow can come with uz, right, but don't say nothin'"
> → In 'Anita and Me', Meena uses Midlands dialect words, slang and non-standard grammar to try to fit in and impress Anita.

Characters' Thoughts are often described

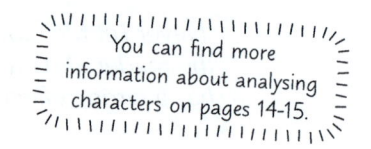

You can find more information about analysing characters on pages 14-15.

1) Novels give descriptions of characters' thoughts and behaviour.
2) Look out for those bits, quote them, and comment on how they help answer the question.

> The head, he thought, appeared to agree with him. Run away, said the head silently...
> → The narrator of 'Lord of the Flies' describes Simon's thoughts and imagined conversation with the pig's head. This allows the reader to experience Simon's hallucinations.

Don't be afraid to be original...

When it comes to language and structure, there are no wrong points (as long as you have evidence to back them up). If you think of something original about a text, remember it in case you can use it in the exam.

Section Four — Prose

Analysing Narrators

The narrator is the person telling the story — they are the link between the reader and the plot.

There are **Different Types** of **Narrator**

1) All prose texts have a narrator — a voice that's telling the story.

2) A first-person narrator is a character who tells the story from their perspective, e.g. Jane narrates 'Jane Eyre' and Kathy narrates 'Never Let Me Go'. You get a first-hand description of exactly what the character sees, does and thinks all the way through the story.

> *What a consternation of soul was mine that dreary afternoon! How all my brain was in tumult, and all my heart in insurrection!*
>
> → In 'Jane Eyre', Jane's narration is very personal and appeals to the reader's emotions. This helps the reader to empathise with her.

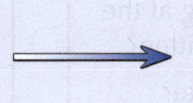

3) A third-person narrator is a separate voice, created by the author to tell the story — this type of narrator is used in 'A Christmas Carol' and 'Pride and Prejudice'. They usually describe the thoughts and feelings of several different characters, making them more of a storyteller than a character.

4) Third-person narrators can be omniscient (all-knowing) or limited (only aware of the thoughts and feelings of one character).

> *To Catherine and Lydia, neither the letter nor its writer were in any degree interesting.*
>
> → The omniscient, third-person narrator of 'Pride and Prejudice' gives the reader an insight into the thoughts of many of the characters, even though the story follows Elizabeth most closely.

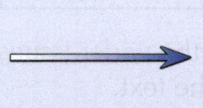

Not all narrators are **Reliable**

1) Don't automatically trust what a narrator says — they may be unreliable. This is particularly common with first-person narrators, who see things from their own point of view.

> *I have recorded in detail the events of my insignificant existence...*
>
> → The first-person narrator of 'Jane Eyre' calls herself "insignificant", but the fact that she's the main character in the book suggests this isn't true.

2) The narrator is not the same person as the author, but watch out for examples of the writer's viewpoint being revealed through the narrator. For example:

> *Scrooge! a squeezing, wrenching, grasping, scraping, clutching, covetous old sinner!*
>
> → The third-person narrator of 'A Christmas Carol' has strong opinions on Scrooge, which seem to be Dickens's views.

EXAM TIP — The narrator and the writer are not the same person...
In the exam, keep in mind that what the narrator thinks isn't necessarily the same as what the writer thinks. Refer to how the writer uses the narrator, rather than just what the narrator says.

19th-Century Context

Texts are influenced by the time and place they're written and set in, as well as by the person who wrote them. There are marks in the exam for writing about these influences on the 19th-century text you study.

Texts are shaped by the Context they were written in

1) Think about the setting of the text and what was happening when it was written.
2) Here are a few questions you should ask yourself when thinking about context:

Where is the text set?
Did the writer base the setting on their own experiences?

When was the text written?
- What was happening at the time the text was written?
- What was society like?

When does the story take place?
Did the writer base the story in the time in which they lived or a different time?

What do you know about the writer?
- Where is the writer from?
- What is their background?

What genre is the text part of?
- Is the text part of a literary movement?
- Was the writer influenced by other texts?

Show you're aware of the Issues the text raises

1) You need to show the examiner that you're aware of the wider issues raised by the text, and comment on how these issues are portrayed in the text.
2) Here are some of the issues that you should look out for:

Social or cultural issues
Authors often comment on the society they're living in, particularly the faults they associate with it. → 'Jane Eyre' challenges 19th-century attitudes towards gender by portraying Jane as independent and strong-willed.

Historical or political issues
Writers may comment on a particular historical situation or political issue. → In 'The War of the Worlds', the Martian invasion is an allegory for the brutality of European empires in the 19th century.

Moral issues
Sometimes a text aims to challenge the reader with a moral message. → 'A Christmas Carol' promotes the idea of social responsibility, especially the need for wealthy people to support people who are poorer than them.

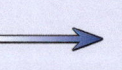

Philosophical issues
Some writers explore a philosophical question through their texts. → In 'Dr Jekyll and Mr Hyde', Stevenson raises questions about the nature of evil.

Reactions to texts can change over time...
When writing about context, think about whether attitudes toward certain issues have changed over time. The original audience of a text may have viewed a text very differently to how an audience would today.

Section Four — Prose

19th-Century Context

The next three pages contain some useful background information on 19th-century life. Reading this should help you understand the texts better — and don't forget, there are marks available for context in the exam.

There was a Big Gap between the Upper and Lower Classes

1) Class was important in the 19th century — your class determined what kind of life you had.

2) Early 19th-century society was divided between the rich upper classes (who owned the land, didn't need to work and so socialised a lot) and the poorer working classes (who relied on the upper classes for work, and were often looked down on because of it).

3) The Industrial Revolution created opportunities for more people to make money, meaning that the middle classes grew in size and influence throughout the century.

4) However, the fact that the middle classes relied on a profession or trade for their wealth meant that they were looked down on by the upper classes.

In the Industrial Revolution, technological advances meant that goods could be produced by machines in factories, rather than by hand in people's homes. This resulted in many people moving from working in farming (and living in the countryside) to working in manufacturing (and living in cities).

'Pride and Prejudice' examines and criticises judgements based on social status. Austen mocks 19th-century class prejudices by showing that characters' behaviour is down to personality, not class.

Many cities were Overcrowded and had Terrible Living Conditions

1) In the 19th century, millions of people moved from the countryside to the cities in search of work in the new factories. As a result, the population of cities grew rapidly and uncontrollably.

2) Most of these people ended up living in slums of cheap, overcrowded housing. There was often no proper drainage or sewage system, and many families had to share one tap and toilet. Overcrowding led to hunger, disease and crime.

Dickens uses 'A Christmas Carol' to highlight the problems and poverty of working-class London. He contrasts the wealth of Scrooge with the poverty of the Cratchit family.

Women were often Dependent on men

1) During the 19th century, women were normally dependent on the men in their family, especially in the upper classes. It was usually men who earned a living or owned land which generated income from rent.

2) Boys' education was more of a priority, and many girls weren't educated at all. An academic education was seen as unnecessary for women — girls from rich families were taught art, music and dance as this would help them to get a husband, and girls from poorer families were expected to go straight into a job that didn't require an education.

3) A woman's best chance of a stable future was a good marriage — there were very few job options available for upper and middle-class women, and women often weren't allowed to inherit land or money.

4) Women didn't have the vote, and generally had to do what their husband told them — they were expected to stay at home and look after children.

'Jane Eyre' was unusual at the time of publication not only because it was written by a woman, but also because its main character is a determined and sometimes outspoken woman. By the end of the novel, Jane is both emotionally and financially independent.

Section Four — Prose

19th-Century Context

Reputation was important

1) For the middle and upper classes, it was important to be respectable. They were expected to have strong morals, keep their emotions under strict control and hide their desire for things like sex and alcohol.

2) If someone was seen doing anything which wasn't considered respectable, their reputation could be ruined. To protect their reputation, people often kept their sinful behaviour and desires secret.

> The gentlemen in 'Jekyll and Hyde' are concerned with their reputations. Jekyll creates Hyde in order to hide his sins and preserve his reputation, and Utterson consistently tries to protect Jekyll's reputation. The book explores how this obsession with reputation can actually be destructive.

Victorian society was very Religious

1) Christianity strongly influenced life in Victorian Britain. To be good Christians, many people believed they should live by a strict moral code — for example, attending church regularly and working hard.

2) However, others believed that being a good Christian meant being charitable and forgiving.

> At the end of 'A Christmas Carol', Scrooge resolves to "honour Christmas" and to continue his generosity and goodwill "all the year". This appears to be Dickens's view of being a good Christian.

Darwin's theory of Evolution was Controversial

1) In the early 1800s, Christianity taught that God created every species to be perfectly adapted to its environment, and that humans were made in God's image, different from animals and ruling over them.

2) In contrast, some scientists, including Charles Darwin, claimed that all creatures evolved from common ancestors through a process called 'natural selection'.

3) Darwin also claimed that humans shared a common ancestor with apes. This went against the Christian idea that man's nature was different from that of other animals. People found this unsettling because it means there may be an animalistic side to everyone, capable of uncivilised acts and violent crimes.

> In 'Dr Jekyll and Mr Hyde', Hyde is described as the "animal within" Jekyll, and Poole says he is "like a monkey". Stevenson may be hinting that Hyde is a less evolved version of Jekyll.

Many texts were influenced by the Gothic genre or by Realism

1) Many 19th-century writers were influenced by the Gothic genre — this generally involved a mysterious location, supernatural elements, troubling secrets and elements of madness.

2) Some writers were more interested in Realism. They tried to accurately portray the lives of ordinary people in their writing.

> In 'Silas Marner', Eliot includes Warwickshire dialect words to show how characters would really speak.

Make sure you understand the text's context...

REVISION TASK Make a list of relevant context points for the 19th-century prose text you've studied (use these pages to get you started). Then jot down a sentence explaining why each point is relevant to the text.

Section Four — Prose

Warm-Up Questions

When you're writing an exam answer about prose texts, always think about the language, the structure and the issues raised in the texts. You also need to remember to focus on the detail and to choose your quotes wisely. Start with the questions on this page, and the exam questions on p.54 should be no problem at all.

Warm-Up Questions

1) Choose a prose text that you have studied. Open it at the first page and read the opening paragraph. Write down three things that you notice about the way the author has written the paragraph.

2) Using a prose text you have studied in class, find a passage that uses descriptive language to set the scene. Write a short paragraph explaining how the writer makes this description vivid. (Hint: think about their use of imagery, interesting vocabulary and appeals to the senses.)

3) Think about a central character in one of the prose texts you have studied, and write a short paragraph for each of the following questions.
   a) Why is this character important to the novel?
   b) Do you sympathise with this character? Why or why not?
   c) How does this character change over the course of the text?

4) Choose a prose text you have studied. Does the text have a first-person or third-person narrator? Write a short paragraph about the effect this narrator has on the text.

5) Read the passage below from Chapter 47 of 'Pride and Prejudice'.
   a) Make a list of all of the words and phrases that are about reputation.
   b) Using your list from part a), write a short paragraph about the importance of reputation for women in 19th-century Britain.

> "This is a most unfortunate affair, and will probably be much talked of. But we must stem the tide of malice, and pour into the wounded bosoms of each other the balm of sisterly consolation."
> Then, perceiving in Elizabeth no inclination of replying, she added, "Unhappy as the event must be for Lydia, we may draw from it this useful lesson: that loss of virtue in a female is irretrievable; that one false step involves her in endless ruin; that her reputation is no less brittle than it is beautiful; and that she cannot be too much guarded in her behaviour towards the undeserving of the other sex."

Section Four — Prose

Worked Exam-Style Question

Take a look at this worked answer for an essay about 'A Christmas Carol'. It will give you some ideas for how to structure your own answers, as well as the sort of points you could include.

0 1 Read the extract from Chapter 1 of 'A Christmas Carol' which begins "At this festive season of the year, Mr. Scrooge..." and ends "Good afternoon, gentlemen!", then answer the question.

Using this part of the novel as a starting point, write about how Dickens presents Scrooge.

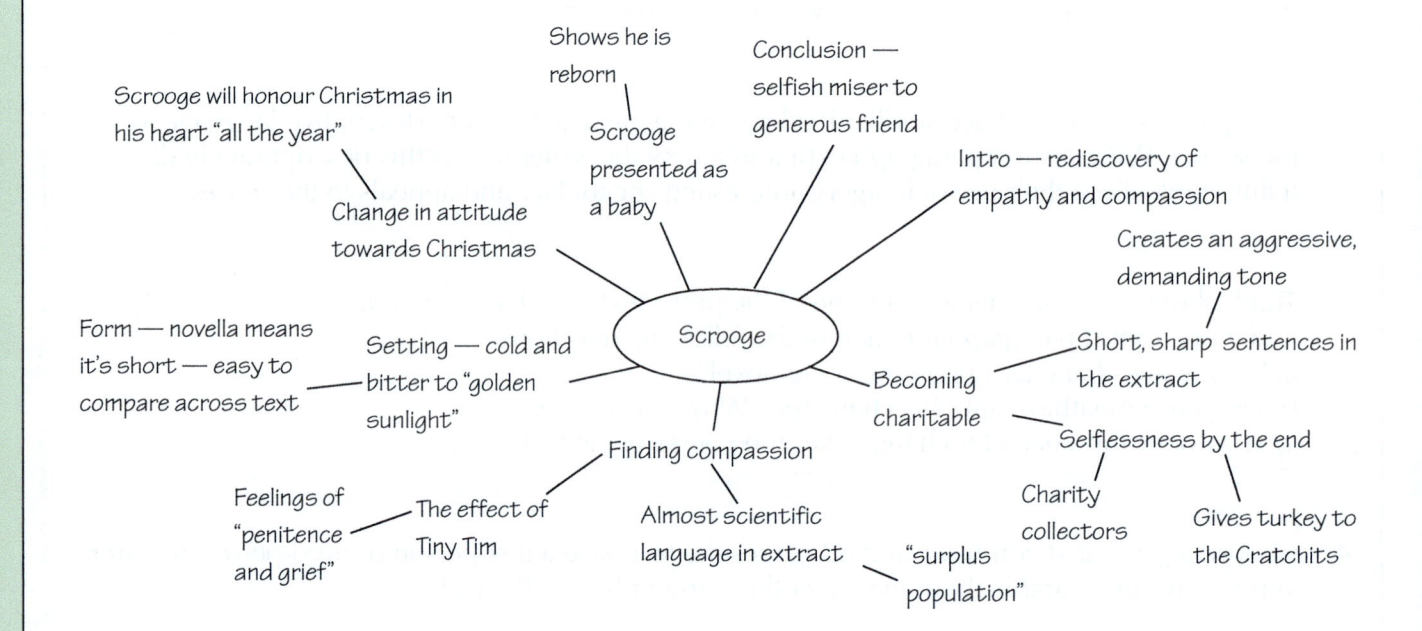

Mind map around "Scrooge":
- Scrooge will honour Christmas in his heart "all the year"
- Change in attitude towards Christmas
- Shows he is reborn
- Scrooge presented as a baby
- Conclusion — selfish miser to generous friend
- Intro — rediscovery of empathy and compassion
- Creates an aggressive, demanding tone
- Short, sharp sentences in the extract
- Becoming charitable
- Selflessness by the end
- Charity collectors
- Gives turkey to the Cratchits
- "surplus population"
- Almost scientific language in extract
- Finding compassion
- The effect of Tiny Tim
- Feelings of "penitence and grief"
- Setting — cold and bitter to "golden sunlight"
- Form — novella means it's short — easy to compare across text

Charles Dickens's 'A Christmas Carol' presents Scrooge as a character who transforms during the novel. The text's structure follows Scrooge as he undergoes a fundamental change of character, rediscovering empathy, compassion and human emotion. He is transformed from a "covetous, old sinner" into someone who keeps the Christmas spirit "all the year". <u>This change is emphasised through Dickens's use of language, setting and structure, as well as how he presents Scrooge's attitude towards Christmas.</u>

The question asks <u>how</u> Scrooge is presented — refer to the <u>techniques</u> Dickens uses to do this.

One of the most obvious changes in Scrooge is his discovery of charity. <u>His conversation with the charity collectors in the extract highlights his selfishness and greed.</u> When asked to make a "slight provision" to help the poor, he responds with a series of short, sharp questions. These give his speech an aggressive and demanding tone, which highlights his lack of sympathy for other people. <u>However, after the visitation of the three ghosts, Scrooge makes active choices to share his wealth, such as making a generous donation to the charity collectors</u> and buying a "prize Turkey" for Bob and his family. The fact that Scrooge sends the turkey anonymously shows that he doesn't expect anything in return, emphasising his newfound selflessness.

Comparing Scrooge in different parts of the novel helps to show how he's presented overall.

It's important to write about the extract given in the question.

Section Four — Prose

Worked Exam-Style Question

Use <u>quotes</u> from the <u>extract</u> in your answer.

Scrooge is presented as uncompassionate towards the poor in the extract, saying that if the poor would rather die than go to the workhouses then they should "do it" and <u>"decrease the surplus population". Dickens's use of cold, almost scientific language shows how cold-hearted and distanced Scrooge is from the poor.</u> However, this attitude changes over the course of the novel. For example, when the Ghost of Christmas Present tells Scrooge that Tiny Tim may die, he repeats Scrooge's exact words. Hearing his own words applied specifically to Bob's son causes Scrooge to feel "penitence and grief", showing that he regrets his earlier lack of compassion, and contrasting his cold-hearted behaviour at the beginning.

This sentence <u>explains</u> the <u>effect</u> that Dickens's language has.

Dickens uses the setting of the text to reinforce the changes in Scrooge's character. In the first chapter, the narrator describes Scrooge as carrying "his own low temperature always about with him", implying that his heart is as cold as the "biting" weather outside. However, by the end of the text the fog and mist have been replaced with "golden sunlight". This change in the weather reflects the change Scrooge has gone through; from a cold-hearted miser to a man of warmth and generosity. By changing elements of the setting for different effects at the start and end of the text, Dickens invites the reader to make a direct comparison across the story about how Scrooge has changed. <u>The text's form makes it even more likely that readers would draw these comparisons, because as a short novel it would often have been read from beginning to end in one sitting.</u>

Don't forget to mention how the <u>form</u> of the text is relevant.

A further change in Scrooge is his attitude to Christmas. In Chapter 1, Scrooge represents solitude and frugality. His repeated shouts of "Humbug" in response to his nephew's festivity show that he denounces Christmas and therefore the values it represents. However, his attitude in the final chapter is a strong contrast: he says that he will honour Christmas in his heart "all the year". By keeping it in his "heart", an organ that is not only associated with love but that is also crucial for life, it suggests that he will make the positive values of Christmas a vital part of who he is. <u>By the end of the nineteenth century, Christmas had come to represent family and feasting</u>; in showing that Scrooge has embraced Christmas, Dickens further emphasises that Scrooge's solitude and frugality have been overcome.

Use <u>context</u> to support your points where possible.

At the end of the text, Dickens presents Scrooge as if he has been reborn. He refers to himself as "quite a baby", and <u>this is emphasised by his enthusiastic language, such as his shouts of "Whoop" and "Hallo", which make him sound young and excited.</u> This emphasis on youth and rebirth shows that Scrooge has changed so much that it is as though he has begun a new life.

When writing about <u>language</u>, make sure you write about the <u>effect</u> it has.

In conclusion, Dickens presents Scrooge as a character on a journey from selfish miser to generous man. <u>Dickens uses language, setting and the structure of the text to show that Scrooge has learnt to be compassionate to the poor, and has fully embraced the Christmas spirit and the values of kindness, charity and family that it represents.</u>

The conclusion should <u>sum up</u> the <u>main points</u> of the answer.

Section Four — Prose

Worked Exam-Style Question

It can be tricky to fit language, structure, form and context into just one answer. Luckily, these pages show how to include all these things in an answer about a modern prose text.

0 1   Read the extract from Chapter 11 of 'Lord of the Flies' which begins "Piggy held up the conch..." and ends "I'm Chief!", then answer the question.

Using this part of the novel as a starting point, write about how Golding presents civilisation and savagery in 'Lord of the Flies'.

In your answer, make sure you:
- write about both the extract and the novel as a whole;
- show that you understand the events and characters in the novel.

Mind map — Civilisation and savagery

- Represents democracy, law etc
- Destroyed — just like civilisation
- Roger's enjoyment — embracing savagery
- Intro — battle between civilisation and savagery, Golding's message
- Civilisation — the conch
- Savagery — taunting and killing Piggy
- Described as weapons — group no longer human
- Conclusion — the conflict represents human nature
- Savagery — acting as a tribe
- Savagery — pig's head
- Wider world parallels — backdrop of war, Golding's beliefs
- Represents evil and the 'beast within'
- Simon's understanding and resulting death — breakdown of civilisation

---

Commenting on the type of novel is a good way to write about form in your answers.

'Lord of the Flies' is an allegorical novel that explores the battle between civilisation and savagery. Throughout the novel, the boys start to lose their sense of civilisation and descend into savagery. The characters, objects and events in the novel act as an allegory for society as a whole, ultimately conveying the author's message that all humans, no matter how civilised, have savagery within them.

It's good to think about how the question relates to the novel's message.

The conch reflects the decline of civilisation in the novel. At first, it is used to summon the boys to meetings, and because only the boy holding it is allowed to speak, it comes to represent democracy and the rules of society. As savagery starts to replace civilisation, the conch begins to lose its power for all of the boys except Piggy and Ralph. This becomes evident in the extract when the other boys' respect for the conch is easily overwhelmed by their newfound savagery: "Piggy held up the conch and the booing sagged a little, then came up again to strength." This hesitation highlights the conflict between this and their more civilised start on the island. The conch is then shattered "into a thousand white fragments" by the same rock that kills Piggy. This marks the end of civilisation on the island. From this point forward, Jack's tribe lose any semblance of civility and even Ralph acts like an animal, obeying "an instinct that he did not know he possessed" to escape, running and hiding from the hunt.

This gives a good introduction to the subject by discussing large-scale points like the conch's role in the novel, before going into more detail.

Think about how objects and characters change through the novel, and what these changes mean.

Section Four — Prose

Worked Exam-Style Question

The killing of Piggy in the extract reflects the complete savagery that has consumed most of the boys. When he releases the rock that kills Piggy, Roger leans "all his weight" on the lever which suggests he has no doubts about killing Piggy. The use of the phrase "delirious abandonment" hints that he is even excited at the prospect of killing Piggy. Roger's implied enjoyment of murder shows a lack of compassion and an embracement of his new savagery.

Don't forget to put in quotes from the extract to support your points.

In the extract, Jack's tribe are made to sound inhuman. They are described as "a solid mass of menace that bristled with spears". This metaphor dehumanises the tribe, suggesting that they are more like weapons than human beings, which emphasises their descent from human civility into savagery. Additionally, Piggy's death is described in a straightforward, unemotional way, with "stuff" coming out of his head which "turned red". This creates a detached tone which highlights the boys' lack of emotion.

You need to think about the language the writer uses and the effect it has.

The pig's head, the Lord of the Flies, represents the savagery and evil inside each human being. The pig's head is most clearly linked to the savagery within humanity when it 'talks' to Simon, telling him that the beast is inside them: "You knew, didn't you? I'm part of you?". Its words foreshadow Simon's death because, when he tries to explain what he has learned to the others, they fear that he is the beast, which drives them to kill him with "teeth and claws". This marks a major turning point in the boys' descent from civilisation to savagery. At the end of the novel, Ralph uses the stick from the Lord of the Flies as a weapon. This shows that civilisation has been completely overcome by savagery, and that even Ralph has become corrupted by the power of evil.

This makes it obvious what the paragraph will be about and gives the answer a clear structure.

Details like this show that you know the text really well and have given it a lot of thought.

The naval officer who rescues the boys at the end of the novel can be seen as an adult representation of the conflict between civilisation and savagery. Despite his smart uniform and politeness, he is still associated with war, which shows the reader that civilisation and savagery are also in conflict in the adult world. Ralph's father also highlights this conflict, as he is portrayed as a caring figure, but is also associated with the war through his job as a "commander in the Navy".

Golding explores the conflict between civilisation and savagery throughout the entire novel. He uses the characters and events in the novel to show how civilisation gives way to savagery, and that anybody can become savage and commit evil acts if the rules of civilisation are removed. In this way, Golding draws parallels with historical events and questions the assumption that people can be fully 'good' or that society can be completely 'civilised'.

Remember to write a brief conclusion to sum up your answer.

Section Four — Prose

Exam-Style Questions

Answering the questions on this page should give you a good chance to practise what you've learned ready for the exam. Whatever text you've studied, there's at least one question for you.

Q1 Read **one** of the following extracts, then answer the question below:

- Chapter 8 of 'Anita and Me', from "It was all falling into place now..." to "...packed up their cases and followed them back here."
- Chapter 1 ('Genesis') of 'Oranges Are Not the Only Fruit', from "My mother and I walked..." to "...chemicals in their sweets."
- Chapter 56 of 'Pride and Prejudice', from "I will not be interrupted..." to "Are the shades of Pemberley to be thus polluted?"

Using this part of the novel as a starting point, explore how prejudice is presented in the novel.

Q2 Choose **one** of the following themes. Starting with one passage from a prose text you have studied, explore how this theme is presented in the extract and the rest of the text.

- marriage and relationships
- power
- reputation
- social class

Q3 Choose a passage from a prose text you have studied which you find particularly frightening. Using this part of the novel as a starting point, explore how the writer creates a sense of fear at different points in the novel.

Q4 Read **one** of the following extracts:

- Chapter 8 of 'Lord of the Flies', from "You are a silly little boy" to the end of the chapter.
- 'Henry Jekyll's Full Statement of the Case' from 'The Strange Case of Dr Jekyll and Mr Hyde', from "I must here speak by theory alone" to "was pure evil".

Using this part of the text as a starting point, explore how the nature of evil is presented in the text.

Q5 Choose a character from a prose text you have studied, then choose one passage in the text which features that character. Using this passage as a starting point, write about the character and the way they are presented at different points in the text.

Section Four — Prose

Section Five — Poetry

Poetry — What You Have To Do

Poetry is an important part of your English Literature GCSE. The next three sections will get you up to speed with what you need to do to write cracking poetry essays.

You'll write about poetry in **Both** of your Literature exams

The poetry aspect of your GCSE English Literature course is divided into two main sections:

1) Poetry anthology (see Section Six) — you'll study a group (or 'anthology') of poems in class. You could be asked about any of the poems from the group you've studied, so you need to know them all well.

2) Unseen poetry (see Section Seven) — in the exam, you have to write about two poems that you've never seen before. You'll get a copy of them in your exam paper and have to analyse them on the spot.

Think about **Language**, **Structure** and **Form**

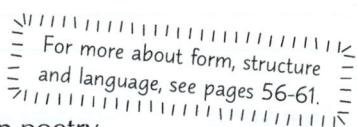

For more about form, structure and language, see pages 56-61.

You should always write about language, structure and form in your answers on poetry.

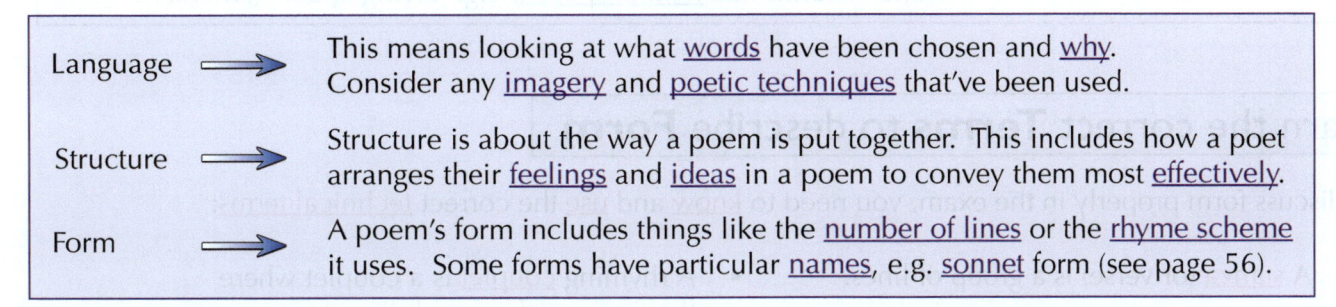

Language →	This means looking at what words have been chosen and why. Consider any imagery and poetic techniques that've been used.
Structure →	Structure is about the way a poem is put together. This includes how a poet arranges their feelings and ideas in a poem to convey them most effectively.
Form →	A poem's form includes things like the number of lines or the rhyme scheme it uses. Some forms have particular names, e.g. sonnet form (see page 56).

You must show you **Appreciate** what the **Poet** is doing

1) Once you've identified points about language, structure and form, think about the effects that these features create.

2) To get the top marks, you need to consider what these effects suggest about the speaker, or how they make the reader feel.

3) You're the reader, so you should include your personal opinion — you can be as creative as you like, as long as you back up your idea with a relevant quote from the poem.

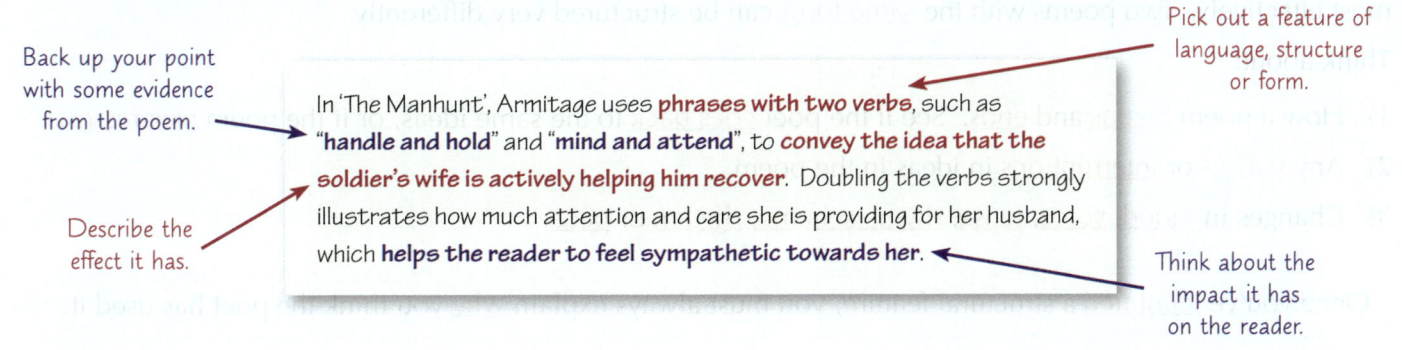

Back up your point with some evidence from the poem.

Pick out a feature of language, structure or form.

In 'The Manhunt', Armitage uses **phrases with two verbs**, such as "**handle and hold**" and "**mind and attend**", to **convey the idea that the soldier's wife is actively helping him recover**. Doubling the verbs strongly illustrates how much attention and care she is providing for her husband, which **helps the reader to feel sympathetic towards her**.

Describe the effect it has.

Think about the impact it has on the reader.

REVISION TIP — **Go over the poem several times to properly understand it...**
Don't be put off if you feel like you don't understand a poem. Go over it a few more times and start to look at language, structure and form — they often give you a clue about the poem's meaning.

Form and Structure

Form and structure are all about the way a poem is put together. Have a look at this page to find out more.

Poetry comes in Different Forms

Different forms (or types) of poems follow different rules. You need to be able to recognise common forms of poetry for your exam.

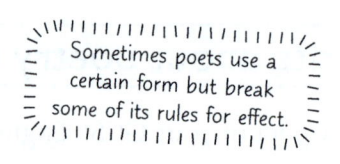

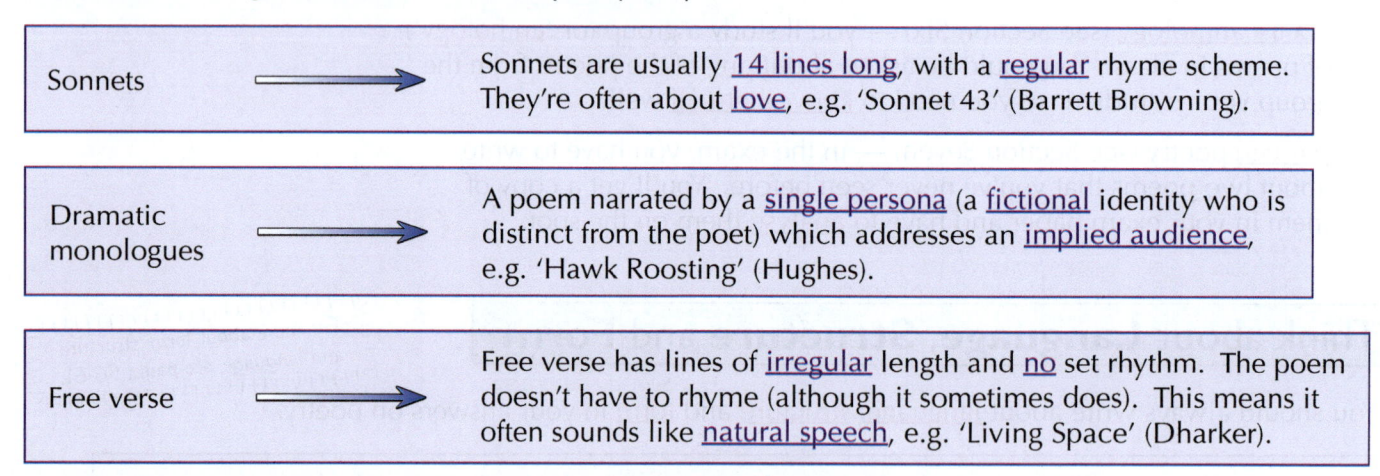

Sometimes poets use a certain form but break some of its rules for effect.

Sonnets →	Sonnets are usually 14 lines long, with a regular rhyme scheme. They're often about love, e.g. 'Sonnet 43' (Barrett Browning).
Dramatic monologues →	A poem narrated by a single persona (a fictional identity who is distinct from the poet) which addresses an implied audience, e.g. 'Hawk Roosting' (Hughes).
Free verse →	Free verse has lines of irregular length and no set rhythm. The poem doesn't have to rhyme (although it sometimes does). This means it often sounds like natural speech, e.g. 'Living Space' (Dharker).

Learn the correct Terms to describe Form

To discuss form properly in the exam, you need to know and use the correct technical terms:

- A stanza (or verse) is a group of lines.
- A tercet is a three-line stanza.
- A quatrain is a four-line stanza.
- A couplet is a pair of lines, usually with the same metre (see p.59).
- A rhyming couplet is a couplet where the final words of each line rhyme.
- A rhyming triplet is where the final words of three successive lines rhyme with each other.

Structure is how a poem is arranged

Structure is how the poet arranges their feelings or ideas in a poem to convey them most effectively. Two poems with the same form can be structured very differently.

Think about:

1) How a poem begins and ends. See if the poet goes back to the same ideas, or if the poem progresses.
2) Any pauses or interruptions in ideas in the poem.
3) Changes in mood, voice, tense, rhyme scheme, rhythm or pace.

Once you've identified a structural feature, you must always explain why you think the poet has used it.

Don't ignore form and structure...

It can be easy to concentrate on language, but you need to write about structure and form as well to get top marks. You can write about any poem's form, even if it's to say that it doesn't have a regular one.

Section Five — Poetry

Poetic Techniques

Poets use lots of techniques to get their message across. Here are the ones you need to know.

A poem's Voice is Who's Speaking and How

1) A poem's voice can affect how the poet's message is conveyed.
2) The narrator might speak in the first person ('I') or the third person ('he' or 'she').
3) A first-person voice gives you one person's perspective. It often makes the poem more personal.

> The use of a first-person voice in Owen's 'Dulce et Decorum Est' allows the narrator to speak personally about the horrors of war. Phrases such as "In all my dreams" show how deeply affected the narrator is by the things that he has witnessed.

4) A third-person voice is often more detached from the action. It can give an outside perspective.

> The third-person narrator of Hardy's 'A Wife in London' acts as an observer. Having a distanced viewpoint means the reader doesn't hear the woman's thoughts, which creates a detached tone. This emphasises the loneliness and anxiety the woman is experiencing.

5) Even though a poem is written in the first person, be careful not to assume that it is the poet speaking. For example, Hughes's 'Hawk Roosting' is written in the first person, but the narrator is a hawk.

Think about who the poem is Addressed To

1) Some poems are written as if the speaker is talking to a specific person — this is called direct address.
2) Direct address can often give the reader hints about the speaker's relationship with another person.

> In 'Valentine', direct address is used to show the personal relationship between the speaker and the person they are addressing. Duffy suggests that there is both certainty and uncertainty in their relationship through the use of the forceful imperative, "Take it", followed by the slight hesitation of "if you like".

Some poems include features of Spoken Language

1) Poems sometimes reproduce spoken language. For example, dialect words can be used to show the narrator's background, emphasise differences between people or reinforce the poet's message. Phonetic spellings show the pronunciation of a word or can be used for emphasis.
2) Some poets use features of spoken language to make the poem more natural and personal.

> In 'Cozy Apologia', Dove uses contractions such as "you'll", and brackets, "(call it blues)", to mimic natural speech and show that the narrator is spontaneously expressing their thoughts. This gives the poem a informal mood, and suggests to the reader that the narrator isn't overly serious.

Section Five — Poetry

Poetic Techniques

Rhyme can add Power to the poet's message

1) Rhyme helps a poem develop its beat or rhythm. Poets can also use it to reinforce the poem's message.
2) Rhyme can be regular (occurring in a set pattern), irregular (with no pattern) or absent from a poem.
3) This creates different effects — regular rhyme schemes can create a sense of control, whereas an irregular rhyme scheme might show chaos or unpredictability. These effects can link to the poem's themes or messages.

> "I met a traveller from an antique land
> Who said: Two vast and trunkless legs of stone
> Stand in the desert ... Near them, on the sand,
> Half sunk, a shattered visage lies, whose frown..."
> ('Ozymandias' — Percy Bysshe Shelley)

→ The poem has a disrupted rhyme scheme, as shown through the half-rhymes "stone" and "frown", and an irregular rhythm. The disorder of the poem mirrors how the statue has been eroded over time, and the collapse of Ozymandias's power.

4) Sometimes rhymes occur within lines, too. These are called internal rhymes.

> "There were dragon-flies, spotted butterflies"
> ('Death of a Naturalist' — Seamus Heaney)

→ The internal rhyme of "dragon-flies" and "butterflies" creates a sense of repetition, which gives the reader the impression that there are many insects in the flax-dam.

Rhythm alters the Pace and Mood of a poem

1) Rhythm is the arrangement of beats within a line. It's easier to feel a rhythm than to see it on the page.
2) Like rhyme, rhythm can be regular or irregular. A strong rhyme scheme often creates a regular rhythm.
3) Rhythm can affect the pace (speed) and mood of a poem — a fast rhythm can make a poem seem rushed and frantic, whereas a slow and regular rhythm can make a poem seem calm.
4) Sometimes poets use rhythm to imitate sounds related to the poem, e.g. a heartbeat or beating drums.

> "In every cry of every Man,
> In every Infant's cry of fear,
> In every voice, in every ban"
> ('London' — William Blake)

→ Blake uses a regular rhythm in these lines to create a steady pace. This imitates the sound of a heartbeat, presenting the city and its people as one living entity.

5) The rhythm often reflects the poem's themes, how the narrator is feeling or the overall message.

> "Behind them, at intervals,
> Stand husbands in skilled trades"
> ('Afternoons' — Philip Larkin)

→ Larkin uses an irregular rhythm which changes every line. This lack of fixed pace could represent his view on the meaninglessness of the subjects' lives.

Section Five — Poetry

Poetic Techniques

Metre is the Pattern of Syllables in a line

A syllable is a single unit of sound, for example, 'beat' has one syllable and 'sonnet' has two syllables.

1) In poetry, the rhythm of a line is created by <u>patterns</u> of <u>syllables</u>. If the patterns are <u>consistent</u>, then the poem's rhythm is <u>regular</u>.

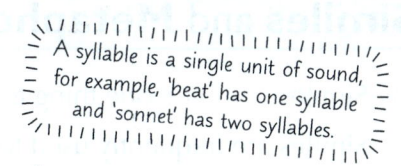

2) <u>Metre</u> is the technical term for these patterns. There are different types of metre, depending on which syllables are <u>stressed</u> (emphasised) and which are <u>unstressed</u>.

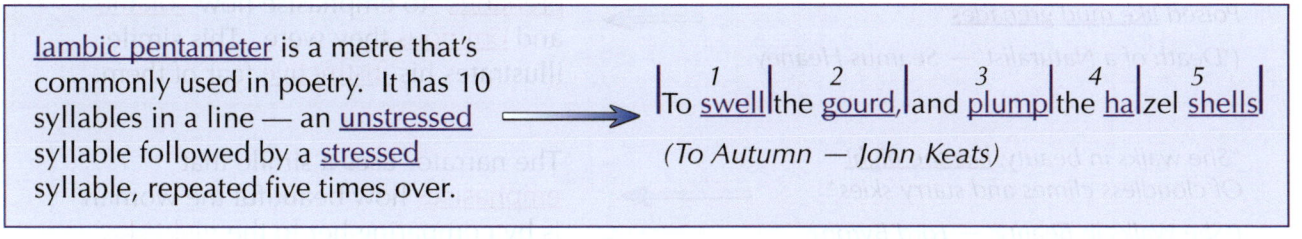

> <u>Iambic pentameter</u> is a metre that's commonly used in poetry. It has 10 syllables in a line — an <u>unstressed</u> syllable followed by a <u>stressed</u> syllable, repeated five times over.
>
> | 1 | 2 | 3 | 4 | 5 |
> |To <u>swell</u>|the <u>gourd</u>,|and <u>plump</u>|the <u>ha</u>zel|<u>shells</u>|
>
> (To Autumn — John Keats)

Punctuation affects how a poem Flows

Punctuation can affect the <u>pace</u> of a poem, emphasise <u>specific words</u>, or <u>interrupt</u> a poem's <u>rhythm</u>.

1) When punctuation creates a <u>pause</u> during a line of poetry, this is called a <u>caesura</u>.

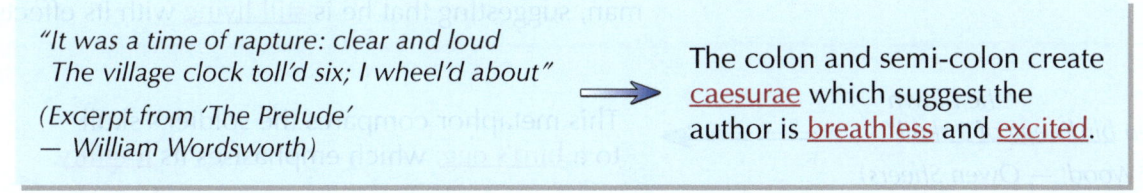

> *"It was a time of rapture: clear and loud*
> *The village clock toll'd six; I wheel'd about"*
>
> (Excerpt from 'The Prelude'
> — William Wordsworth)
>
> → The colon and semi-colon create <u>caesurae</u> which suggest the author is <u>breathless</u> and <u>excited</u>.

2) <u>Enjambment</u> is when a <u>sentence</u> or <u>phrase</u> runs over from <u>one line</u> of poetry into the <u>next one</u>. Often, enjambment puts emphasis on the <u>last word</u> of the first line or on the <u>first word</u> of the next line.

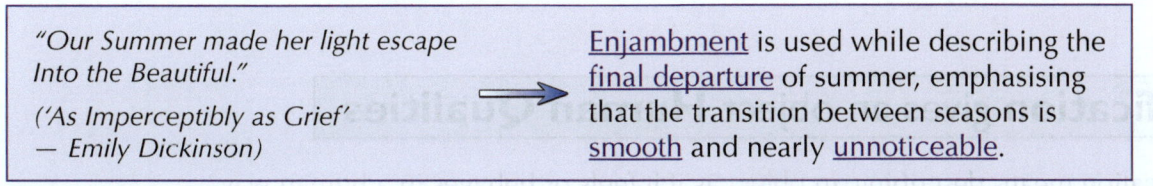

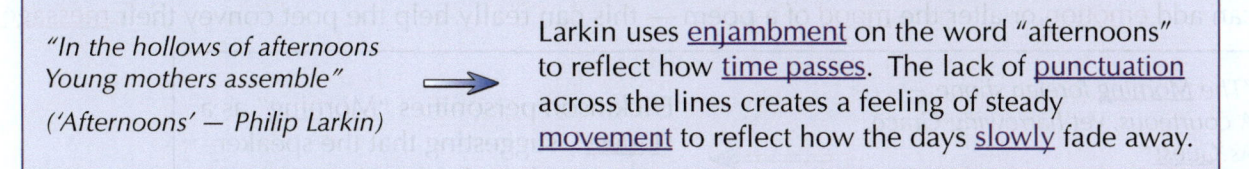

> *"Our Summer made her light escape*
> *Into the Beautiful."*
>
> ('As Imperceptibly as Grief'
> — Emily Dickinson)
>
> → <u>Enjambment</u> is used while describing the <u>final departure</u> of summer, emphasising that the transition between seasons is <u>smooth</u> and nearly <u>unnoticeable</u>.

> *"In the hollows of afternoons*
> *Young mothers assemble"*
>
> ('Afternoons' — Philip Larkin)
>
> → Larkin uses <u>enjambment</u> on the word "afternoons" to reflect how <u>time passes</u>. The lack of <u>punctuation</u> across the lines creates a feeling of steady <u>movement</u> to reflect how the days <u>slowly</u> fade away.

3) An <u>end-stopped line</u> is a line of poetry that ends in a <u>definite pause</u>, usually created by <u>punctuation</u>. End-stopped lines can help to maintain a <u>regular rhythm</u> and can also affect the <u>pace</u> of a poem.

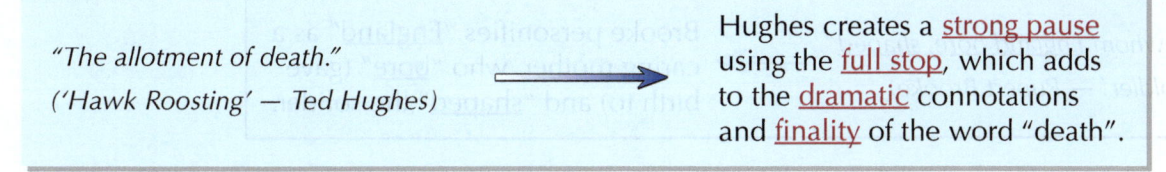

> *"The allotment of death."*
>
> ('Hawk Roosting' — Ted Hughes)
>
> → Hughes creates a <u>strong pause</u> using the <u>full stop</u>, which adds to the <u>dramatic</u> connotations and <u>finality</u> of the word "death".

Section Five — Poetry

Poetic Techniques

Similes and Metaphors add power to Descriptions

1) Similes <u>compare</u> one thing to another — they often contain the words '<u>like</u>' or '<u>as</u>'.
2) Similes are frequently used to <u>exaggerate</u> — the poet usually wants to <u>emphasise</u> something.

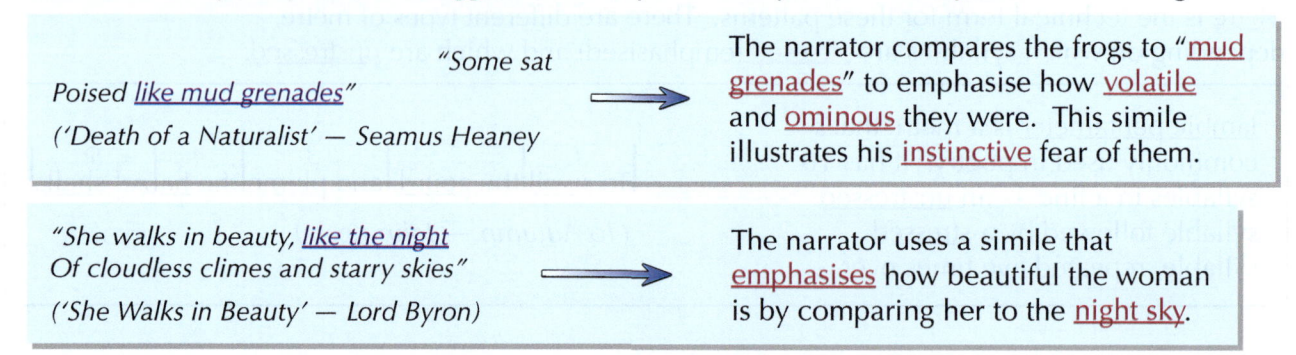

"Some sat
Poised <u>like mud grenades</u>"
('Death of a Naturalist' — Seamus Heaney)

→ The narrator compares the frogs to "<u>mud grenades</u>" to emphasise how <u>volatile</u> and <u>ominous</u> they were. This simile illustrates his <u>instinctive</u> fear of them.

"She walks in beauty, <u>like the night</u>
Of cloudless climes and starry skies"
('She Walks in Beauty' — Lord Byron)

→ The narrator uses a simile that <u>emphasises</u> how beautiful the woman is by comparing her to the <u>night sky</u>.

3) Metaphors describe something as though it <u>is</u> something else.
4) They take an object or person and give it the <u>qualities</u> of something else. This means that the poet can put a lot of <u>meaning</u> into a few words.

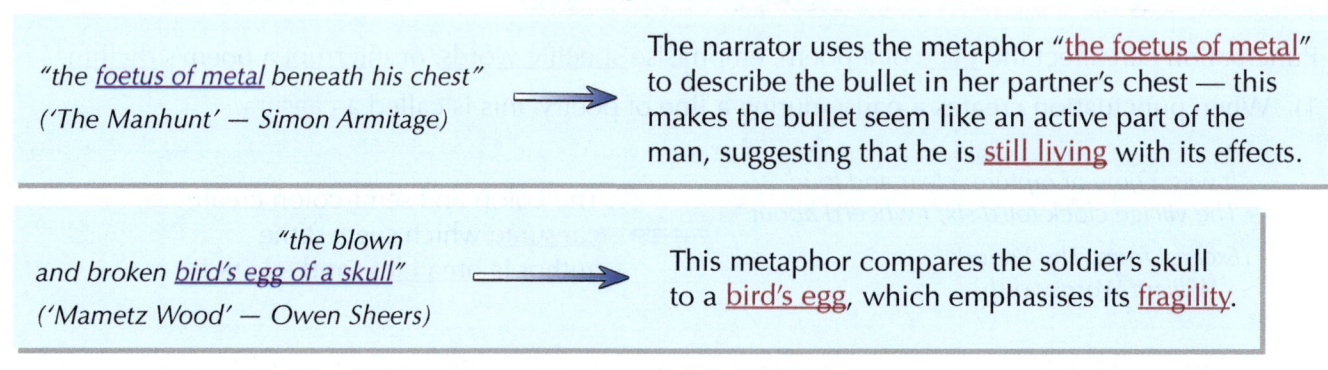

"the <u>foetus of metal</u> beneath his chest"
('The Manhunt' — Simon Armitage)

→ The narrator uses the metaphor "<u>the foetus of metal</u>" to describe the bullet in her partner's chest — this makes the bullet seem like an active part of the man, suggesting that he is <u>still living</u> with its effects.

"the blown
and broken <u>bird's egg of a skull</u>"
('Mametz Wood' — Owen Sheers)

→ This metaphor compares the soldier's skull to a <u>bird's egg</u>, which emphasises its <u>fragility</u>.

Personification gives an object Human Qualities

1) Personification means describing an <u>object</u> as if it feels or behaves in a <u>human way</u>.
2) It can add <u>emotion</u> or alter the <u>mood</u> of a poem — this can really help the poet convey their <u>message</u>.

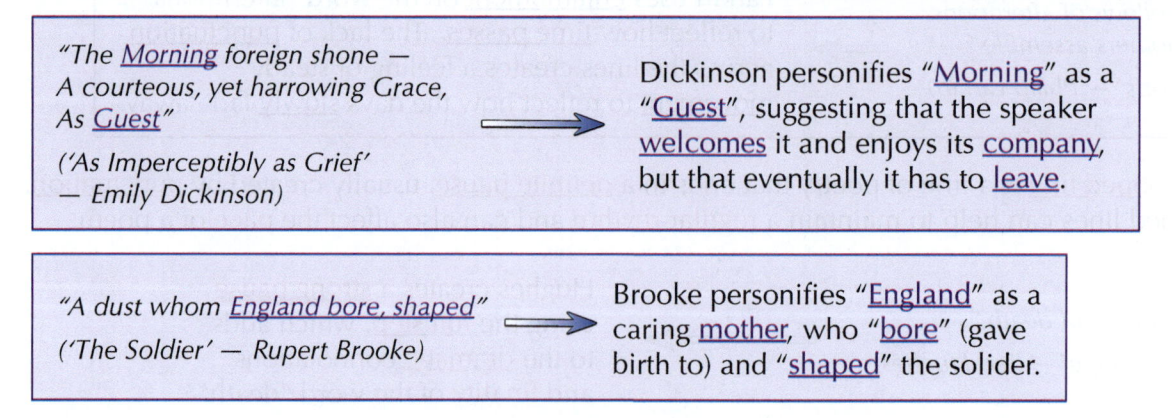

"The <u>Morning</u> foreign shone —
A courteous, yet harrowing Grace,
As <u>Guest</u>"
('As Imperceptibly as Grief'
— Emily Dickinson)

→ Dickinson personifies "<u>Morning</u>" as a "<u>Guest</u>", suggesting that the speaker <u>welcomes</u> it and enjoys its <u>company</u>, but that eventually it has to <u>leave</u>.

"A dust whom <u>England bore, shaped</u>"
('The Soldier' — Rupert Brooke)

→ Brooke personifies "<u>England</u>" as a caring <u>mother</u>, who "<u>bore</u>" (gave birth to) and "<u>shaped</u>" the solider.

Section Five — Poetry

Poetic Techniques

Imagery isn't just visual

1) Poets often appeal to all the senses (touch, sight, sound, smell and taste) — this is called <u>sensory imagery</u>.
2) Sensory imagery helps to create a <u>vivid image</u> in the reader's mind.

"She sits in the <u>tawny vapour</u>"
('A Wife in London' — Thomas Hardy)
→ Hardy uses the <u>sensory</u> imagery of thick, yellow fog enveloping the soldier's wife to create a sense of <u>foreboding</u>. She "sits" <u>motionless</u> in the fog, suggesting that she is <u>powerless</u> in her situation.

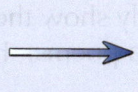

"And full-grown lambs loud <u>bleat</u> from hilly bourn; Hedge-crickets <u>sing</u>; and now with treble soft The red-breast <u>whistles</u> from a garden-croft;"
('To Autumn' — John Keats)
→ Keats highlights the <u>richness</u> of autumn with <u>detailed</u>, <u>sensory</u> descriptions. The focus on <u>animal noises</u> in this stanza completes the picture and allows the <u>reader</u> to <u>imagine</u> themselves on the hillside.

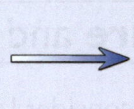

Poets use the Sounds of words for effect

The sounds words create can alter the <u>mood</u>, <u>pace</u> and <u>tone</u> of a poem. Here are some of the most common <u>techniques</u> that use sound for effect:

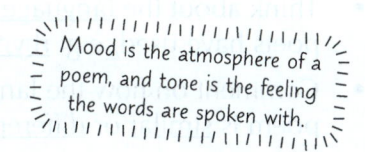

Mood is the atmosphere of a poem, and tone is the feeling the words are spoken with.

1) <u>Alliteration</u> is where words that are close together <u>start</u> with the <u>same sound</u>.

"Not a <u>c</u>ute <u>c</u>ard or a <u>k</u>issogram."
('Valentine' — Carol Ann Duffy)
→ The repeated, <u>plosive</u> '<u>c</u>' and '<u>k</u>' sounds are <u>harsh</u> and emphasise the narrator's <u>dislike</u> for stereotypical gifts.

2) <u>Assonance</u> is when <u>vowel</u> sounds are <u>repeated</u>.

"I love th<u>ee</u> fr<u>ee</u>ly"
('Sonnet 43' — Elizabeth Barrett Browning)
→ The <u>assonant long</u> '<u>ee</u>' sounds <u>draw out</u> each word — this reflects the <u>depth</u> and extent of the narrator's <u>love</u>.

3) <u>Sibilance</u> is when sounds create a '<u>hissing</u>' or '<u>shushing</u>' effect.

"We hi<u>ss</u>'d along the poli<u>sh</u>'d i<u>ce</u>"
(Excerpt from 'The Prelude' — William Wordsworth)
→ The '<u>ss</u>' and '<u>sh</u>' sounds mimic those of the ice skates.

4) <u>Onomatopoeia</u> is when a word <u>mimics</u> the sound it's describing.

"If you could hear, at every jolt, the blood Come <u>gargling</u>"
('Dulce et Decorum Est' — Wilfred Owen)
→ The word "<u>gargling</u>" imitates the <u>sound</u> of the soldier's <u>violent</u> death, highlighting the devastating effects of the chlorine gas.

Try to learn some technical terms...

REVISION TASK — Write down some technical terms on separate pieces of card, and write the meaning on the back of each one. Then, for each card, read the meaning and guess what the technical term is without looking.

Comparing Poems

In the exam you'll have to compare poems — they could be seen or unseen. Here are some general tips.

Compare both poems in Every Paragraph

1) When you're asked to compare poems, you need to find similarities and differences between them.
2) This means you need to discuss both poems in every paragraph. There's a lot to squeeze in, so it's important to structure your paragraphs well.
3) Comparative words help you to do this. They clearly show the examiner if the point you're making is a similarity or difference between the two poems. Here are a few examples:

| similarly | equally | in contrast | however | conversely |

Compare Language, Structure and Form

When you plan your answer, make sure you consider language, structure and form — that way you won't forget to write about them in your essay.

Language

- Think about the language techniques the poets have used, e.g. rhyme, imagery, sound.
- Comment on how the language used in each poem is similar or different, and explain why.

→ Both 'Mametz Wood' and 'The Soldier' personify earth as a protector. Sheers describes how the earth "stands sentinel" over the fallen soldiers, guarding their bodies. Similarly, Brooke's extended metaphor of England as a mother illustrates the country's care and guardianship of the soldier.

Structure

- Compare the beginnings and endings of the poems, and how the ideas and feelings presented are developed.
- Comment on changes in mood, voice, tense and tone — think about the effect this has.

→ The poets' messages in 'Dulce et Decorum Est' and 'A Wife in London' are emphasised by the way they order their ideas. Owen's uninterrupted description of the horrors of war creates a strong contrast with "The old Lie" that war is noble at the end of the poem. Hardy, meanwhile, structures his poem to reveal news of the soldier's death before the arrival of the soldier's letter, which contains his hopes for the future. This makes his death seem more tragic.

Form

- See if the poems have a specific form and explain why you think the poet has made that choice.
- Compare the effects of form in each poem. Think about how they relate to the themes.
- Check if any rules are broken for effect, e.g. a sonnet with 15 lines instead of 14.

→ 'Sonnet 43' is written as a conventional sonnet. By choosing a regular form, traditionally used for love poems, Barrett Browning stresses the strength of the love between the narrator and her beloved. In contrast, 'Living Space' has a completely irregular, free verse form. Inconsistent line lengths and a lack of regular rhyme and rhythm reflect the disorder and instability of the buildings.

EXAM TIP: Compare the poems in every paragraph...
The examiner wants to see you're comparing both poems. Make it easy for them — write one point of comparison in each paragraph and use comparative words to show your comparisons clearly.

Section Five — Poetry

Warm-Up Questions

When it comes to poetry, you need to look at the overall message of the poem — but don't forget to focus on smaller things too, such as line endings, punctuation and even the vowel sounds in the middle of words. They all have a part to play. To see if you've got to grips with this section, have a go at these questions.

Warm-Up Questions

1) Write a brief definition of each of the following poetic techniques:
   a) Onomatopoeia b) Caesura c) Enjambment

2) Write out the sentences below. For each sentence, underline the letters or words that are used to create the effect in brackets.
   Write a sentence for each example explaining the effect of the technique used.

   "A messenger's knock cracks smartly" (**onomatopoeia**)
   (A Wife in London, Thomas Hardy)

   "bluebottles / Wove a strong gauze of sound around the smell" (**sibilance**)
   (Death of a Naturalist, Seamus Heaney)

   "Which waves in every raven tress" (**assonance**)
   (She Walks in Beauty, Lord Byron)

   "The lone and level sands stretch far away" (**alliteration**)
   (Ozymandias, Percy Bysshe Shelley)

3) The extract below personifies a Valentine's Day gift — "an onion".
   Explain the effect of personifying the onion.

   > I give you an onion.
   > Its fierce kiss will stay on your lips
   > *Valentine*, Carol Ann Duffy

4) Read the extract below. Write a sentence explaining the effect of each of the following features of the extract:
   a) The rhyme scheme.
   b) End-stopping.
   c) Emotive language.

   > Gas! GAS! Quick, boys! – An ecstasy of fumbling,
   > Fitting the clumsy helmets just in time;
   > But someone still was yelling out and stumbling,
   > And flound'ring like a man in fire or lime ...
   >
   > *Dulce et Decorum Est*, Wilfred Owen

Section Five — Poetry

Revision Summary

This section should give you a good basic knowledge of the things you need to cover when you write about poems. So, if you can answer the questions on this page you should be well on the way to getting some great marks in your exam. If not, look back over the section until you get them right.

- Try these questions and tick off each one when you get it right.
- When you've done all the questions under a heading and are completely happy with it, tick it off.

Poetry — What You Have To Do (p.55)

1) There are three main elements of a poem that you have to write about in the exam. One is the language of the poem. What are the other two?
2) What should you include to back up each of your ideas about the poem?

Form and Structure (p.56)

3) What is the difference between form and structure?
4) Write a sentence describing each of these forms of poem:
   a) dramatic monologue b) sonnet c) free verse
5) What is:
   a) a stanza? b) a couplet? c) a quatrain?

Poetic Techniques (p.57-61)

6) Write down whether each of these descriptions refers to the first- or third-person narrative voice:
   a) is more detached b) gives you one person's point of view
7) Why might a poet include features of spoken language in their poem? Give one reason.
8) Write a brief explanation of what an irregular rhyme scheme is.
9) What two aspects of a poem does the rhythm alter?
10) Below are two lines from a poem. What is the metre? How can you tell?

    Shall I compare thee to a summer's day?
    Thou art more lovely and more temperate.
    (Sonnet 18 — William Shakespeare)

11) What is the difference between enjambment and end-stopping?
12) Find one simile and one metaphor from the poems you have studied.
13) Find two examples of sensory imagery from the poems you have studied. Explain their effect on the reader.
14) Write a sentence explaining what each of these technical terms means:
    a) alliteration b) sibilance c) assonance
15) What are "boom", "splash" and "crunch" all examples of?

Comparing Poems (p.62)

16) Give two examples for each of the following:
    a) comparative words you could use when explaining the similarity between two poems.
    b) comparative words you could use when explaining the difference between two poems.
17) Is the following statement true or false?
    "It's best to compare two poems by writing several paragraphs about one and then several paragraphs about the other."

Section Five — Poetry

Section Six — Poetry Anthology

The Poetry Anthology

You'll have to study a collection of poems in class, which you'll write about in Paper 1, Section B of your exam.

This is what you'll have to do in the Exam

1) You will be asked to answer two questions in the poetry anthology part of the exam.
2) In the first part of the exam, you'll get a copy of a named poem which you'll have to analyse on the spot. In the second part, you'll be asked to compare the first poem with another poem of your choice.
3) Your comparison will based on something the two poems have in common, e.g. a particular theme. Choose your second poem carefully so you'll have lots of comparison points to make in your answer.
4) Your answers to both questions should discuss the poems' context, key ideas and how they use language, structure and form.
5) You won't have a copy of the anthology in the exam, so make sure you know all the poems really well.

Read the Question carefully and Underline key words

1) In the exam, read each question carefully. Underline the theme and any other key words.
2) Here are a couple of examples of the kind of question you might get:

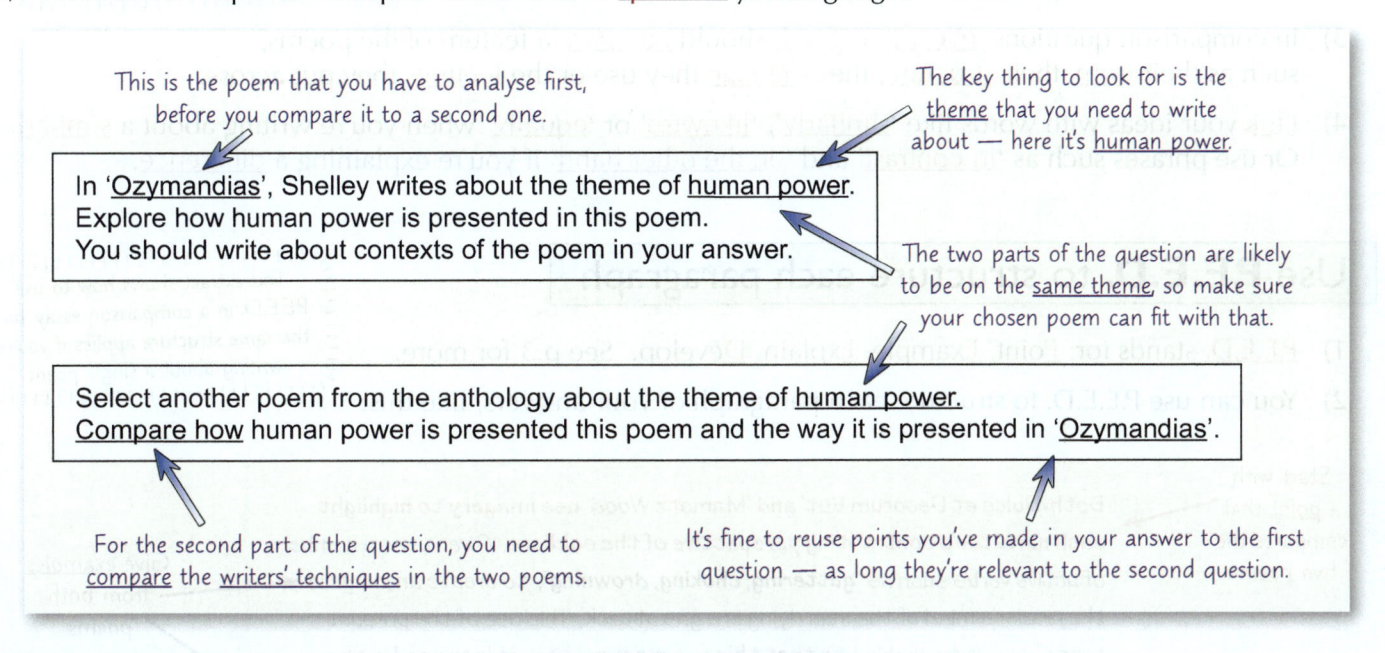

This is the poem that you have to analyse first, before you compare it to a second one.

> In 'Ozymandias', Shelley writes about the theme of human power. Explore how human power is presented in this poem. You should write about contexts of the poem in your answer.

The key thing to look for is the theme that you need to write about — here it's human power.

The two parts of the question are likely to be on the same theme, so make sure your chosen poem can fit with that.

> Select another poem from the anthology about the theme of human power. Compare how human power is presented this poem and the way it is presented in 'Ozymandias'.

For the second part of the question, you need to compare the writers' techniques in the two poems.

It's fine to reuse points you've made in your answer to the first question — as long they're relevant to the second question.

There are Three Main Ways to get marks

There are three main things to keep in mind when you're planning and writing your answer:

- Give your own thoughts and opinions on the poems and support them with quotes from the text.
- Explain features like form, structure and language.
- Describe the similarities and differences between poems and their contexts.

REVISION TASK — Make sure you have a good knowledge of all your poems...
Draw a mindmap for every poem you've studied — add branches for relevant themes and then add short quotes to each branch. You can then use these quotes to back up your points in the exam.

How to Structure Your Answer

A solid structure is essential — it lets the examiner follow your argument nice and easily.

Start with an **Introduction** and end with a **Conclusion**

1) Your introduction should begin by giving a clear answer to the question in a sentence or two. Use the rest of the introduction to briefly develop this idea — try to include some of the main ideas from your plan.

2) The main body of your essay should be three to five paragraphs of analysis.

3) Finish your essay with a conclusion — this should summarise your answer to the question. It's also your last chance to impress the examiner, so try to make your final sentence memorable.

Compare the two poems throughout the **Second Question**

1) In the second question, don't just write several paragraphs about one poem, followed by several paragraphs about the other.

2) Instead, structure each paragraph of your essay by writing about one poem and then explaining whether the other poem is similar or different.

3) In comparison questions, every paragraph should compare a feature of the poems, such as their form, their structure, the language they use or the feelings they put across.

4) Link your ideas with words like 'similarly', 'likewise' or 'equally' when you're writing about a similarity. Or use phrases such as 'in contrast' and 'on the other hand' if you're explaining a difference.

Remember to start a new paragraph every time you start comparing a new feature of the poems.

Use **P.E.E.D.** to structure each paragraph

1) P.E.E.D. stands for: Point, Example, Explain, Develop. See p.3 for more.

2) You can use P.E.E.D. to structure each paragraph of your answers, like this:

This extract shows how to use P.E.E.D. in a comparison essay, but the same structure applies if you're writing about a single poem.

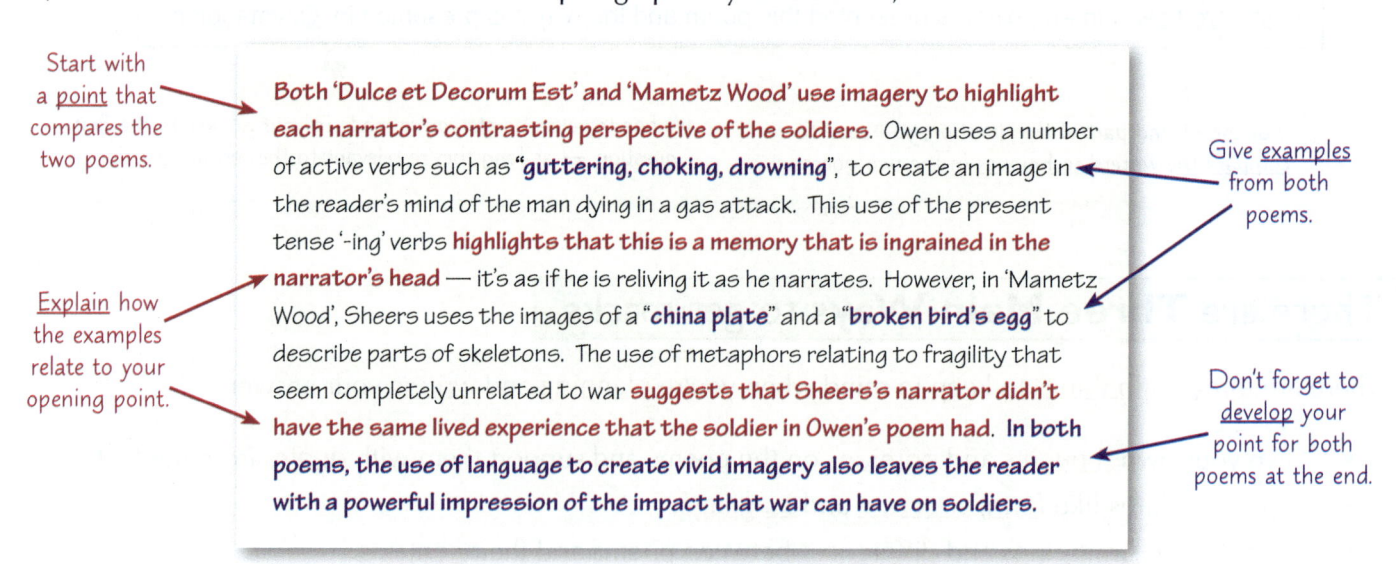

Start with a point that compares the two poems. →

Both 'Dulce et Decorum Est' and 'Mametz Wood' use imagery to highlight each narrator's contrasting perspective of the soldiers. Owen uses a number of active verbs such as **"guttering, choking, drowning"**, to create an image in the reader's mind of the man dying in a gas attack. This use of the present tense '-ing' verbs **highlights that this is a memory that is ingrained in the narrator's head** — it's as if he is reliving it as he narrates. However, in 'Mametz Wood', Sheers uses the images of a **"china plate"** and a **"broken bird's egg"** to describe parts of skeletons. The use of metaphors relating to fragility that seem completely unrelated to war **suggests that Sheers's narrator didn't have the same lived experience that the soldier in Owen's poem had. In both poems, the use of language to create vivid imagery also leaves the reader with a powerful impression of the impact that war can have on soldiers.**

← Explain how the examples relate to your opening point.

Give examples from both poems. →

Don't forget to develop your point for both poems at the end. →

P.E.E.D. is a good way to structure an essay, but it's not essential...
P.E.E.D. is a framework you can use to make sure your paragraphs have all the features they need to pick up marks — it's a useful structure to bear in mind, but you don't have to follow it rigidly in every paragraph.

Section Six — Poetry Anthology

How to Answer the Question

Now you're up to speed with how to structure your answer, there are a few other things you should keep in mind when answering an exam question on your anthology poems.

Look closely at **Language**, **Form** and **Structure**

1) To get top marks, you need to pay close attention to the techniques the poets use.
2) Analyse the form and structure of the poems, which includes their rhyme scheme and rhythm.
3) Explore language — think about why the poets have used certain words and language techniques.
4) You also need to comment on the effect that these techniques have on the reader. The examiner wants to hear what you think of a poem and how it makes you feel.
5) This is the kind of thing you could write about language:

> In 'As Imperceptibly as Grief', Dickinson associates the passing of time with grieving. This association is explored through the continued use of symbolism related to light throughout the poem, such as "Dusk", "Twilight" and "Morning foreign shone". **Using these natural images related to both night and day highlights how the narrator's grief begins in darkness but it gradually lightens like a sunrise. The reader, who has perhaps been through similar stages of grief, can empathise with and understand the implied experiences of the narrator. In contrast, the passing of time is presented in...**

— Analyse the effects of key quotes.
— Always develop your ideas.
— You'd then need to compare this point with another poem.

Always **Support Your Ideas** with **Details** from the **Text**

1) You need to back up your ideas with quotes from or references to the text.
2) Choose your quotes carefully — they have to be relevant to the point you're making.
3) Don't quote large chunks of text — instead, use short quotes and embed them in your sentences.

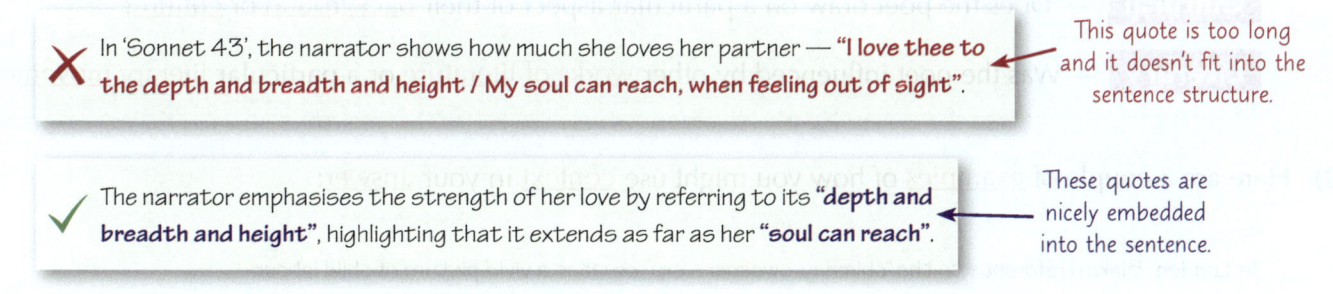

> ✗ In 'Sonnet 43', the narrator shows how much she loves her partner — **"I love thee to the depth and breadth and height / My soul can reach, when feeling out of sight"**.

— This quote is too long and it doesn't fit into the sentence structure.

> ✓ The narrator emphasises the strength of her love by referring to its **"depth and breadth and height"**, highlighting that it extends as far as her **"soul can reach"**.

— These quotes are nicely embedded into the sentence.

4) Don't forget to explain your quotes — you need to use them as evidence to support your argument.

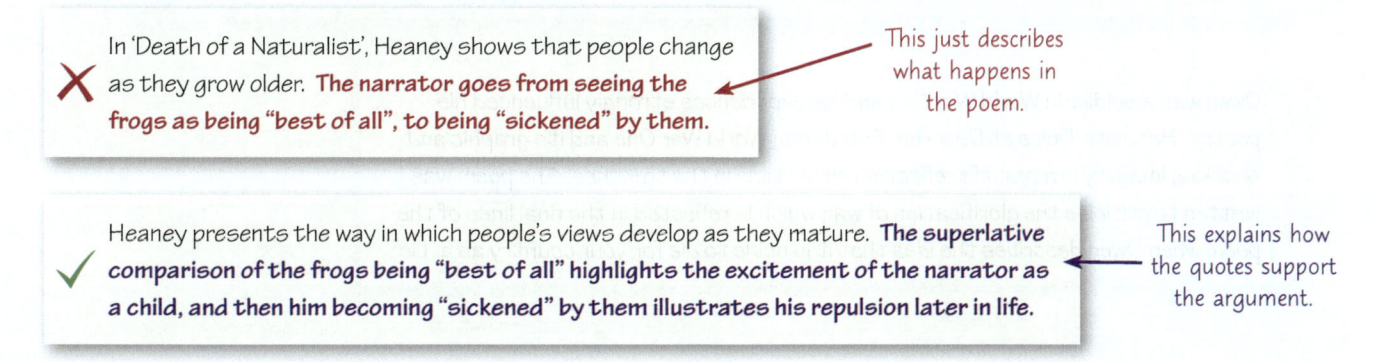

> ✗ In 'Death of a Naturalist', Heaney shows that people change as they grow older. **The narrator goes from seeing the frogs as being "best of all", to being "sickened" by them.**

— This just describes what happens in the poem.

> ✓ Heaney presents the way in which people's views develop as they mature. **The superlative comparison of the frogs being "best of all" highlights the excitement of the narrator as a child, and then him becoming "sickened" by them illustrates his repulsion later in life.**

— This explains how the quotes support the argument.

Section Six — Poetry Anthology

How to Answer the Question

Give Alternative Interpretations

1) You need to show you're aware that poems can be interpreted in more than one way.
2) If a poem is a bit ambiguous, or you think that a particular line or phrase could have several different meanings, then say so.

> In 'Ozymandias', Shelley refers to the sculptor as the "hand that mocked" the statue. On the surface, the word "**mocked**" shows only that the sculptor created the artwork. However, Shelley may also be playing on the second meaning of the word "mocked" (to make fun of); the "**wrinkled lip and sneer**" of the statue suggest that the sculptor disliked Ozymandias, hinting that he may have intended to ridicule the leader by his unflattering depiction.

Remember to support your interpretations with evidence from the poem.

3) Be original with your ideas — just make sure you can back them up with an example from the text.

Show some Wider Knowledge

1) To get a top grade, you need to explain how the ideas in the poems relate to their context.
2) When you're thinking about a particular poem, consider these aspects of context:

> **Historical** — Do the ideas in the poem relate to the time in which it's written or set?
>
> **Geographical** — How is the poem shaped and influenced by the place in which it's set?
>
> **Social** — Is the poet criticising or praising the society or community they're writing about?
>
> **Cultural** — Does the poet draw on a particular aspect of their background or culture?
>
> **Literary** — Was the poet influenced by other works of literature or a particular literary movement?

3) Here are a couple of examples of how you might use context in your answer:

> In 'London', Blake's reference to the "chimney-sweeper's cry" creates a vivid picture of child labour, which was common in the late 18th century. Blake considered child labour to be morally wrong, and he may have included this emotive image in order to boost public sympathy for his views.

> Owen was a soldier in World War One and his experiences strongly influenced his poetry. He wrote 'Dulce et Decorum Est' during World War One and its graphic and shocking imagery is a real-life reflection on his time in the trenches. The poem was written to criticise the glorification of war, which is reflected in the final lines of the poem when Owen describes the idea that it is noble to die for your country as a "Lie".

How to Answer the Question

Use Sophisticated Language

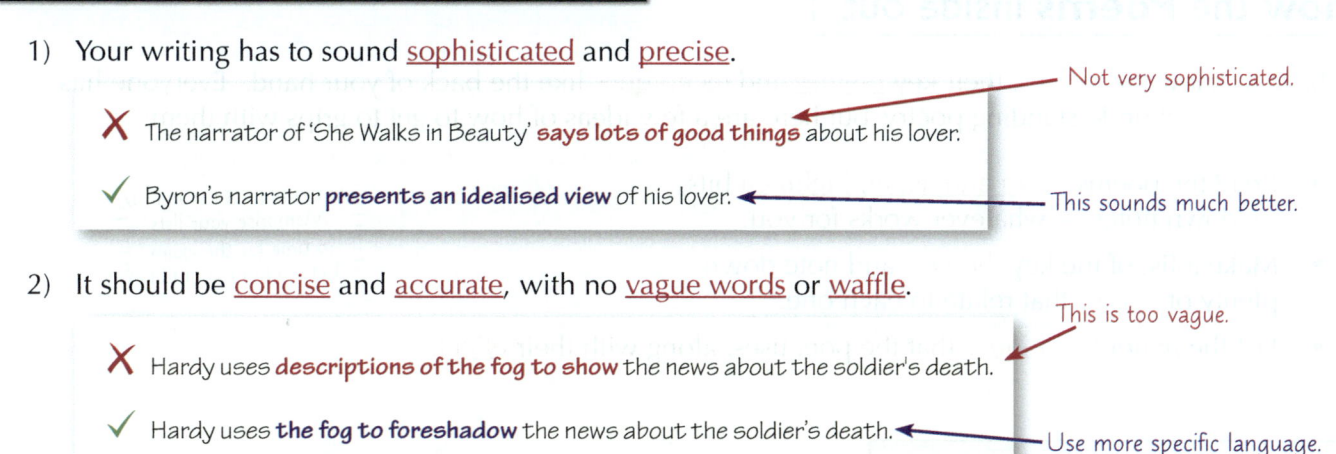

1) Your writing has to sound **sophisticated** and **precise**.

   ✗ The narrator of 'She Walks in Beauty' **says lots of good things** about his lover. — Not very sophisticated.

   ✓ Byron's narrator **presents an idealised view** of his lover. — This sounds much better.

2) It should be **concise** and **accurate**, with no **vague words** or **waffle**.

   ✗ Hardy uses **descriptions of the fog to show** the news about the soldier's death. — This is too vague.

   ✓ Hardy uses **the fog to foreshadow** the news about the soldier's death. — Use more specific language.

3) Your writing should also show an **impressive range** of **vocabulary**.

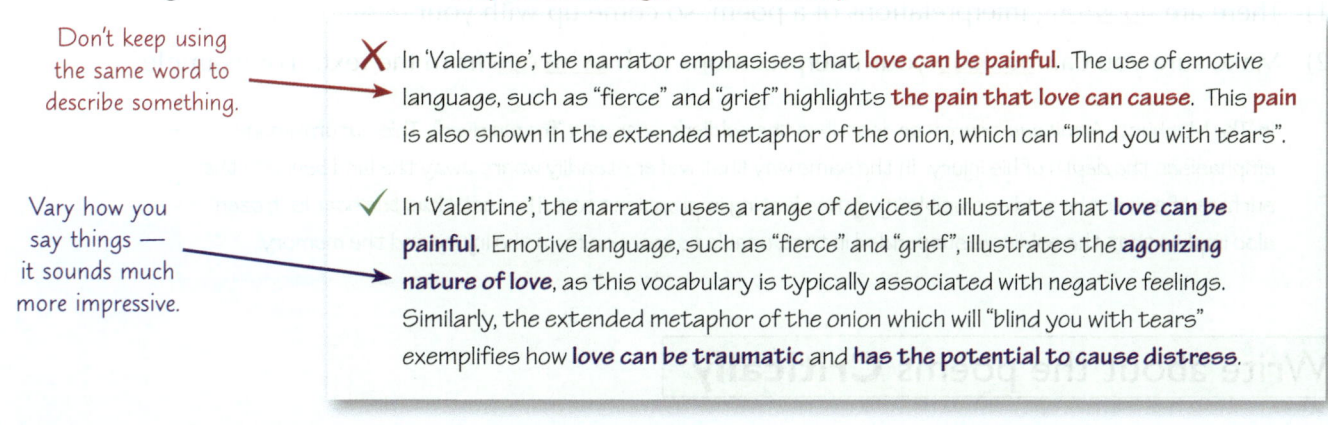

   Don't keep using the same word to describe something.

   ✗ In 'Valentine', the narrator emphasises that **love can be painful**. The use of emotive language, such as "fierce" and "grief" highlights **the pain that love can cause**. This **pain** is also shown in the extended metaphor of the onion, which can "blind you with tears".

   Vary how you say things — it sounds much more impressive.

   ✓ In 'Valentine', the narrator uses a range of devices to illustrate that **love can be painful**. Emotive language, such as "fierce" and "grief", illustrates the **agonizing nature of love**, as this vocabulary is typically associated with negative feelings. Similarly, the extended metaphor of the onion which will "blind you with tears" exemplifies how **love can be traumatic** and **has the potential to cause distress**.

4) However, make sure you **only** use words that you know the **meaning** of. For example, don't say that a poem has a '**volta**' if you don't know what it **really means** — it will be **obvious** to the examiner.

Use Technical Terms where possible

1) To get top marks, you need to use the **correct technical terms** when you're writing about poetry.
2) Flick back to Section Five (p.55-64) for more on these terms, or have a look at the **glossary** at the back of the book.

Don't write

✗ Simon Armitage uses *good images*.

✗ The poet uses *words that sound similar*.

✗ The *sentences run on from line to line*.

Write

✓ Simon Armitage uses *effective metaphors*.

✓ The poet uses *half-rhyme*.

✓ The poet uses *enjambment*.

EXAM TIP — **It's not just what you write...**
... it's also how you write it. In the exam, think about your writing style — you should be clear and precise, and you'll need to use the correct terms to show the examiner you know your stuff.

Section Six — Poetry Anthology

How to Write a Top Grade Answer

If you're aiming for a grade 9, you're going to have to do a little bit extra. Here are a few tips...

Know the Poems inside out

You have to know the poems, their key themes and techniques like the back of your hand. Everyone has their own ways of understanding poetry, but here are a few ideas of how to get to grips with them:

- Read the poems again and again, highlight bits, jot down notes — whatever works for you.
- Make a list of the key themes, and note down plenty of quotes that relate to each one.
- List the major techniques that the poet uses, along with their effect.

Memorise your lists in time for the exam.

Be as Original as you can

1) There are no wrong interpretations of a poem, so come up with your own ideas.
2) Make sure you can back up your interpretations with evidence from the text. For example:

> In 'The Manhunt', Armitage's narrator describes the soldier's scar as a "frozen river". This natural image emphasises the depth of his injury. In the same way that water steadily wears away the land beneath the surface of a river, the soldier's visible injury has lasting implications too. The fact that the scar is "frozen" also implies that the soldier is suspended in time, unable to move on from the injury and the memory.

Write about the poems Critically

1) Being critical means giving your own opinions about the poems — e.g. how effective you think the poet's techniques are, and why you think this.
2) You need to phrase your opinions in a sophisticated way. For example:

> In 'Living Space', the phrase "slanted universe" compels the reader to experience the setting as Dharker's narrator does: a vast, unstable and chaotic place.

Get to grips with Context

It's not enough just to mention a link to context — you need to really explore the effect it has on the poem, or on your understanding of it. For example:

> Like other Romantic poets, Wordsworth often explored the relationship between humans and nature. This is evident in the excerpt from his autobiographical poem 'The Prelude', in which he uses imagery throughout to illustrate the connection he felt as a child to nature. For example, he compares himself to "an untir'd horse", and expresses his growing awareness of the natural world's vast scale by referencing "distant hills".

For a top grade, think originally and critically...

When it comes to grade 9, the examiner wants your interpretation and your opinion of the poems. Have a look at the sample answers on pages 72-75 for some ideas of how to write a great poetry essay.

Warm-Up Questions

For a poetry essay, you need to know what to write about and how to write it. When you answer the questions on this page, practise using sophisticated language so it becomes second nature by the time the exam comes round. Remember to use technical terms whenever possible as well.

Warm-Up Questions

1) In your anthology, find a poem that rhymes.
   What effect does the use of rhyme have in this poem?

2) Choose a poem from your anthology that is written in the first person and one that is written in the third person. Do you find it easier to empathise with the first-person narrator or the characters described by the third-person narration? Write a paragraph explaining your answer.

3) For each of the following aspects of form and structure, find an example from any of the poems in your anthology. Write a sentence explaining the effect each example has on the reader.
   a) End-stopping.
   b) Caesurae.
   c) Enjambment.

4) Using two of your answers to question 3, write a paragraph comparing the form and structure of two of the poems, and explaining how the poets use form and structure to help convey their messages.

5) For each of the following language techniques, find an example from any of the poems in your anthology. Write a sentence explaining the effect each example has on the reader.
   a) Repetition.
   b) Onomatopoeia.
   c) Alliteration.
   d) Sibilance.

6) Using two of your answers to question 5, write a paragraph comparing the language of two of the poems, and explaining how the poets use language to help convey their messages.

7) Pick one more poem from your anthology. How does the poet use imagery in the poem? Write a paragraph about your favourite image, explaining what effect it has on you.

Section Six — Poetry Anthology

Worked Exam-Style Questions

Here's an example of how you might answer a question that asks you to analyse a single poem from your anthology. Have a read, then flick over to page 74 to see an example answer for a comparison question.

| 1 | 1 | In 'She Walks in Beauty', Byron writes about the theme of feelings for another person. Explore how feelings for another person are presented in this poem. You should write about contexts of the poem in your answer. |

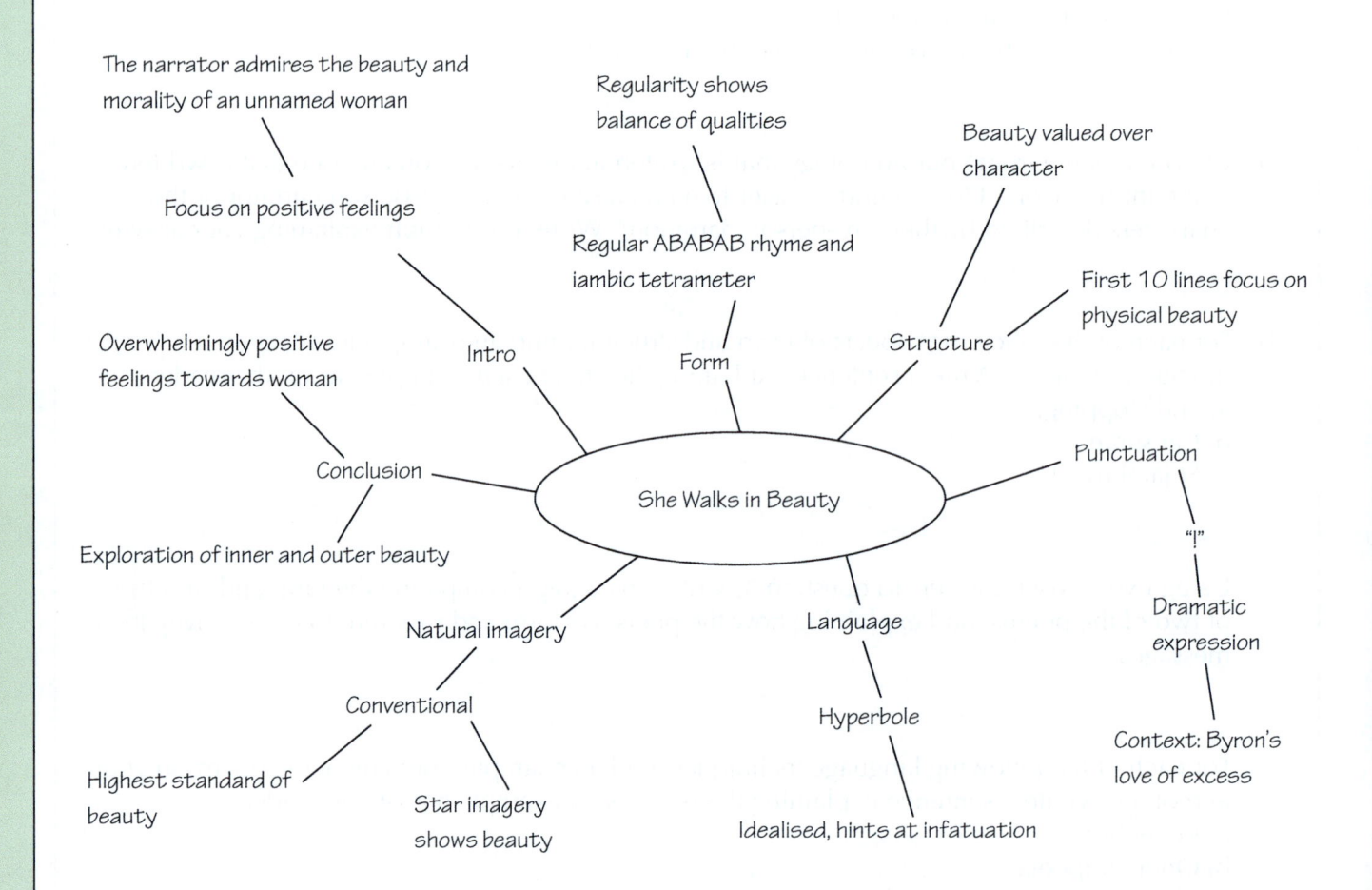

Mind map — She Walks in Beauty:

- **Intro**
  - The narrator admires the beauty and morality of an unnamed woman
  - Focus on positive feelings
- **Form**
  - Regularity shows balance of qualities
  - Regular ABABAB rhyme and iambic tetrameter
- **Structure**
  - Beauty valued over character
  - First 10 lines focus on physical beauty
- **Punctuation**
  - "!"
  - Dramatic expression
  - Context: Byron's love of excess
- **Language**
  - Hyperbole
  - Idealised, hints at infatuation
- **Natural imagery**
  - Conventional
  - Highest standard of beauty
  - Star imagery shows beauty
- **Conclusion**
  - Overwhelmingly positive feelings towards woman
  - Exploration of inner and outer beauty

'She Walks in Beauty' by Lord Byron presents feelings for another person in a positive way. In the poem, the narrator admires an unnamed woman, discussing both her beauty and morality in turn. The narrator explores the relationship between these two attributes, and uses it to express his feelings for her.

→ Show the examiner that you *understand* the question by *addressing* it at the beginning.

It's important to write about *form* in your answers. →

The rhyme scheme and meter of the poem are intended to reflect the beauty which the narrator sees in the woman. Byron uses an ABAB rhyme scheme and iambic tetrameter throughout to give the poem a sense of regularity and harmony. This reflects the narrator's feeling that the woman is a perfect balance of different qualities. Byron could be suggesting that, just like the harmony of the poem, the woman's beauty is also harmonious — perhaps all her features complement each other perfectly.

→ Make sure you *develop your points* clearly.

Section Six — Poetry Anthology

Worked Exam-Style Questions

Embedding short quotes helps to keep your sentences **clear** and **easy to understand**.

At the beginning of the poem, Byron's description of the woman is dominated by her looks: he describes her "eyes" and "raven" hair. It is only after line 10 that he mentions elements of her personality. This suggests that her physical appearance is the strongest attraction for the narrator, and that it has defined his feelings for her. Because the narrator discusses her beauty before discussing her personality, the reader gets the impression that he values her appearance more than her character.

Byron uses punctuation effectively to convey the narrator's feelings for the woman he admires. Each stanza is made up of a single sentence, most of which end with a full stop at the end of the stanza. However, the sentence in the final stanza then ends with an exclamation mark rather than a full stop: the poem builds towards a final, dramatic expression of emotion. This reflects the excitement that the narrator experiences as he thinks and writes about the woman. Byron himself was a flamboyant man, known for his love of excess, and this is reflected in the narrator's lavish and enthusiastic praise for the unnamed woman.

Each paragraph should mark the start of a **new point**.

Show that you can apply **your own knowledge** to the poem.

The narrator of 'She Walks in Beauty' presents an idealised picture of the woman, using hyperbole to describe her "pure" mind and "innocent" heart. This makes his love for her seem unrealistic, because he does not see any flaws in her personality. His focus on her perfection gives the impression that his feelings for her are those of infatuation, rather than of love.

It's good to show the examiner that you can analyse the effect of **specific words**.

The beauty of the woman in the poem is emphasised through the use of natural imagery. By comparing her to "starry skies", the narrator shows her beauty is timeless, but like the stars, this perhaps also hints that she is out of reach. As an important figure in the Romantic movement, which held nature as the highest standard of beauty, Byron's use of natural imagery in the poem gives the reader the impression that Byron is giving the woman the highest form of praise.

Context is critical to include if you want the highest marks.

'She Walks in Beauty' clearly presents the narrator's feelings of adoration for the woman in question and his admiration of her outer and inner beauty is central to the poem. Although the enthusiastic and hyperbolic presentation of these feelings may lead the reader to question the depth and permanence of them, by the end of the poem it is nevertheless clear that the narrator feels very positively towards the woman.

Keep linking your answer back to the **question** to stay on topic.

Section Six — Poetry Anthology

Worked Exam-Style Questions

Here's another example answer. This time it's for the comparison question. Have a good read of it, then when you're happy flick over to page 76 and try some exam-style questions for yourself.

> **1 2** Select another poem from the anthology about the theme of feelings for another person. Compare how feelings for another person are presented in this poem and the way they are presented in 'She Walks in Beauty'. You should compare:
> - what the poems are about and the way they are organised
> - how the poets create effects in the poems
> - the poems' contexts, and how the poems are influenced by these contexts.

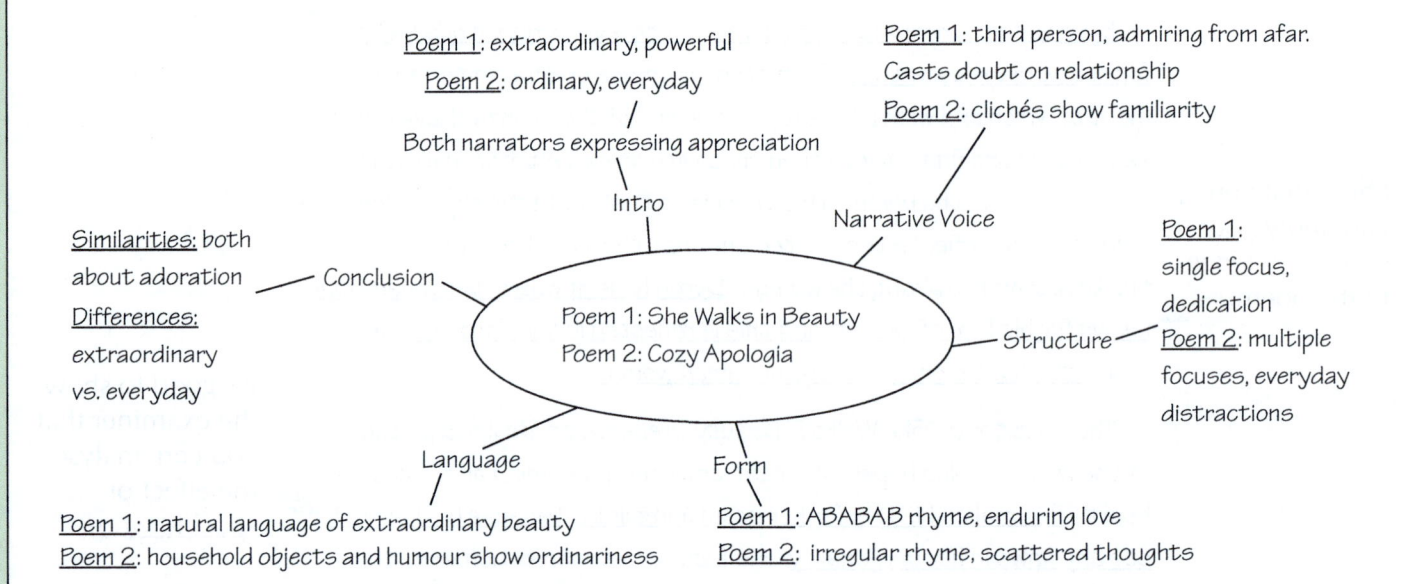

Mind map around central topic: Poem 1: She Walks in Beauty / Poem 2: Cozy Apologia

- **Intro** — Both narrators expressing appreciation
  - Poem 1: extraordinary, powerful
  - Poem 2: ordinary, everyday
- **Narrative Voice**
  - Poem 1: third person, admiring from afar. Casts doubt on relationship
  - Poem 2: clichés show familiarity
- **Structure**
  - Poem 1: single focus, dedication
  - Poem 2: multiple focuses, everyday distractions
- **Form**
  - Poem 1: ABABAB rhyme, enduring love
  - Poem 2: irregular rhyme, scattered thoughts
- **Language**
  - Poem 1: natural language of extraordinary beauty
  - Poem 2: household objects and humour show ordinariness
- **Conclusion**
  - Similarities: both about adoration
  - Differences: extraordinary vs. everyday

Compare the poems in your opening sentence. → Although both 'She Walks in Beauty' and 'Cozy Apologia' are poems which feature feelings of appreciation towards their subjects, they vary considerably in the way that those feelings are presented. Byron uses regular form and natural imagery to present his narrator's feelings as intense and extraordinary. Dove's presentation of feelings is disrupted and irregular in order to convey the sense of ordinary, typical appreciation which her narrator feels. *Sum up the main argument of your essay.* → The two poems both describe feelings of adoration and appreciation, but they are presented in different ways, which highlights the difference between idealised and realistic love.

The poems use different narrative voices to show each narrator's feelings of appreciation. *Use the correct technical terms.* → 'She Walks in Beauty' is written with a formal narrative voice, seen in the use of the third person ("Meet in her aspect"). This suggests that the narrator is distanced from the subject of his affections, as though he is admiring her from afar, which suggests that they might not even have a relationship. Dove uses an informal narrative voice in 'Cozy Apologia', as shown when the narrator uses clichés such as "chain mail glinting, to set me free". These traditional stereotypes of a romantic hero and a damsel in distress give the narrator's voice a tongue-in-cheek tone, which suggests much of her appreciation is based on how playful she and her lover can be together. *Bring in some contextual details to your answer.* → This could be a reflection of Dove's relationship with her husband Fred, who the poem is dedicated to.

Section Six — Poetry Anthology

Worked Exam-Style Questions

Explain the effect of the examples you give.

The narrators' levels of appreciation are shown through the way each poem is structured. In 'She Walks in Beauty', the woman is the narrator's focus throughout, which shows the intensity of his affections. In 'Cozy Apologia', the focus begins on her lover but then changes to her memories, "the post-post-modern age" and Hurricane Floyd. <u>This change in focus suggests that the narrator's appreciation is disrupted by other thoughts about her past and the weather</u>. She does return to thoughts of her lover though, which ends the poem on a note of familiarity. The changing focus in Dove's poem gives the reader the sense that the relationship is more grounded in reality than the relationship in Byron's poem, and therefore more likely to endure.

Compare the poems' form.

<u>Rhyme schemes are used in different ways in the poems to support the narrators' different feelings</u>. In 'She Walks in Beauty', Byron utilises a regular ABABAB rhyme to create a sense of uniformity, which reflects the narrator's appreciation for her perfect beauty. In contrast, 'Cozy Apologia' has a varying rhyme scheme which reflects the narrator's changing focus. Dove uses rhyming couplets at the start of the poem to reflect the focus on traditional romantic imagery. This is disrupted in the second stanza, as the narrator becomes preoccupied with things outside of her relationship. In the third stanza, the poem returns to a stable ABABAB rhyme scheme, which creates a sense of security and comfort once more. This emphasises that even though the narrator is often distracted by other things, her relationship provides a safe and stable place for her to return to. <u>This makes the narrator's feelings for her partner seem less intense but more comforting than the feelings expressed by the narrator in Byron's poem</u>.

Try to develop your ideas.

Compare the language used in the two poems.

<u>The language used in the two poems reflects each narrator's appreciation</u>. Byron's narrator uses natural imagery of the "Heavens" and "starry skies" to emphasise her beauty by comparing her to beautiful aspects of nature. These images are also symbolic of the divine and things beyond the comprehension of man, suggesting his admiration borders on worship. The narrator in 'Cozy Apologia' utilises more mundane and sometimes humorous language instead. <u>She likens her partner to everyday objects like "This lamp" or "My pen" to show how their relationship is decidedly normal and regular</u>. Her humour ("They all had sissy names") and simple language illustrate the realistic and ordinary side of a relationship, which could arguably make the poem more relatable for a reader. <u>Dove dedicating her poem to her husband suggests that it is a personal account of her own feelings, and 'Cozy Apologia' is more down-to-earth than 'She Walks in Beauty'</u>.

Use quotes to support your argument.

You can give more than one interpretation in your answer.

Both 'She Walks in Beauty' and 'Cozy Apologia' present strong feelings for another person, but in very different ways. Byron does so in a classical Romantic way, using a regular rhyme scheme and natural imagery to present a narrator who is overwhelmed by and overjoyed with his feelings. On the other hand, Dove's use of irregular form and everyday language present feelings which are typical and realistic, but nonetheless are important to the narrator. <u>Although each poem is a dedication to the person that each narrator admires, the poems are both products of their contexts, and therefore offer contrasting presentations of these people</u>.

Your last sentence should sum up your argument, and it needs to be memorable.

Section Six — Poetry Anthology

Exam-Style Questions

Now it's time to put all you've learned about how to write a great answer into practice.
Make sure you think carefully about each question before you start writing.

Q1 a) In 'The Soldier', Brooke writes about the theme of admiration.
Explore how admiration is presented in this poem.
You should write about the contexts of the poem in your answer.

Q1 b) Select another poem from the anthology about the theme of worship.
Compare how worship is presented in this poem and the way it is presented in 'The Soldier'.

Q2 a) In 'Dulce et Decorum Est', Owen writes about the theme of war.
Explore how war is presented in this poem.
You should write about the contexts of the poem in your answer.

Q2 b) Select another poem from the anthology about the theme of war.
Compare how war is presented in this poem and the way it is presented in 'Dulce et Decorum Est'.

Q3 a) In 'London', Blake writes about the theme of freedom and constraint.
Explore how freedom and constraint is presented in this poem.
You should write about the contexts of the poem in your answer.

Q3 b) Select another poem from the anthology about the theme of freedom and constraint.
Compare how the theme of freedom and constraint is presented in this poem
and the way it is presented in 'London'.

Q4 a) In 'Sonnet 43', Barrett Browning writes about the theme of relationships.
Explore how the theme of relationships is presented in this poem.
You should write about the contexts of the poem in your answer.

Q4 b) Select another poem from the anthology about the theme of relationships.
Compare how the theme of relationships is presented in this poem
and the way it is presented in the 'Sonnet 43'.

Section Six — Poetry Anthology

Section Seven — Unseen Poetry

Five Steps to Analysing a Poem

In the final section of Paper 2, you're going to have to analyse some unseen poetry — here's how to do it.

The examiner is looking for Four Main Things

You'll have to answer <u>two questions</u> in this section — one on an <u>unseen poem</u>, and one where you <u>compare</u> the poem with another unseen poem. To impress the examiner, you need to:

1) Show that you <u>understand</u> what the poems are <u>about</u>.
2) Write about the <u>techniques</u> used in the poems.
3) Use the <u>correct technical terms</u> to describe the techniques in the poems.
4) <u>Support</u> every point you make with <u>quotes</u> or <u>examples</u> from the poems.

Five Steps to analysing an unseen poem

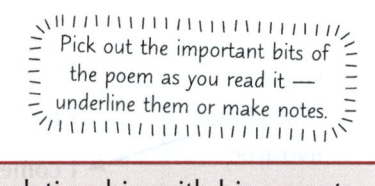

Pick out the important bits of the poem as you read it — underline them or make notes.

1) Work out what the poem's about

- Work out the <u>subject</u> of the poem, e.g. the poem is about the narrator's relationship with his parents.
- Think about <u>who</u> is <u>speaking</u>, and <u>who</u> the poem is <u>addressing</u> — e.g. the narrator's lover, the reader...

2) Identify the purpose, theme or message

- Think about <u>what</u> the poet is saying, <u>why</u> they've written the poem, or what <u>ideas</u> they're using.
- The poem could be an <u>emotional response</u> to something. It might aim to <u>get a response</u> from the <u>reader</u>, or put across a message or an opinion about something.

3) Explore the emotions, moods or feelings

- Consider the <u>different emotions or feelings</u> in the poem and identify its <u>mood</u>.
- Look at how the poet <u>shows</u> these emotions (see step 4).

4) Identify the techniques used in the poem

- Find the <u>different techniques</u> the poet has used and how they create <u>emotions</u>, <u>moods</u> or <u>feelings</u>. Think about <u>why</u> the poet has used them, and what <u>effect</u> they create.
- Techniques can be related to <u>language</u> (<u>alliteration</u>, <u>onomatopoeia</u>, <u>imagery</u> etc.), <u>structure</u> (the order of <u>ideas</u> and any changes in <u>mood</u> or <u>tone</u>) and <u>form</u> (<u>line</u> and <u>stanza</u> length, <u>rhyme schemes</u> etc.).

5) Include your thoughts and feelings about the poem

- Examiners love to hear what <u>you think</u> of a poem and how it makes <u>you feel</u>. Think about how well the poem gets its <u>message</u> across and what <u>impact</u> it has on you.
- Try <u>not</u> to use "I" though — don't say "I felt sad that the narrator's brother died", it's much <u>better</u> to say "It makes the reader feel the narrator's sense of sadness at the death of his brother."
- Think about any <u>other ways</u> that the poem could be <u>interpreted</u>.

Always read the poem with the question in mind...

The first thing to do when you're analysing a poem is to read the question carefully and underline the key words. That'll help you to identify aspects of the poem that are directly relevant to the question.

Worked Exam-Style Question

On the next three pages is a step-by-step guide to answering an unseen poetry question in the exam. The first stage is to read the question carefully and annotate the relevant parts of the poem.

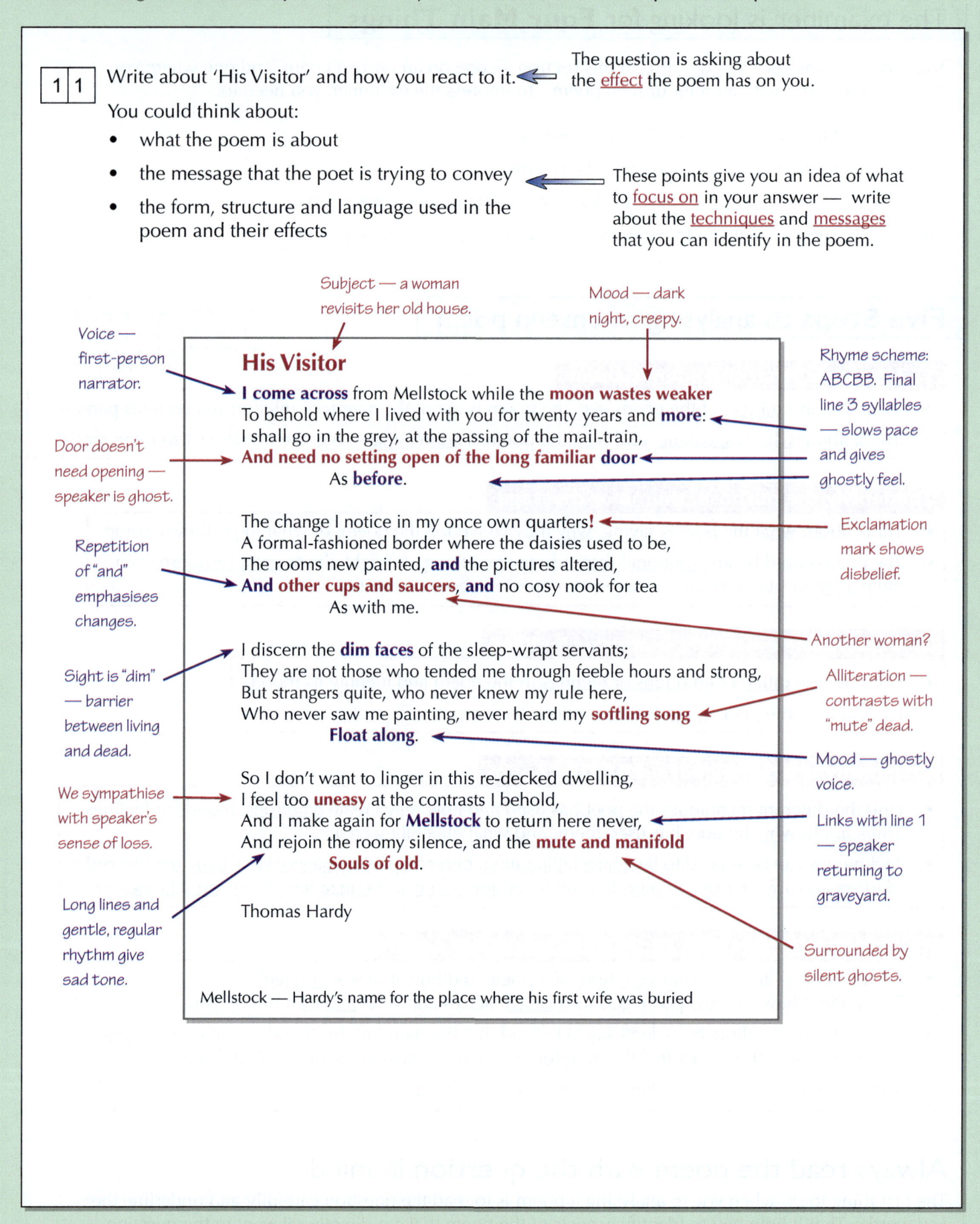

1 1 Write about 'His Visitor' and how you react to it.

You could think about:
- what the poem is about
- the message that the poet is trying to convey
- the form, structure and language used in the poem and their effects

The question is asking about the <u>effect</u> the poem has on you.

These points give you an idea of what to <u>focus on</u> in your answer — write about the <u>techniques</u> and <u>messages</u> that you can identify in the poem.

His Visitor

I come across from Mellstock while the **moon wastes weaker**
To behold where I lived with you for twenty years and **more**:
I shall go in the grey, at the passing of the mail-train,
And need no setting open of the long familiar door
    As **before**.

The change I notice in my once own quarters**!**
A formal-fashioned border where the daisies used to be,
The rooms new painted, **and** the pictures altered,
And other cups and saucers, **and** no cosy nook for tea
    As with me.

I discern the **dim faces** of the sleep-wrapt servants;
They are not those who tended me through feeble hours and strong,
But strangers quite, who never knew my rule here,
Who never saw me painting, never heard my **softling song**
    Float along.

So I don't want to linger in this re-decked dwelling,
I feel too **uneasy** at the contrasts I behold,
And I make again for **Mellstock** to return here never,
And rejoin the roomy silence, and the **mute and manifold**
    Souls of old.

Thomas Hardy

Mellstock — Hardy's name for the place where his first wife was buried

---

Annotations:

- Voice — first-person narrator.
- Door doesn't need opening — speaker is ghost.
- Repetition of "and" emphasises changes.
- Sight is "dim" — barrier between living and dead.
- We sympathise with speaker's sense of loss.
- Long lines and gentle, regular rhythm give sad tone.
- Subject — a woman revisits her old house.
- Mood — dark night, creepy.
- Rhyme scheme: ABCBB. Final line 3 syllables — slows pace and gives ghostly feel.
- Exclamation mark shows disbelief.
- Another woman?
- Alliteration — contrasts with "mute" dead.
- Mood — ghostly voice.
- Links with line 1 — speaker returning to graveyard.
- Surrounded by silent ghosts.

Section Seven — Unseen Poetry

Worked Exam-Style Question

PAPER 2

Once you've got to grips with the poem, spend five minutes planning your answer.
Then get writing your answer — just make sure you refer back to your plan and the question as you write.

Plan:

1. Intro
   - Subject — a ghost visits her former home.
   - Sorrow of dead.

2. Makes reader think about life after death
   - Ghost narrator.
   - Ghost is sad, not scary — reader sympathises with her.

3. Feeling of sorrow
   - She is "uneasy" at the changes, but can't do anything about them.
   - Her only choice is to "rejoin the roomy silence".
   - Sad tone (reinforced by gentle, regular rhythm) — living move on, dead don't.

4. Separation between dead and living
   - She doesn't need the door opened — she's formless.
   - Living are unaware of her.
   - Living are "dim faces" — indistinct.
   - Living are vocal — "softling song". Dead are "mute".

5. Effect of death on the living
   - Poet vs. narrator. He imagines her response.
   - Hints to reader of guilt at the changes/new wife?

6. Conclusion
   - Reader impression that dead always with us.
   - Living and dead are separate but impact on each other.

Don't spend *too long* on your plan. It's only *rough work*, so you don't need to write in full sentences.

Focus on three or four key points about the poem.

Remember to write about *what* the poet says, *how* they say it and what *effect* it has — don't just discuss it in the conclusion.

The poem 'His Visitor' describes the *return of a ghost to the home she shared with her partner for "twenty years and more"*. In it, the poet imagines the narrator's resentment of the changes that have occurred since her death, indirectly revealing his own guilt at allowing these changes to take place. The poem suggests that *although the living can affect the dead, and vice versa, ultimately they are separate states with no point of contact.*

The poet encourages the reader to think about life after death. Although the narrator of the poem never explicitly states that she is a ghost, it is made clear when she says, for instance, that she arrives by night and needs *"no setting open"* of the door. *The use of the first person makes the reader empathise with the sadness of the narrator, breaking down the stereotype of ghosts being frightening.*

Clear start, showing that you've *understood* the poem.

Write about the poem's main *messages* early on in your essay.

Always use *quotes* to back up points.

Give a *personal response* to the poem — think about how it might make the reader *feel*.

Section Seven — Unseen Poetry

Worked Exam-Style Question

Write about feelings and mood, and use quotes to back up your points.

The feeling of sorrow is emphasised to the reader by the powerlessness of the narrator. Although she is "uneasy" at the changes that have been made to her former home, the only way she can ease her discomfort is to leave and "return here never". Death therefore involves giving up a loved home and all that is familiar, and instead accepting the loneliness that comes with joining the "roomy silence". The gentle rhythm of the poem reinforces the narrator's loneliness. The three-syllable lines that end each stanza are separated from the rest of the stanza by the change in rhythm, but they are linked to it by rhyme. They have the effect of making each stanza seem to tail off wistfully, reinforcing the narrator's sorrow, while their content shows her fixation on "before". This gives the reader the impression that, while the living are able to move forward, the dead are trapped in the past.

Comment on form and the effect it has.

Make sure you discuss the reader's reaction to the poem.

The poet also suggests that death divides the narrator from the living world. The colours of the poem are muted: the "grey" of night and the moon that "wastes weaker" create a feeling of unreality that contrasts with the "cosy nook" of the past. The "dim faces" of the sleeping servants may be shadowy because it is night, or because the narrator exists in the spiritual world, so to her, the material world is vague and unclear. Although the narrator is aware of her surroundings, the reader sees that she cannot interact with them, instead passing through the "long familiar door". The silence of the dead is emphasised by the alliteration of "mute and manifold", which contrasts with the "softling song" of the narrator when she was alive.

Write about any imagery in the poem.

Think about different interpretations to help you get top marks.

Mention and explain any poetic devices that you spot.

Think about any hidden meanings the poem might contain.

The poem also gives clues about the impact of death on the living. By imagining how "uneasy" the narrator feels at the "contrasts" she sees, Hardy gives the reader a hint of the guilt he feels at moving on while she cannot. The changes described are not large, but the use of an exclamation mark and the repetition of "and" in the second stanza shows how significant the poet believes they would have been to the narrator. The mention of "other cups and saucers", traditionally chosen by women, hint that the dead woman's place may have been taken by another woman. This may explain the poet's guilt. However, the fact that he is so concerned with what the ghost would feel suggests, ironically, that he has not really moved on.

Give a good personal response wherever you can.

Mention specific language features and explain why the poet used them.

Sum up the what and how in your final paragraph.

The main message of the poem is that the living and the dead inhabit two separate worlds. Hardy presents this idea to the reader through the ghostly first-person narrator, a gentle regular rhythm which reflects her sad drifting around the house and her eventual return to "roomy silence".

Section Seven — Unseen Poetry

Comparing Two Poems

To do well in the exam, you'll need to be able to compare two unseen poems. Here are a few tips...

You'll have to Compare Two unseen poems

1) In the exam, you're going to have to compare two unseen poems.
2) This means that you need to write about the similarities and differences between them.
3) You'll need to discuss the techniques the poets use and their effect on the reader, so focus on the structure, form and language used in the two poems.

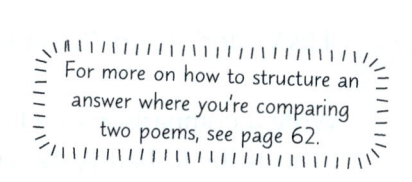

For more on how to structure an answer where you're comparing two poems, see page 62.

Four Steps to answering a comparison question

Don't start writing without thinking about what you're going to say — follow these four steps to organise your ideas:

You can re-use points from your first answer for the comparison question — you don't have to analyse the first poem again from scratch.

1) Read the question

- Read the question carefully and underline the key words.
- The poems will be linked by a common theme — make sure you identify and understand it before you start.

2) Annotate the poems

- Go through and annotate the poems, focusing on the techniques used and the effect they have on the reader.
- As you're annotating the second poem, look for similarities and differences with the techniques and effects you picked out in the first poem.

Read, Annotate, Plan, Write. To help you remember these four steps, try: Really Angry Penguins Wobble.

3) Plan your answer

- Identify three or four key similarities and/or differences that you're going to write about.
- Write a short plan that outlines the structure of your answer.

4) Write your answer

- Use your plan to make sure that every paragraph you write discusses one similarity or difference between the two poems. This could be in their themes and ideas, their mood or their form, structure and language.
- Use linking words and phrases, e.g. 'in contrast' or 'similarly', to make it really clear that you're comparing the two poems.

EXAM TIP

You need to write about both poems in your answer...

The examiner wants to see that you can discuss the similarities and differences between the two poems — make this easy for them by including at least one clear comparison in every paragraph.

Section Seven — Unseen Poetry

Worked Exam-Style Question

Here's another worked example. Use it to get some ideas about how to approach a comparison question.

12 'His Visitor' (see p.78) and 'Ghosts' both portray <u>people's feelings on visiting a former home</u>. ← This is the <u>theme</u> that the poems share.

Write a comparison of 'His Visitor' by Thomas Hardy and 'Ghosts' by Robert W. Service.

You should write about:
- what the poems are about and how you react to them ← Use these bullet points to help you <u>identify</u> specific <u>similarities</u> and <u>differences</u> between the poems.
- the messages that the poets are trying to convey
- the form, structure and language used in the poems and their effects

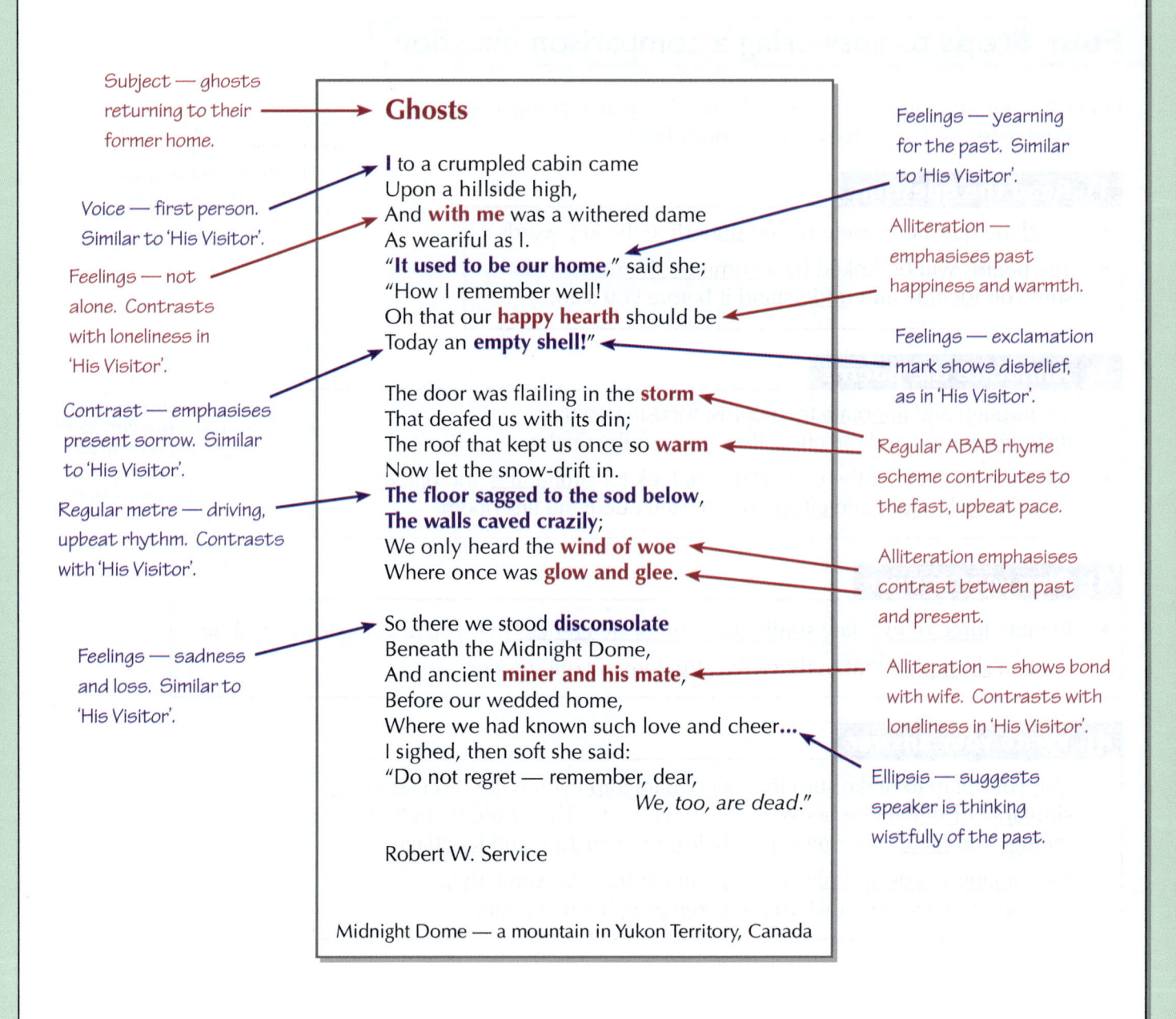

Ghosts

I to a crumpled cabin came
Upon a hillside high,
And **with me** was a withered dame
As wearifu' as I.
"**It used to be our home**," said she;
"How I remember well!
Oh that our **happy hearth** should be
Today an **empty shell!**"

The door was flailing in the **storm**
That deafed us with its din;
The roof that kept us once so **warm**
Now let the snow-drift in.
The floor sagged to the sod below,
The walls caved crazily;
We only heard the **wind of woe**
Where once was **glow and glee**.

So there we stood **disconsolate**
Beneath the Midnight Dome,
And ancient **miner and his mate**,
Before our wedded home,
Where we had known such love and cheer**...**
I sighed, then soft she said:
"Do not regret — remember, dear,
　　　　　We, too, are dead."

Robert W. Service

Midnight Dome — a mountain in Yukon Territory, Canada

Annotations (left side):
- Subject — ghosts returning to their former home.
- Voice — first person. Similar to 'His Visitor'.
- Feelings — not alone. Contrasts with loneliness in 'His Visitor'.
- Contrast — emphasises present sorrow. Similar to 'His Visitor'.
- Regular metre — driving, upbeat rhythm. Contrasts with 'His Visitor'.
- Feelings — sadness and loss. Similar to 'His Visitor'.

Annotations (right side):
- Feelings — yearning for the past. Similar to 'His Visitor'.
- Alliteration — emphasises past happiness and warmth.
- Feelings — exclamation mark shows disbelief, as in 'His Visitor'.
- Regular ABAB rhyme scheme contributes to the fast, upbeat pace.
- Alliteration emphasises contrast between past and present.
- Alliteration — shows bond with wife. Contrasts with loneliness in 'His Visitor'.
- Ellipsis — suggests speaker is thinking wistfully of the past.

Section Seven — Unseen Poetry

Worked Exam-Style Question

Plan:

1. Intro
- Subject — ghosts visit their former homes.
- Melancholy tone and longing for past in both poems.

2. Voice
- Both poems written in the first person.
- Poem 1: ghost alone and lonely.
- Poem 2: ghost with wife, not lonely.

Structuring your plan as 'Poem 1... / Poem 2...' is helpful so that you remember to compare both poems throughout.

3. Titles
- Different attitudes towards death.
- Poem 1: ambiguous title, avoidance of reality, regret.
- Poem 2: very clear from the start, more accepting of the situation.

Split your essay into sensible sections to keep it as clear as possible.

4. Language
- Used to show past happiness vs. present sorrow.
- Poem 1: "cosy nook" vs. "roomy silence".
- Poem 2: "happy hearth" vs. "empty shell".

5. Symbolism
- State of former homes shows how narrators are being forgotten.
- Poem 1: "re-decked dwelling" shows how life has moved on without her.
- Poem 2: home is "crumpled", disappearing, symbolises memory of them fading.

6. Form
- Poem 1: 3-syllable lines heighten sadness.
- Poem 2: metre and rhyme lighten mood.

7. Conclusion
- Poem 1: darker and more melancholy.

Make sure you summarise concisely in your conclusion.

'His Visitor' and 'Ghosts' are both melancholy poems in which a ghostly narrator returns to their former home and is distressed to find that it has changed dramatically. Although the poems convey similar feelings about visiting a former home, the poets use narrative voice, language and form in different ways to put these feelings across.

Both poems use a first-person narrator. This makes the narrators' feelings seem more real and immediate, and encourages the reader to empathise with them. In 'His Visitor', the narrator's isolation is conveyed by her repeated use of the first-person singular pronoun "I", which emphasises her loneliness as she revisits the once-familiar house that's now filled with "strangers". In 'Ghosts', however, the narrator is accompanied by his wife. The collective pronouns "we" and "us" highlight their close connection and contrast with the loneliness of the narrator in 'His Visitor'.

Show that you've understood the question.

Explain how the techniques in the poems affect the reader.

Embed short quotes into your writing.

Section Seven — Unseen Poetry

Worked Exam-Style Question

The two poets present varying attitudes towards death. In 'His Visitor', Hardy discusses death ambiguously, as the dead narrator is referred to as a 'visitor' in the title, who belongs with the "Souls of old". The reader knows that the narrator is Hardy's wife, so these euphemisms might indicate that he cannot fully accept her death. That said, a 'visitor' has a fleeting presence, so this choice of words might imply that he knows this attitude cannot last. Conversely, Service is much more direct in 'Ghosts', explicitly referencing death in his title and ending the poem with the wife's statement that "We, too, are dead". The woman's attempt to reassure her husband, the narrator, reveals her acceptance of their deaths. She encourages him to have no "regret" but instead to "remember".

(Show that you can develop both sides of an idea.)
(Show that you understand the imagery in the poems.)

Both poets use language to emphasise the contrast between past happiness and present sorrow. In 'His Visitor', the "cosy nook" that symbolises the warmth and comfort the house once offered is replaced with the afterlife's "roomy silence", and the "happy hearth" in 'Ghosts' contrasts with the now "empty shell" of the cabin. This highlights the narrators' yearning for the past, something that is emphasised to the reader by the repeated use of phrases associated with the past, such as "As before" in 'His Visitor' and "used to be" in 'Ghosts', suggesting that both narrators are fixated on the way things were.

(Introduce your paragraphs with a comparison.)
(Use quotes to support your argument.)

In both poems, the former homes symbolise how the narrators have been left behind. In 'His Visitor', the narrator describes the "re-decked dwelling" that has been "new painted" in her absence. The way the house has been "altered" suggests to the reader that life has moved on without her and all trace of her has been erased. The house in 'Ghosts' is in much worse condition, with "sagged" floors and "caved" walls. The house has become an "empty shell", which is a metaphor for the way all evidence of the happy life the couple lead there has disappeared.

(Remember to compare the two poems.)

The form of 'His Visitor' helps to convey the narrator's feelings. The three-syllable lines that end each stanza slow the poem's pace and give it an irregular rhythm, with each stanza trailing off wistfully. This creates a powerful sense of sadness and melancholy. In contrast, the regular metre and simple ABAB rhyme scheme of 'Ghosts' give the poem a faster pace and a driving, upbeat rhythm which lightens the mood and makes the poem seem less bleak and melancholy than 'His Visitor'.

(Write about how form conveys meaning.)

'His Visitor' and 'Ghosts' both use language to convey similar feelings of sadness, loss and longing for the past, and regret at the changes to their former homes. However, differences in the poets' use of narrative voice and form mean that, overall, the tone of 'His Visitor' is darker and more melancholy than that of 'Ghosts'.

(Summarise the similarities and differences in your conclusion.)

Section Seven — Unseen Poetry

Warm-Up Questions

Before you answer the questions at the bottom of the page, read the poem all the way through and annotate anything you think is important. Once you've got an idea of what the poem's about, the techniques the poet uses and why she uses them, you'll be ready to answer the questions.

Warm-Up Questions

Spring in War-Time

Now the sprinkled blackthorn snow
Lies along the lovers' lane
Where last year we used to go—
Where we shall not go again.

In the hedge the buds are new,
By our wood the violets peer—
Just like last year's violets, too,
But they have no scent this year.

Every bird has heart to sing
Of its nest, warmed by its breast;
We had heart to sing last spring,
But we never built our nest.

Presently red roses blown
Will make all the garden gay...
Not yet have the daisies grown
On your clay.

Edith Nesbit

1) Write down what you think the poem is about, in just one sentence.

2) What do you think the narrator means by "we never built our nest" in the 3rd stanza?

3) How does the poet create a contrast between the signs of spring and the narrator's feelings in the poem?

4) What is the rhyme scheme of this poem and why do you think that the poet chose it?

5) The last line of the poem has a different rhythm. Why do you think that the poet has done this?

Section Seven — Unseen Poetry

Exam-Style Questions

On the next two pages are questions about two poems that you probably won't have read before. They'll test your ability to analyse and compare unseen poetry, just like you'll have to do in the exam.

Q1a) Both 'At Sea' and 'The Sands of Dee' (p.87) describe the power of the sea.

Write about 'At Sea' by Jennifer Copley and how you react to it.

You could think about:
- what the poem is about
- the message that the poet is trying to convey
- the form, structure and language used in the poem and their effects

At Sea

With nothing to do now he's gone,
she dusts the house,
sweeps the bleached verandah clear of sand.
The broom leaves a trail of grit on the step,
a sprinkling under the hook where it hangs.

A coat for a pillow,
she sleeps downstairs,
dreams the loathed ocean is coming for her,
climbing the cliffs,
creeping in through the door.

She wakes to the screaming gulls,
his shirts on the line
and the high tide's breakers'
chill in her arms.

Jennifer Copley

Section Seven — Unseen Poetry

Exam-Style Questions

Q1b) Write a comparison of 'At Sea' by Jennifer Copley and 'The Sands of Dee' by Charles Kingsley.

You should write about:

- what the poems are about and how you react to them
- the messages that the poets are trying to convey
- the form, structure and language used in the poems and their effects

The Sands of Dee

'O Mary, go and call the cattle home,
And call the cattle home,
And call the cattle home
Across the sands of Dee;'
The western wind was wild and dank with foam,
And all alone went she.

The western tide crept up along the sand,
And o'er and o'er the sand,
And round and round the sand,
As far as eye could see.
The rolling mist came down and hid the land:
And never home came she.

'Oh! is it weed, or fish, or floating hair—
A tress of golden hair,
A drowned maiden's hair
Above the nets at sea?
Was never salmon yet that shone so fair
Among the stakes on Dee.'

They rowed her in across the rolling foam,
The cruel, crawling foam,
The cruel, hungry foam,
To her grave beside the sea:
But still the boatmen hear her call the cattle home,
Across the sands of Dee.

Charles Kingsley

Section Seven — Unseen Poetry

Practice Papers

Here are some practice papers to test how well-prepared you are for your GCSE English Literature exams.
- There are two practice papers in this section:
  Paper 1: Shakespeare and Poetry (pages 88-95)
  Paper 2: Post-1914 Prose/Drama, 19th-Century Prose and Unseen Poetry (pages 96-108)
- Before you start each exam, read through all the instructions and information on the front.
- You'll need some paper to write your answers on.
- When you've finished, have a look at the answers starting on page 122 — they'll give you some ideas of the kind of things you should have included in your answers.
- Don't try to do both of the exams in one sitting.

CGP Practice Exam Paper: GCSE English Literature

General Certificate of Secondary Education

GCSE English Literature

Surname
Other names
Candidate signature

Centre name
Centre number
Candidate number

Paper 1: Shakespeare and Poetry

Time allowed: 2 hours

Instructions to candidates
- Answer **both** questions on the **one** text you have studied in **Section A** (p.89-94).
- Answer **both** questions in Section B (p.95).
- Write your answers in black ink or ball-point pen.
- Write your name and other details in the boxes **above**.

Information for candidates
- The marks available are given in brackets.
- There are 80 marks available for this exam paper — 40 marks for Section A and 40 marks for Section B.
- The marks for Section A include 5 marks for accuracy in spelling, punctuation and the use of vocabulary and sentence structures. These are available for the second part of Section A only.

Practice Papers — Paper 1

Section A: Shakespeare

For the **one** text you have studied, answer **both** questions.
Spend about **20** minutes on the **first** question and **40** minutes on the **second**.

Romeo and Juliet

1 1 Read the extract below. You should only write about the extract in your answer to this question.

Paying close attention to the characters' actions and dialogue, write about how an audience could react to this extract.

(15 marks)

1 2 Write about the theme of romantic love in the play. In your response, you should focus on how Shakespeare presents characters and events from the play.

(20 marks)
(+5 marks for spelling, punctuation and grammar)

Friar Lawrence's Cell.
[*Enter Friar Lawrence and Romeo.*]

Friar Lawrence: So smile the heavens upon this holy act,
That after hours with sorrow chide us not!

Romeo: Amen, amen! But come what sorrow can,
It cannot countervail the exchange of joy
That one short minute gives me in her sight.
Do thou but close our hands with holy words,
Then love-devouring death do what he dare,
It is enough I may but call her mine.

Friar Lawrence: These violent delights have violent ends
And in their triumph die, like fire and powder,
Which as they kiss consume: the sweetest honey
Is loathsome in his own deliciousness
And in the taste confounds the appetite.
Therefore love moderately, long love doth so;
Too swift arrives as tardy as too slow.
[*Enter Juliet.*]
Here comes the lady. O, so light a foot
Will ne'er wear out the everlasting flint.
A lover may bestride the gossamers
That idles in the wanton summer air,
And yet not fall; so light is vanity.

Juliet: Good even to my ghostly confessor.

Friar Lawrence: Romeo shall thank thee, daughter, for us both.

Juliet: As much to him, else is his thanks too much.

Practice Papers — Paper 1

Macbeth

2 1 Read the extract below. You should only write about the extract in your answer to this question.

Paying close attention to the characters' actions and dialogue, write about how an audience could react to this extract.

(15 marks)

2 2 Write about the theme of masculinity in the play.
In your response, you should focus on how Shakespeare presents this theme.

(20 marks)
(+5 marks for spelling, punctuation and grammar)

Macbeth: Speak if you can: what are you?
First Witch: All hail Macbeth! Hail to thee, Thane of Glamis!
Second Witch: All hail Macbeth! Hail to thee, Thane of Cawdor!
Third Witch: All hail Macbeth that shalt be king hereafter!
Banquo: Good sir, why do you start, and seem to fear
Things that do sound so fair? I'th'name of truth
Are ye fantastical, or that indeed
Which outwardly ye show? My noble partner
You greet with present grace and great prediction
Of noble having and of royal hope,
That he seems rapt withal. To me you speak not.
If you can look into the seeds of time
And say which grain will grow and which will not,
Speak then to me, who neither beg nor fear
Your favours nor your hate.
First Witch: Hail!
Second Witch: Hail!
Third Witch: Hail!
First Witch: Lesser than Macbeth, and greater.
Second Witch: Not so happy, yet much happier.
Third Witch: Thou shalt get kings, though thou be none.
So all hail Macbeth and Banquo!
First Witch: Banquo and Macbeth, all hail!
Macbeth: Stay, you imperfect speakers. Tell me more.
By Sinel's death, I know I am Thane of Glamis,
But how of Cawdor? The Thane of Cawdor lives
A prosperous gentleman, and to be king
Stands not within the prospect of belief,
No more than to be Cawdor. Say from whence
You owe this strange intelligence, or why
Upon this blasted heath you stop our way
With such prophetic greeting? Speak, I charge you.
[*Witches vanish.*]

Othello

3 1 Read the extract below.

Write about what this part of the play reveals about Othello's state of mind, referring to examples from the extract in your response.

(15 marks)

3 2 Write about the character of Cassio and how Shakespeare presents him at different points in *Othello*.

(20 marks)
(+5 marks for spelling, punctuation and grammar)

Othello:	It is the cause, it is the cause, my soul:
	Let me not name it to you, you chaste stars,
	It is the cause. Yet I'll not shed her blood;
	Nor scar that whiter skin of hers than snow
	And smooth as monumental alabaster.
	Yet she must die, else she'll betray more men.
	Put out the light, and then put out the light:
	If I quench thee, thou flaming minister,
	I can again thy former light restore
	Should I repent me; but once put out thy light,
	Thou cunning'st pattern of excelling nature,
	I know not where is that Promethean heat
	That can thy light relume. When I have pluck'd the rose
	I cannot give it vital growth again.
	It must needs wither: I'll smell it on the tree.
	[*Kissing her*]
	Ah balmy breath, that dost almost persuade
	Justice to break her sword! One more, one more:
	Be thus when thou art dead, and I will kill thee,
	And love thee after. One more, and this the last.
	So sweet was ne'er so fatal. I must weep,
	But they are cruel tears: this sorrow's heavenly;
	It strikes where it doth love. She wakes.
Desdemona:	Who's there? Othello?
Othello:	Ay. Desdemona.
Desdemona:	Will you come to bed, my lord?
Othello:	Have you pray'd tonight, Desdemona?
Desdemona:	Ay, my lord.
Othello:	If you bethink yourself of any crime
	Unreconciled as yet to heaven and grace,
	Solicit for it straight.
Desdemona:	Alas, my lord, what do you mean by that?
Othello:	Well, do it, and be brief; I will walk by.
	I would not kill thy unprepared spirit;
	No; heaven forfend, I would not kill thy soul.

Much Ado About Nothing

4 1 Read the extract below. You should only write about the extract in your answer to this question.

Paying close attention to Benedick and Beatrice's actions and dialogue, write about how an audience could react to this extract.

(15 marks)

4 2 Explore how Shakespeare presents the character of Dogberry in *Much Ado About Nothing*.

(20 marks)
(+5 marks for spelling, punctuation and grammar)

[*Enter Beatrice*]

Benedick:	Sweet Beatrice, wouldst thou come when I called thee?
Beatrice:	Yea, signior, and depart when you bid me.
Benedick:	O, stay but till then!
Beatrice:	'Then' is spoken — fare you well now, and yet, ere I go, let me go with that I came, which is, with knowing what hath passed between you and Claudio.
Benedick:	Only foul words; and thereupon I will kiss thee.
Beatrice:	Foul words is but foul wind, and foul wind is but foul breath, and foul breath is noisome — therefore I will depart unkissed.
Benedick:	Thou hast frighted the word out of his right sense, so forcible is thy wit. But I must tell thee plainly, Claudio undergoes my challenge, and either I must shortly hear from him, or I will subscribe him a coward. And, I pray thee now, tell me for which of my bad parts didst thou first fall in love with me?
Beatrice:	For them all together, which maintained so politic a state of evil that they will not admit any good part to intermingle with them. But for which of my good parts did you first suffer love for me?
Benedick:	Suffer love! A good epithet! I do suffer love indeed, for I love thee against my will.
Beatrice:	In spite of your heart, I think. Alas, poor heart! If you spite it for my sake, I will spite it for yours, for I will never love that which my friend hates.
Benedick:	Thou and I are too wise to woo peaceably.

Henry V

5 1 Read the extract below. You should only write about the extract in your answer to this question.

Paying close attention to Henry's behaviour and speech, write about how an audience could react to this extract.

(15 marks)

5 2 Write about the character of Pistol and how Shakespeare presents him at different points in *Henry V*.

(20 marks)
(+5 marks for spelling, punctuation and grammar)

King Henry V: Upon the king! Let us our lives, our souls,
Our debts, our careful wives,
Our children and our sins lay on the king!
We must bear all. O hard condition,
Twin-born with greatness, subject to the breath
Of every fool whose sense no more can feel
But his own wringing. What infinite heart's-ease
Must kings neglect, that private men enjoy!
And what have kings, that privates have not too,
Save ceremony, save general ceremony?
And what art thou, thou idle ceremony?
What kind of god art thou, that suffer'st more
Of mortal griefs than do thy worshippers?
What are thy rents? What are thy comings-in?
O ceremony, show me but thy worth!
What is thy soul of adoration?
Art thou aught else but place, degree and form,
Creating awe and fear in other men?
Wherein thou art less happy, being fear'd,
Than they in fearing?
What drink'st thou oft, instead of homage sweet,
But poison'd flattery? O, be sick, great greatness,
And bid thy ceremony give thee cure!
Think'st thou the fiery fever will go out
With titles blown from adulation?
Will it give place to flexure and low bending?
Canst thou, when thou command'st the beggar's knee,
Command the health of it?

The Merchant of Venice

6 1 Read the extract below. You should only write about the extract in your answer to this question.

Paying close attention to Portia's actions and dialogue,
write about how an audience could react to this extract.

(15 marks)

6 2 Using evidence from the text, write about points in the play when
the audience might feel sympathetic towards Antonio.

(20 marks)
(+5 marks for spelling, punctuation and grammar)

Portia: The quality of mercy is not strained;
It droppeth as the gentle rain from heaven
Upon the place beneath. It is twice blest;
It blesseth him that gives and him that takes.
'Tis mightiest in the mightiest; it becomes
The thronèd monarch better than his crown.
His sceptre shows the force of temporal power,
The attribute to awe and majesty,
Wherein doth sit the dread and fear of kings;
But mercy is above this sceptred sway;
It is enthronèd in the hearts of kings;
It is an attribute to God himself,
And earthly power doth then show likest God's
When mercy seasons justice. Therefore, Jew,
Though justice be thy plea, consider this:
That, in the course of justice, none of us
Should see salvation: we do pray for mercy,
And that same prayer doth teach us all to render
The deeds of mercy. I have spoke thus much
To mitigate the justice of thy plea,
Which if thou follow, this strict court of Venice
Must needs give sentence 'gainst the merchant there.

Section B: Poetry Anthology
Answer **both** questions from this section.
Spend about **20** minutes on the **first** question and **40** minutes on the **second**.

The poems in this anthology are:
- *The Manhunt* (Simon Armitage)
- *Sonnet 43* (Elizabeth Barrett Browning)
- *London* (William Blake)
- *The Soldier* (Rupert Brooke)
- *She Walks in Beauty* (Lord Byron)
- *Living Space* (Imtiaz Dharker)
- *As Imperceptibly as Grief* (Emily Dickinson)
- *Cozy Apologia* (Rita Dove)
- *Valentine* (Carol Ann Duffy)
- *A Wife in London* (Thomas Hardy)
- *Death of a Naturalist* (Seamus Heaney)
- *Hawk Roosting* (Ted Hughes)
- *To Autumn* (John Keats)
- *Afternoons* (Philip Larkin)
- *Dulce et Decorum Est* (Wilfred Owen)
- *Ozymandias* (Percy Bysshe Shelley)
- *Mametz Wood* (Owen Sheers)
- Excerpt from '*The Prelude*' (William Wordsworth)

7 1 In the excerpt from 'The Prelude', Wordsworth writes about the theme of childhood.
Explore how childhood is presented in this excerpt.
You should write about the contexts of the excerpt in your answer.
(15 marks)

7 2 Select another poem from the anthology about the theme of childhood.
Compare how childhood is presented in this poem and
the way it is presented in the excerpt from 'The Prelude'.

You should compare:
- what the poems are about and the way they are organised
- how the poets create effects in the poems
- the poems' contexts, and how the poems are influenced by these contexts.

Remember to use subject-specific terminology in your response.
(25 marks)

Excerpt from 'The Prelude' by William Wordsworth

And in the frosty season, when the sun
Was set, and visible for many a mile
The cottage windows through the twilight blaz'd,
I heeded not the summons: – happy time
It was, indeed, for all of us; to me
It was a time of rapture: clear and loud
The village clock toll'd six; I wheel'd about,
Proud and exulting, like an untir'd horse,
That cares not for his home. – All shod with steel,
We hiss'd along the polish'd ice, in games
Confederate, imitative of the chace
And woodland pleasures, the resounding horn,
The Pack loud bellowing, and the hunted hare.
So through the darkness and the cold we flew,
And not a voice was idle; with the din,
Meanwhile, the precipices rang aloud,
The leafless trees, and every icy crag
Tinkled like iron, while the distant hills
Into the tumult sent an alien sound
Of melancholy, not unnoticed, while the stars,
Eastward, were sparkling clear, and in the west
The orange sky of evening died away.

Practice Papers — Paper 1

96

CGP Practice Exam Paper: GCSE English Literature

General Certificate of Secondary Education

GCSE
English Literature

Surname

Other names

Candidate signature

Centre name

Centre number

Candidate number

Paper 2:
Post-1914 Prose/Drama,
19th-Century Prose and
Unseen Poetry

Time allowed: 2 hours 30 minutes
Instructions to candidates
- You should answer **one** question from **Section A** (p.97-100), **one** question from **Section B** (p.101-106) and **both** questions in **Section C** (p.107-108).
- Write your answers in black ink or ball-point pen.
- Write your name and other details in the boxes **above**.

Information for candidates
- The marks available are given in brackets.
- There are 120 marks available for this exam paper — 40 marks for each section.
- The marks for Section A include 5 marks for accuracy in spelling, punctuation and the use of vocabulary and sentence structures.

Section A: Post-1914 Prose/Drama

Answer **one** question from this section.
Spend about **45** minutes on this section.

Lord of the Flies

0 1 Read the extract from Chapter 5 which begins "The thing is — fear can't hurt you..." and ends "Unless we get frightened of people", then answer the question.

Using this part of the novel as a starting point, write about how fear is presented in *Lord of the Flies*.

In your answer, make sure you:
- write about both the extract and the novel as a whole;
- show that you understand the events and characters in the novel.

(35 marks)
(+5 marks for spelling, punctuation and grammar)

Anita and Me

0 2 Read the extract from Chapter 6 which begins "When I said that we talked..." and ends "...and buying me stuff", then answer the question.

Using this part of the novel as a starting point, explore how Syal portrays the relationship between Meena and Anita, and the ways in which it is important to the novel as a whole.

In your answer, make sure you:
- write about both the extract and the novel as a whole;
- show that you understand the events and characters in the novel.

(35 marks)
(+5 marks for spelling, punctuation and grammar)

Practice Papers — Paper 2

Never Let Me Go

0 3 Read the extract from Chapter 23 which begins "I was talking to one of my donors..." and ends "...no one can take away", then answer the question.

Using this part of the novel as a starting point, write about memory and the way it is presented in *Never Let Me Go*.

In your answer, make sure you:

- write about both the extract and the novel as a whole;
- show that you understand the events and characters in the novel.

(35 marks)
(+5 marks for spelling, punctuation and grammar)

The Woman In Black

0 4 Read the extract from 'Mr Jerome is Afraid' which begins "I intended to cycle" to the end of the chapter, then answer the question.

Using this part of the novel as a starting point, write about the character of Arthur and the way he is presented in *The Woman in Black*.

In your answer, make sure you:

- write about both the extract and the novel as a whole;
- show that you understand the events and characters in the text.

(35 marks)
(+5 marks for spelling, punctuation and grammar)

Oranges are not the Only Fruit

0 5 Read the extract from 'Joshua' which begins "Over breakfast the next morning..." and ends "I hardly heard what she said", then answer the question.

Using this part of the novel as a starting point, write about how Melanie and the way she is presented in *Oranges are not the Only Fruit*.

In your answer, make sure you:

- write about both the extract and the novel as a whole;
- show that you understand the events and characters in the text.

(35 marks)
(+5 marks for spelling, punctuation and grammar)

Practice Papers — Paper 2

The Curious Incident of the Dog in the Night-Time

0 6 Read the extract from Part One which begins "ED: Christopher? Christopher?" and ends "So... I killed Wellington, Christopher", then answer the question.

Using this part of the play as a starting point, write about honesty and dishonesty and the way they are presented in *The Curious Incident of the Dog in the Night-Time*.

In your answer, make sure you:
- write about both the extract and the play as a whole;
- show that you understand the events and characters in the play.

(35 marks)
(+5 marks for spelling, punctuation and grammar)

A Taste of Honey

0 7 Read the extract from Act 2, Scene 1 which begins "JO: Please stay, Geof." and ends "There's plenty of time.", then answer the question.

Using this part of the play as a starting point, write about Jo and the way she is presented in *A Taste of Honey*.

In your answer, make sure you:
- write about both the extract and the play as a whole;
- show that you understand the events and characters in the play.

(35 marks)
(+5 marks for spelling, punctuation and grammar)

An Inspector Calls

0 8 Read the extract from near the end of Act 2 which begins "SHEILA [*with feeling*]: Mother, I think it was cruel and vile." and ends "...wasn't his money", then answer the question.

Using this part of the play as a starting point, write about the theme of social class and how it is presented in *An Inspector Calls*.

In your answer, make sure you:
- write about both the extract and the play as a whole;
- show that you understand the events and characters in the play.

(35 marks)
(+5 marks for spelling, punctuation and grammar)

Practice Papers — Paper 2

The History Boys

0 9 Read the extract from Act 1 which begins "IRWIN: "It's just that the boys seem to know..." and ends "Life goes on. Gobbets!"

Using this part of the play as a starting point, write about education and how it is presented in *The History Boys*.

In your answer, make sure you:
- write about both the extract and the play as a whole;
- show that you understand the events and characters in the play.

(35 marks)
(+5 marks for spelling, punctuation and grammar)

Blood Brothers

1 0 Read the extract from Act 2 which begins "MICKEY: *[enters his house]*" and ends "Now give me them", then answer the question.

Using this part of the play as a starting point, write about the character of Mickey and the way he changes during the course of *Blood Brothers*.

In your answer, make sure you:
- write about both the extract and the play as a whole;
- show that you understand the events and characters in the play.

(35 marks)
(+5 marks for spelling, punctuation and grammar)

Section B: 19th-Century Prose

Answer **one** question from this section.
Spend about **45** minutes on this section.

A Christmas Carol

2 1 Read the extract below, then answer the question.

Using this part of the text as a starting point, write about how Dickens presents poverty in *A Christmas Carol*.

In your answer, make sure you:
- write about both the extract below and the text as a whole;
- show that you understand the events and characters in the text;
- write about the text's contexts.

(40 marks)

From the foldings of its robe, it brought two children; wretched, abject, frightful, hideous, miserable. They knelt down at its feet, and clung upon the outside of its garment.

"Oh, Man! look here. Look, look, down here!" exclaimed the Ghost.

They were a boy and girl. Yellow, meagre, ragged, scowling, wolfish; but prostrate, too, in their humility. Where graceful youth should have filled their features out, and touched them with its freshest tints, a stale and shrivelled hand, like that of age, had pinched, and twisted them, and pulled them into shreds. Where angels might have sat enthroned, devils lurked, and glared out menacing. No change, no degradation, no perversion of humanity, in any grade, through all the mysteries of wonderful creation, has monsters half so horrible and dread.

Scrooge started back, appalled. Having them shown to him in this way, he tried to say they were fine children, but the words choked themselves, rather than be parties to a lie of such enormous magnitude.

"Spirit! are they yours?" Scrooge could say no more.

"They are Man's," said the Spirit, looking down upon them. "And they cling to me, appealing from their fathers. This boy is Ignorance. This girl is Want. Beware them both, and all of their degree, but most of all beware this boy, for on his brow I see that written which is Doom, unless the writing be erased. Deny it!" cried the Spirit, stretching out its hand towards the city. "Slander those who tell it ye! Admit it for your factious purposes, and make it worse. And bide the end!"

"Have they no refuge or resource?" cried Scrooge.

"Are there no prisons?" said the Spirit, turning on him for the last time with his own words. "Are there no workhouses?"

The bell struck twelve.

Silas Marner

2 2 Read the extract below, then answer the question.

Using this part of the novel as a starting point, write about how Eliot presents Dolly Winthrop.

In your answer, make sure you:

- write about both the extract below and the novel as a whole;
- show that you understand the events and characters in the novel;
- write about the novel's contexts.

(40 marks)

"I'd a baking yisterday, Master Marner, and the lard-cakes turned out better nor common, and I'd ha' asked you to accept some, if you'd thought well. I don't eat such things myself, for a bit o' bread's what I like from one year's end to the other; but men's stomichs are made so comical, they want a change — they do, I know, God help 'em."

Dolly sighed gently as she held out the cakes to Silas, who thanked her kindly and looked very close at them, absently, being accustomed to look so at everything he took into his hand — eyed all the while by the wondering bright orbs of the small Aaron, who had made an outwork of his mother's chair, and was peeping round from behind it.

"There's letters pricked on 'em," said Dolly. "I can't read 'em myself, and there's nobody, not Mr. Macey himself, rightly knows what they mean; but they've a good meaning, for they're the same as is on the pulpit-cloth at church. What are they, Aaron, my dear?"

Aaron retreated completely behind his outwork.

"Oh, go, that's naughty," said his mother, mildly. "Well, whativer the letters are, they've a good meaning; and it's a stamp as has been in our house, Ben says, ever since he was a little un, and his mother used to put it on the cakes, and I've allays put it on too; for if there's any good, we've need of it i' this world."

"It's I. H. S.," said Silas, at which proof of learning Aaron peeped round the chair again.

"Well, to be sure, you can read 'em off," said Dolly. "Ben's read 'em to me many and many a time, but they slip out o' my mind again; the more's the pity, for they're good letters, else they wouldn't be in the church; and so I prick 'em on all the loaves and all the cakes, though sometimes they won't hold, because o' the rising — for, as I said, if there's any good to be got we've need of it i' this world — that we have; and I hope they'll bring good to you, Master Marner, for it's wi' that will I brought you the cakes; and you see the letters have held better nor common."

Silas was as unable to interpret the letters as Dolly, but there was no possibility of misunderstanding the desire to give comfort that made itself heard in her quiet tones. He said, with more feeling than before — "Thank you — thank you kindly." But he laid down the cakes and seated himself absently — drearily unconscious of any distinct benefit towards which the cakes and the letters, or even Dolly's kindness, could tend for him.

War of the Worlds

2 3 Read the extract below, then answer the question.

Using this extract as a starting point, write about how Wells presents humans in the novel, and the ways in which they are important to the novel as a whole.

In your answer, make sure you:
- write about both the extract below and the novel as a whole;
- show that you understand the events and characters in the novel.
- write about the novel's contexts.

(40 marks)

There were sad, haggard women tramping by, well dressed, with children that cried and stumbled, their dainty clothes smothered in dust, their weary faces smeared with tears. With many of these came men, sometimes helpful, sometimes lowering and savage. Fighting side by side with them pushed some weary street outcast in faded black rags, wide-eyed, loud-voiced, and foul-mouthed. There were sturdy workmen thrusting their way along, wretched, unkempt men, clothed like clerks or shopmen, struggling spasmodically; a wounded soldier my brother noticed, men dressed in the clothes of railway porters, one wretched creature in a nightshirt with a coat thrown over it.

But varied as its composition was, certain things all that host had in common. There were fear and pain on their faces, and fear behind them. A tumult up the road, a quarrel for a place in a waggon, sent the whole host of them quickening their pace; even a man so scared and broken that his knees bent under him was galvanised for a moment into renewed activity. The heat and dust had already been at work upon this multitude. Their skins were dry, their lips black and cracked. They were all thirsty, weary, and footsore. And amid the various cries one heard disputes, reproaches, groans of weariness and fatigue; the voices of most of them were hoarse and weak. Through it all ran a refrain:

"Way! Way! The Martians are coming!"

Few stopped and came aside from that flood. The lane opened slantingly into the main road with a narrow opening, and had a delusive appearance of coming from the direction of London. Yet a kind of eddy of people drove into its mouth; weaklings elbowed out of the stream, who for the most part rested but a moment before plunging into it again. A little way down the lane, with two friends bending over him, lay a man with a bare leg, wrapped about with bloody rags. He was a lucky man to have friends.

A little old man, with a grey military moustache and a filthy black frock coat, limped out and sat down beside the trap, removed his boot — his sock was blood-stained — shook out a pebble, and hobbled on again; and then a little girl of eight or nine, all alone, threw herself under the hedge close by my brother, weeping.

"I can't go on! I can't go on!"

My brother woke from his torpor of astonishment and lifted her up, speaking gently to her, and carried her to Miss Elphinstone. So soon as my brother touched her she became quite still, as if frightened.

"Ellen!" shrieked a woman in the crowd, with tears in her voice — "Ellen!" And the child suddenly darted away from my brother, crying "Mother!"

"They are coming," said a man on horseback, riding past along the lane.

Pride and Prejudice

2 4 Read the extract below, then answer the question.

Using this part of the novel as a starting point, explore how Austen portrays the relationship between Mr and Mrs Bennet.

In your answer, make sure you:
- write about both the extract below and the novel as a whole;
- show that you understand the events and characters in the novel;
- write about the novel's contexts.

(40 marks)

"I see no occasion for that. You and the girls may go, or you may send them by themselves, which perhaps will be still better, for as you are as handsome as any of them, Mr. Bingley may like you the best of the party."

"My dear, you flatter me. I certainly have had my share of beauty, but I do not pretend to be anything extraordinary now. When a woman has five grown-up daughters, she ought to give over thinking of her own beauty."

"In such cases, a woman has not often much beauty to think of."

"But, my dear, you must indeed go and see Mr. Bingley when he comes into the neighbourhood."

"It is more than I engage for, I assure you."

"But consider your daughters. Only think what an establishment it would be for one of them. Sir William and Lady Lucas are determined to go, merely on that account, for in general, you know, they visit no newcomers. Indeed you must go, for it will be impossible for us to visit him if you do not."

"You are over-scrupulous, surely. I dare say Mr. Bingley will be very glad to see you; and I will send a few lines by you to assure him of my hearty consent to his marrying whichever he chooses of the girls; though I must throw in a good word for my little Lizzy."

"I desire you will do no such thing. Lizzy is not a bit better than the others; and I am sure she is not half so handsome as Jane, nor half so good-humoured as Lydia. But you are always giving her the preference."

"They have none of them much to recommend them," replied he; "they are all silly and ignorant like other girls; but Lizzy has something more of quickness than her sisters."

"Mr. Bennet, how can you abuse your own children in such a way? You take delight in vexing me. You have no compassion for my poor nerves."

"You mistake me, my dear. I have a high respect for your nerves. They are my old friends. I have heard you mention them with consideration these last twenty years at least."

Jane Eyre

2 5 Read the extract below, then answer the question.

Using this part of the novel as a starting point, write about Mr Rochester and the ways in which he changes throughout the novel.

In your answer, make sure you:
- write about both the extract below and the novel as a whole;
- show that you understand the events and characters in the novel;
- write about the novel's contexts.

(40 marks)

"Jane! you think me, I daresay, an irreligious dog: but my heart swells with gratitude to the beneficent God of this earth just now. He sees not as man sees, but far clearer: judges not as man judges, but far more wisely. I did wrong: I would have sullied my innocent flower — breathed guilt on its purity: the Omnipotent snatched it from me. I, in my stiff-necked rebellion, almost cursed the dispensation: instead of bending to the decree, I defied it. Divine justice pursued its course; disasters came thick on me: I was forced to pass through the valley of the shadow of death. His chastisements are mighty; and one smote me which has humbled me for ever. You know I was proud of my strength: but what is it now, when I must give it over to foreign guidance, as a child does its weakness? Of late, Jane — only — only of late — I began to see and acknowledge the hand of God in my doom. I began to experience remorse, repentance, the wish for reconcilement to my Maker. I began sometimes to pray: very brief prayers they were, but very sincere.

"Some days since: nay, I can number them — four; it was last Monday night, a singular mood came over me: one in which grief replaced frenzy — sorrow, sullenness. I had long had the impression that since I could nowhere find you, you must be dead. Late that night — perhaps it might be between eleven and twelve o'clock — ere I retired to my dreary rest, I supplicated God, that, if it seemed good to Him, I might soon be taken from this life, and admitted to that world to come, where there was still hope of rejoining Jane.

"I was in my own room, and sitting by the window, which was open: it soothed me to feel the balmy night-air; though I could see no stars, and only by a vague, luminous haze, knew the presence of a moon. I longed for thee, Janet! Oh, I longed for thee both with soul and flesh! I asked of God, at once in anguish and humility, if I had not been long enough desolate, afflicted, tormented; and might not soon taste bliss and peace once more. That I merited all I endured, I acknowledged — that I could scarcely endure more, I pleaded; and the alpha and omega of my heart's wishes broke involuntarily from my lips in the words, 'Jane! Jane! Jane!'"

The Strange Case of Dr Jekyll and Mr Hyde

2 6 Read the extract below, then answer the question.

Using this part of the novel as a starting point, write about how Stevenson presents morality in the *The Strange Case of Dr Jekyll and Mr Hyde*.

In your answer, make sure you:
- write about both the extract below and the novel as a whole;
- show that you understand the events and characters in the novel;
- write about the novel's contexts.

(40 marks)

I was the first that could thus plod in the public eye with a load of genial respectability, and in a moment, like a schoolboy, strip off these lendings and spring headlong into the sea of liberty. But for me, in my impenetrable mantle, the safety was complete. Think of it — I did not even exist! Let me but escape into my laboratory door, give me but a second or two to mix and swallow the draught that I had always standing ready; and whatever he had done, Edward Hyde would pass away like the stain of breath upon a mirror; and there in his stead, quietly at home, trimming the midnight lamp in his study, a man who could afford to laugh at suspicion, would be Henry Jekyll.

The pleasures which I made haste to seek in my disguise were, as I have said, undignified; I would scarce use a harder term. But in the hands of Edward Hyde, they soon began to turn towards the monstrous. When I would come back from these excursions, I was often plunged into a kind of wonder at my vicarious depravity. This familiar that I called out of my own soul, and sent forth alone to do his good pleasure, was a being inherently malign and villainous; his every act and thought centred on self; drinking pleasure with bestial avidity from any degree of torture to another; relentless like a man of stone. Henry Jekyll stood at times aghast before the acts of Edward Hyde; but the situation was apart from ordinary laws, and insidiously relaxed the grasp of conscience. It was Hyde, after all, and Hyde alone, that was guilty. Jekyll was no worse; he woke again to his good qualities seemingly unimpaired; he would even make haste, where it was possible, to undo the evil done by Hyde. And thus his conscience slumbered.

Section C: Unseen Poetry

Answer **both** questions from this section.

For a Five-Year-Old

A snail is climbing up the window-sill
into your room, after a night of rain.
You call me in to see, and I explain
that it would be unkind to leave it there:
it might crawl to the floor; we must take care
that no one squashes it. You understand,
and carry it outside, with careful hand,
to eat a daffodil.

I see, then, that a kind of faith prevails:
your gentleness is moulded still by words
from me, who have trapped mice and shot wild birds,
from me, who drowned your kittens, who betrayed
your closest relatives, and who purveyed
the harshest kind of truth to many another.
But that is how things are: I am your mother,
and we are kind to snails.

Fleur Adcock

---

3 1 — 'For a Five-Year-Old' and 'The Beautiful Lie' (p.108) both portray relationships between adults and children.

Write about 'For a Five-Year-Old' and how you react to it.

You could think about:
- what the poem is about
- the message that the poet is trying to convey
- the form, structure and language used in the poem and their effects

(15 marks)

The Beautiful Lie

He was about four, I think… it was so long ago.
In a garden; he'd done some damage
behind a bright screen of sweet-peas
– snapped a stalk, a stake, I don't recall,
but the grandmother came and saw, and asked him
"Did you do that?"

Now, if she'd said *why* did you do that,
he'd never have denied it. She showed him
he had a choice. I could see in his face
the new sense, the possible. That word and deed
need not match, that you could say the world
different, to suit you.

When he said "No", I swear it was as moving
as the first time a baby's fist clenches
on a finger, as momentous as the first
taste of fruit. I could feel his eyes looking
through a new window, at a world whose form
and colour weren't fixed

but fluid, that poured like a snake, trembled
around the edges like northern lights, shape-shifted
at the spell of a voice. I could sense him filling
like a glass, hear the unreal sea in his ears.
*This is how to make songs, create men, paint pictures,
tell a story.*

I think I made up the screen of sweet-peas.
Maybe they were beans, maybe there was no screen:
it just felt as if there should be, somehow.
And he was my – no, I don't need to tell that.
I know I made up the screen. And I recall very well
what he had done.

Sheenagh Pugh

3 2 Write a comparison of 'For a Five-Year-Old' and 'The Beautiful Lie'.

You should write about:
- what the poems are about and how you react to them
- the messages that the poets are trying to convey
- the form, structure and language used in the poems and their effects

(25 marks)

Answers

Section Two — Prose and Drama

Pages 22-23 — Warm-Up Questions

1) a) characterisation
   b) theme
   c) mood/atmosphere

2) Answer depends on chosen text.

3) Answers should focus on what the character is like, how the writer presents them and how this makes you feel about them. Here are some points you could consider:
   - Actions: What does the character do in the text? How does he or she treat other people? How do their actions make you feel about them?
   - Structure: Does the character change over the course of the text? Do they learn anything?
   - Language: How is the character described? How does the character speak? Does this make them likeable or not to you?

4) Answer depends on chosen text. E.g. for 'A Christmas Carol', you could have picked out the following themes:
   - Social responsibility
     It is implied that Scrooge helping the Cratchits at the end of the novel saves Tiny Tim's life. This shows how important social responsibility is — it can save lives.
   - Redemption
     The contrast between Scrooge's behaviour at the beginning and at the end of the novel. This emphasises that anyone, even someone as miserly and mean as Scrooge, has the potential to be redeemed.
   - Family
     The Cratchits are "happy, grateful, pleased with one another, and contented with the time", despite their poverty. This shows that family can bring comfort and joy to life, regardless of the hardships that people have to endure.

5) Answer depends on chosen text. E.g.
   - You might write that the message of 'Macbeth' is: 'Ambition and lust for power can drive the humanity out of a person.'
   - You might write that the message of 'Pride and Prejudice' is: 'Don't judge people on first impressions or superficial qualities.'

6) Answer depends on chosen text. Here are some points you could consider:
   - What did you think about the characters?
   - How did you feel at different points in the text?
   - Did you agree with the writer's message?

7) Answer depends on chosen text.

8) Answers should focus on what atmosphere the writer creates, how they create it and the effect it has on the reader. Here are some points you could consider:
   - Structure: Does the writer reveal what's happening gradually or suddenly?
   - Language: What words does the writer use? How do they make you feel? Does the writer use any techniques to create or add to the atmosphere (e.g. imagery)?
   - Form: Are the sentences long or short? Do they vary in length? What effect does this have?

9) a) E.g. "The conch shell represents democracy — it enables the boys to impose a fair system on their meetings that allows them all a chance to put their views across."
   b) E.g. "The old chestnut tree symbolises Jane's relationship with Mr Rochester. Just as the tree is split in two by lightning, Jane and Mr Rochester are separated by the revelation that he is already married."
   c) E.g. "Driving is a symbol for freedom. The students have little control over their lives, but they believe that driving would give them some freedom and a sense of being able to escape from their lives."

10) Answers should focus on what the structural feature is and the effect it creates. Here are some points you could consider:
    - What is the feature? Why do you think the writer chose to use it at this point in the story?
    - Does it add to your enjoyment of the text? If so, how?
    - How would the text be different if the writer had not used this feature or had used a different structure?

11) Paragraph a) shows better use of quotations, because it uses short quotations that are embedded into the text.

Page 24 — Exam-Style Questions

1) For this question, you're asked to focus on one scene. Make sure you pick one that you think shows your chosen character in an interesting light, so you'll have plenty of things to write about. You need to really get to grips with the language, and show how Shakespeare uses words to influence the reader's opinion of the character. This answer is for the character of Beatrice in Act 2, Scene 1 of 'Much Ado About Nothing', but it's worth reading even if you're studying a different play. Here are some things you could mention:
   - Act 2, Scene 1 of 'Much Ado About Nothing' starts with Beatrice criticising Don John because he is "too like an image and says nothing". This shows her to be judgemental and somewhat cruel in her assessment of others.
   - Despite this, however, she appears to be well-liked. Rather than telling her off for her cruelty, Leonato just reminds her that she will never find a husband if she continues to be so "shrewd of tongue". This shows that he is more concerned about the consequences of her behaviour than how rude she is being, which implies that he cares about her future and wellbeing.
   - Beatrice's conversation with Leonato also highlights her wit. For example, she answers Leonato's hope that she will be "fitted with a husband" by arguing that "Adam's sons are my brethren, and truly I hold it a sin to match in my kindred." In this line, she plays on the biblical idea that all men are descended from Adam in order to emphasise her point. This shows her intelligence and ability to think quickly. Jokes about incest would have been considered shocking in Shakespeare's day, so this also shows the extent to which Beatrice flouts convention and ignores the rules of society.
   - When the questioning turns to Hero, Beatrice supports her by suggesting that Hero should have some say in who she marries: "let him be a handsome fellow, or else make another curtsy" and by advising Hero not to rush into marriage: "there is measure in every thing". This shows Beatrice to be loyal to her cousin, but the fact that she repeatedly answers questions addressed to Hero makes her seem over-bearing. This suggests that her intentions are good, but that she can be insensitive in her efforts to protect the people she cares about. Her tendency to talk too much links her to her own assessment of Benedick, "evermore tattling", and hints to the audience that they may be destined for each other.

- However, Beatrice's lack of awareness of how suitable Benedick is for her is highlighted by their exchange. Pretending that she does not know it is Benedick, she calls him "a very dull fool" and says that his only gift is "devising impossible slanders". This shows that she has a cruel gift for finding and playing on people's weaknesses, whilst being unaware of her own.
- The more positive side of Beatrice's personality is shown by Don Pedro's reaction to her: he calls her a "pleasant-spirited lady", says she was "born in a merry hour" and jokingly proposes to her. This shows that, when she does not see men as a threat, Beatrice is capable of being very charming.

2) For this question, you have to focus on a single passage from a prose text you're studying and then write about the rest of the text. You should focus on the way that the author has used language, structure and form to create a feeling of tension or excitement. This answer is about tension in 'The War of the Worlds', focusing on Book 2, Chapter 4, from "Something was moving to and fro" to the end of the chapter, but it's worth reading even if you're studying a different novel. Here are some things you could mention:

- There is a strong sense of tension at the beginning of the extract. The use of "Something" at the start creates a tense atmosphere because neither the narrator nor the reader knows what's moving. This also engages the reader by encouraging them to read on and discover what is moving outside the scullery.
- The contrast between the urgent language of the narrator's thoughts and the tentacle's measured movement creates tension in this extract. The narrator describes himself as being "on the verge of screaming" and "whispered passionate prayers" in his fear, whereas the tentacle's movement make a "slow, deliberate sound". These opposing descriptions emphasise the intensity of the narrator's fear at this point in the novel, creating tension as the reader waits to see if he will survive unscathed.
- Well's animalistic descriptions of the Martians create tension in the extract. The narrator describes the tentacle as "like an elephant's trunk" and a "black worm swaying its blind head to and fro". These animalistic descriptions suggest that the Martians are wild and therefore unpredictable, which increases the tension by implying that neither the reader nor the narrator can be sure about what the Martian will do next.
- Wells also uses the structure of the novel in order to create tension. For example, he ends the first chapter with the narrator describing a pleasant walk with his wife, saying that his situation "seemed so safe and tranquil". The narrator is speaking with hindsight, so ending the chapter with this reflection hints that the narrator's life is about to change for the worse, creating a cliffhanger that builds tension as the reader worries about what will happen to the narrator in the rest of the novel.
- Wells also creates tension when the narrator first sees the Martians. Before describing in detail the Martian who comes out of the cylinder, the narrator says "A sudden chill came over me". This description of his reaction to the creature's appearance creates tension by suggesting something unnatural and sinister is coming out of the cylinder. The use of the sensory word "chill" also gives the reader a powerful impression of the narrator's reaction. This leaves the reader to anticipate the potentially horrifying Martian exiting the cylinder.

3) For this question, you have to focus on a single passage from a prose text you're studying, then write about the rest of the text. You should focus on the way the author has used language, structure and form to present the character. This answer is about Mr Birling in 'An Inspector Calls', focusing on Act 1 from "I just want to say this..." to "absolutely unsinkable", but it's worth reading whatever text you're studying, because it'll give you an idea of the kind of things you should be writing about. Here are some things you could mention:

- Mr Birling is presented in the extract as obsessed with money. He describes Gerald and Sheila's marriage as coming at a "very good time" because it is a time of "steadily increasing prosperity". This shows money is always at the forefront of his mind, even when discussing apparently unrelated topics such as love and marriage. Mr Birling's reference to the miner's strike as something that Gerald and Sheila may "worry" about also hints that he values money and his family's financial security over the welfare of the miners and other struggling workers.
- Priestley uses dramatic irony in this extract to suggest that Birling is foolish: he predicts that there "isn't a chance" of war with Germany and that the Titanic is "unsinkable". These references to famous events that hadn't occurred in early 1912, when the play is set, would have been proven wrong by 1946, when the play was first performed. This makes Birling seem misguided and unintelligent. Birling's inaccurate predictions also imply that he could be wrong about the beliefs he demonstrates later in the play, such as the idea that people shouldn't have responsibility for one another in society.
- Birling's selfish nature first becomes apparent earlier in Act 1, when he says that Sheila and Gerald's marriage means "a tremendous lot" to him because it will bring together his company and a rival company. This suggests that his feelings about the marriage are focused on how it will benefit him in business. This portrays him as an even more self-interested character, who thinks about his own interests even over the needs and interests of his family.
- Birling seems highly focused on his social reputation. He is at first shaken by the Inspector's visit, moving "hesitatingly" after he leaves. However, when Gerald reveals that the Inspector was a "hoax", he decides that the family's problems are "All over now". This shows that he wasn't upset because he and his family had acted in a way that was morally wrong, but because of the "scandal" that the information could have caused and the damage it would have done to his reputation. This shows that the Inspector's visit hasn't made him reconsider his selfishness and lack of social conscience, suggesting that he is incapable of change.

4) This question asks you to focus on a particular theme. Make sure you choose a theme that is relevant to the text you have studied. Focus on how the writer uses language, structure and form to present the theme. This answer is about the lives of women in 'Pride and Prejudice', starting with Chapter 13, from the start of the chapter to "do something or other about it.", but it's worth reading whichever text you're studying, because it'll give you an idea of the kind of things you should be writing about. Here are some things you could mention:

- In the extract, Austen emphasises how important it is that the novel's young female characters find husbands. She describes how Mrs Bennet's eyes "sparkled" at the hope that Mr Bingley may be visiting; the verb shows how excited she is, because she hopes that he will marry Jane. Mrs Bennet's reaction is typical of her excitable and emotional character, but it also shows how important marriage was for women at the time Austen was writing — it wasn't socially acceptable for upper and middle-class women to have jobs, which meant they were unable to earn money for themselves, and so were reliant upon marrying a wealthy husband to ensure their financial security.

- Mr and Mrs Bennet's discussion in the extract of the entailment of the Bennet estate shows how the law treated women unfairly. It means that only a male heir can inherit the property, who in this case is Mr Collins. Mr Bennet explains that Mr Collins could turn the female family members out of the house "as soon as he pleases" when he is the owner. This phrase emphasises how little control the female family members will have when the entailment comes into effect. This highlights the unequal position of women in Regency England, because the law is not set up in their favour.
- Austen also explores some of the unfair expectations of women in Regency society. In Chapter 8, Miss Bingley describes how an "accomplished" woman is expected to have several abilities including "singing" and "drawing", as well as other features including a certain "tone of voice". The large number and specific nature of these requirements makes them seem unachievable, and therefore suggests that they were unfair towards women.
- Austen portrays a strong female character in Elizabeth. She is confident about breaking some social conventions. For example, in Chapter 7, she is not worried about getting "dirty stockings" when walking to see Jane, despite Mrs Bennet saying that she would "not be fit to be seen" in that state. Mrs Bennet's disapproval suggests that Elizabeth's independence and lack of social propriety are unusual, emphasising that women typically had to conform to strict expectations of appearance and behaviour to maintain their reputations.
- Austen also demonstrates how women could suffer harshly for breaking social conventions. Regency society's beliefs about social propriety for women meant that Lydia's elopement with Wickham is viewed as a very serious problem. It destroys her reputation: Mary says that Lydia's virtue is now "irretrievable", and Mr Collins claims that Lydia's death would have been a "blessing" in comparison. This highlights how breaking social conventions regarding marriage could have serious consequences for the woman involved.

Section Three — Drama

Page 37 — Warm-Up Questions

1) E.g. In 'An Inspector Calls', Priestley uses stage directions to help create an atmosphere of stately formality. For example, the furniture is described as "solid" and the room as a whole appears "substantial" but "not cosy and homelike".
2) Monologue — e.g. one person speaking alone for a long period of time. Example depends on chosen text.
   Aside — e.g. a short comment that reveals a character's thoughts to the audience, but not to the other characters. Example depends on chosen text.
   Soliloquy — e.g. when one character speaks their thoughts aloud for a long time, but no other character can hear them. Example depends on chosen text.
3) Answers depend on chosen text.
4) E.g. In Act 2, Scene 4 of 'Romeo and Juliet', Mercutio mocks people who swordfight for being pretentious, calling them "lisping" and "fashion-mongers". This gives the scene a light-hearted tone that reflects the events of the play at this point — Romeo is in love with Juliet and they are due to be married. The humour here suggests to the audience that all is well and things will have a happy ending. This makes the following scenes even more tragic because the audience has been misdirected into thinking the play could end happily.
5) Answers should focus on how the passage makes you feel and how Shakespeare achieves this. Here are some points you could consider:
   - How do you feel when you read the passage? E.g. Is it funny, sad, exciting or frightening?
   - How does Shakespeare convey the characters' feelings? Look at what they say and how they speak.
   - What has happened directly before the passage and what happens next? Does the position of the passage in the text enhance its effect or affect your reading of it?
6) a) Don Pedro's speech — blank verse
      The lines are written in iambic pentameter but they don't rhyme.
      Prince's speech — verse
      The lines are written in rhymed iambic pentameter.
      Iago's speech — prose
      The start of each line doesn't begin with a capital letter.
   b) The Prince's speech is written in verse form with rhymed iambic pentameter, and it has an ABAB rhyme scheme. These combine to make it sound serious and important.

Page 42 — Exam-Style Questions

1) For this question, you'll need to look carefully at the language used in the extract, but keep in mind where the extract fits into the play too. Remember to refer to the plot and characters in your answer, and back your points up with quotes. This answer is for 'Romeo and Juliet', but it's worth reading whichever of Shakespeare's plays you're studying. Here are some things you could mention:
- The prologue sets the scene for the play and captures the audience's attention. Shakespeare summarises the plot in the prologue, informing the audience that the play will involve two "lovers" who "take their life". This gives the audience a taste of the drama and tragedy that will follow, sparking their interest and making them want to find out the details of the story. This is reinforced by the last two lines of the prologue, where the Chorus talks directly to the audience, addressing them as "you" and telling them to pay attention to the play to hear more.
- The prologue introduces the theme of fate in the play. Romeo and Juliet are referred to as "star-cross'd lovers", implying that their lives are controlled by fate, not by their own choices. The prologue also states that their death is the only thing that can "bury their parents' strife", or end the feud between the Montagues and the Capulets, suggesting that there is a purpose to their deaths. In this way, Shakespeare introduces the audience to the idea that Romeo and Juliet's deaths are unavoidably fated. This emphasis on fate makes the audience feel more sympathetic to the characters of Romeo and Juliet, as the knowledge that they will die tragically makes their happiness seem bittersweet.
- The form of the prologue echoes this theme of fate: it is written in iambic pentameter, the steady rhythm of which gives the feeling of a pattern long established, which cannot be changed. The prologue is also written in rhyming verse, ending with a rhyming couplet — "attend" and "mend". This gives the audience the sense that Romeo and Juliet's fate is fixed and final.
- The form of the prologue also hints at the play's main theme of passionate love, since it is a sonnet, a form which audiences associate with love poems. This makes it clear to the audience that love will be a key theme in the play.

2) For this question, you'll need to explain Shakespeare's use of comedy in the play, and pick out specific examples to illustrate this. This answer is for 'The Merchant of Venice', but it's worth reading whichever of Shakespeare's plays you're studying. Here are some things you could mention:
- Shakespeare's use of comedy provides light relief for the audience. For example, Act 3 Scene 5 is a comic scene that comes just before a long, emotional courtroom scene. The comic nature of this scene means that the courtroom scene which follows feels more serious and dramatic to the audience. However, it also highlights themes that are important to the courtroom scene — Launcelot's jokes about the "price of hogs" highlight the conflict between Jews and Christians that forms the backdrop of the play. This shows how Shakespeare uses the placement of comedic scenes within the structure of the play to add to its overall impact.
- Shakespeare uses puns to create humour. For example, Jessica and Launcelot use the word "bastard" to mean both 'illegitimate' and 'pointless' when discussing the "bastard hope" that Shylock might not really be Jessica's father and therefore that she might not be Jewish herself. Since her mother is also Jewish, the word "bastard" also suggests that it is a 'pointless' hope. Shakespeare's audience would likely have been aware of the dual meaning of the word, and so may have been entertained by the cleverness of the characters. However, the pun also shows the prejudice against Jews that existed in Shakespeare's time, because it demonstrates how it was considered better to be a Christian, providing a serious undertone to the humour.
- In Act 1, Scene 2, Shakespeare uses mockery and exaggeration to create humour. Portia and Nerissa discuss the suitors who have tried to win Portia's hand in marriage, and the use of exaggeration makes each sound ridiculous, such as Monsieur le Bon, who is so keen to show off his fencing skills that he would "fence with his own shadow". The portrayal of each man as an over-the-top cliché of a bad suitor would be amusing for the audience, as it emphasises Portia's continuing bad luck in finding an appropriate husband.
- Shakespeare's use of disguise and mistaken identity is also humorous. In Act 2, Scene 2, Launcelot's father, Old Gobbo, is blind and so cannot recognise his son. Launcelot tricks him into thinking that his son has "gone to heaven", before eventually revealing his true identity. This interaction is an example of dramatic irony, as Launcelot's identity would always be clear to the audience, which makes this interaction especially funny on stage. Launcelot's disguise also highlights one of the play's key ideas, that appearances do not always match reality. This is perhaps shown most clearly by the phrase "All that glitters is not gold", which is found inside the gold casket in Act 2, Scene 7, suggesting that something being visually impressive does not make it a good thing. Shakespeare's use of comedic disguise therefore emphasises this serious message that appearances cannot always be trusted.

3) For this question, you have to focus on a single passage from a drama text you're studying and then write about the rest of the play. You should focus on the ways that the author has presented the theme of gender or growing up. This answer is about gender in 'An Inspector Calls', from the start of Act 2 to "I suppose I asked for that", but it's worth reading even if you're studying a different play. Here are some things you could mention:
- Gerald has a stereotypical, often patronising, view of women, which Priestley seeks to highlight and condemn. This is clearly seen in his treatment of Sheila in the extract. For example, Gerald tries to shut Sheila out, stating that she has "obviously had about as much as she can stand" after the questions from the Inspector. He does not make the same comment about himself or the other men, suggesting that he does not consider women capable of coping with difficult issues and that he sees them as mentally weaker than men.
- Priestley uses the character of the Inspector in the extract to challenge the characters' prejudiced views about women. For instance, he questions whether women should really be protected from "unpleasant" things. This repeats the words of Birling from earlier in the play, who wanted to protect Sheila from "unpleasant business". The repetition highlights how the Inspector is presenting a different viewpoint, one which suggests that women are capable of dealing with upsetting things as well as men. The contrast of views makes the attitudes of some of the Birlings seem overprotective and prejudiced.
- Men in the play are held to different moral standards than women. Birling appears to defend Gerald later in Act 2 by implying that a lot of young men have affairs and telling Sheila that she "must understand" this, indicating that he thinks it is acceptable or at least should be quietly ignored. This suggests that infidelity is tolerated for men in a way that it would not be for women. Through this, Priestley reveals the unequal positions of men and women in early 20th-century Britain.
- Priestley also shows female characters who challenge stereotypes about women. For instance, Sheila changes throughout the play and becomes more assertive, insisting that she has "a right to know" about Gerald's behaviour. She takes on a similar role to the Inspector, asking questions of the other characters and trying to get them to see how they have not learnt their lesson — "You're just beginning to pretend all over again". By presenting Sheila as strong and independent, Priestley shows how stereotypes about women can be wrong.

4) For this question, you need to write about the play as a whole. You need to pick out important bits of the play where Shakespeare addresses the theme of conflict, and explain how each bit you write about relates to the question. This answer is for 'Henry V', but it's worth reading whatever play you're studying, because it'll give you an idea of the kind of things you should be writing about. Here are some things you could mention:
- The conflict between England and France is presented as something that causes atrocious and immoral acts. On the verge of defeat, the French army "Kill the poys" (boys) who are guarding the English luggage, and in response Henry decides to "cut the throats" of the French prisoners they have captured. The murder of young people and the specific command from Henry about how to kill the French prisoners present graphic and shocking details of conflict. Having both sides commit acts like this makes the audience question whether Henry and his army are any more heroic than their enemies.

- Conflict in the play is linked to the honour of soldiers. Before the battle at Harfleur, Henry tells his soldiers to "Dishonour not your mothers" and show that they are "worth" their "breeding". This emotive language suggests that victory in conflict is linked to family and national pride. Henry also talks about the idea of earning honour through fighting in his speech before the battle at Agincourt, further emphasising the link between conflict and honour.
- Shakespeare presents some aspects of conflict as being less honourable. In Act 4, Scene 4, Pistol threatens a French soldier in order to extort money from him. The French soldier's description of Pistol as "brave" and "valorous" contrasts with Pistol's actual behaviour, highlighting the lack of honour in his actions. By showing Pistol's dishonourable behaviour, Shakespeare suggests that soldiers during conflict are not always motivated by honour.
- Conflict is also presented as being motivated by politics. In Act 1, Scene 1, the Bishop of Ely and the Archbishop of Canterbury discuss an "offer" of money Canterbury has made to the King. They hope it will encourage him to prevent the passing of a bill that would cause the Church to "lose the better half" of its "possession". The bill was delayed during the "scambling and unquiet time" of civil war in England, so the bishops know that it is likely to be delayed again if they support Henry in declaring war on France. By including this scene before showing Ely and Canterbury's discussion with Henry about his claim to the French throne, Shakespeare makes sure the audience is aware of their ulterior motives.

5) For this question, you have to focus on a single passage from a drama text you're studying and then write about the rest of the play. You should focus on the ways that the author has presented the relationship between two characters. This answer is for 'Blood Brothers', focusing on the end of Act 2, from "I had to start thinkin' again" to "Linda runs down the aisle", but it's worth a read even if you haven't studied the play. Here are some things you could mention:

- Russell uses the recurring motif of 'blood brothers' to show that Edward and Mickey's bond gets weaker as they grow up. In the extract, Mickey reminds Edward that they are supposed to be "Blood brothers" when Edward lies about being "friends" with Linda. This reference to the "Blood brothers" motif introduced in Act 1 reminds the reader that Mickey and Edward's relationship is based on an agreement Edward has broken, reinforcing that adult Edward no longer values his friendship with Mickey in the way that he did as a child.
- Class division contributes to the breakdown of Mickey and Edward's relationship when they are adults. In the extract, Mickey asks why he "got nothin'" while Edward "got everything". This suggests Mickey's resentment of Edward is a result of the differences that Mickey has observed in their quality of life. This resentment contrasts strongly with their earlier friendship, showing that even a strong bond like that of Mickey and Edward can be destroyed by social inequality.
- In Act 2, Russell uses a montage to illustrate the continuing happiness of the relationship between Mickey and Edward as teenagers. The stage directions during the montage say that both characters "smile" frequently, which emphasises the joy and freedom of youth and their pleasure in each other's company. This contrasts with the characters' actions and emotions immediately after Edward returns from university later in the act, where the stage directions say that Edward "laughs" and jokes, but Mickey is "unamused" and suggests that Edward is "still a kid". This contrast emphasises that the turning point in Mickey and Edward's relationship occurs when they begin their 'adult' lives.
- The balance of power in the relationship between Mickey and Edward changes as time goes on. As children, Mickey has the power in the friendship. He has knowledge that Edward wants, and behaves in a way that Edward admires. When Edward shouts at Mrs Lyons, "you're a fuckoff!", it is clear that he's already strongly influenced by what Mickey says, even when he doesn't know what it means. As adults, Edward holds the influence in Mickey's life — he gets Mickey a house and a job. Mickey resents this, feeling that he "didn't sort anythin' out" for himself, and this contributes to the final confrontation between the brothers.

Section Four — Prose

Page 49 — Warm-Up Questions

1) Answer depends on chosen text. Here are some points you could consider:
   - The writer's choice of language — is it formal and written in Standard English, or more informal and written using slang or dialect words?
   - The sentence structures the writer uses — does the writer use long sentences to describe something in detail, or short, punchy sentences to create an exciting beginning for the reader?
   - The writer's tone — what is the overall feeling of the text in the first paragraph? Does it seem particularly cheerful, conversational or melancholy? How is this achieved?

2) Answers should focus on how the writer sets the scene and what effect the description has. Here are some points you could consider:
   - Where is the passage set? What is the place like?
   - How does the passage make you feel? Can you pick out any words or phrases that contribute to this effect?
   - Does the writer use techniques such as imagery to make the description more vivid? If so, what effect does it have on the reader?

3) For example:
   a) Elizabeth Bennet is the central character in Jane Austen's 'Pride and Prejudice'. She is important because she is involved in much of the action, and is portrayed as one of the wisest characters, so we trust her judgement. She has the strongest will of any of the Bennet sisters and she follows her own mind. Because of this, she is responsible for many of the novel's turning points.
   b) Elizabeth is a presented as sympathetic character, which helps the reader to identify with her feelings and decisions. She is presented as a caring, witty character, but her mistakes (e.g. misjudging Darcy and Wickham) make her seem like a real person.
   c) Elizabeth's opinion of Darcy and her sister's suitor, Wickham, changes as she recognises that she has misjudged them. By the end of the novel she has realised that appearances can be deceptive, and that it is wrong to judge people on first impressions.

4) E.g. In 'Anita and Me', the narrator writes in the first person, as an adult looking back on the events of her childhood. This allows the reader to follow her thought processes and empathise with her. The use of a grown-up narrator gives an adult perspective on the events and emotions of childhood, which adds humour and pathos to the narrative.

5) a) For example: "most unfortunate affair", "much talked of", "useful lesson", "loss of virtue in a female is irretrievable", "one false step involves her in endless ruin", "reputation is no less brittle than it is beautiful", "she cannot be too much guarded in her behaviour".

b) For example: "Reputation was extremely important for women in nineteenth-century Britain. Women who damaged their reputation by behaving in an 'improper' way were regarded as having lost their "virtue", a situation that was judged "irretrievable". This shows that, once a woman's good reputation was lost, there was no way of getting it back — she would have been affected for life. Such women were used as a "useful lesson" to prevent other women from behaving in the same way."

Page 54 — Exam-Style Questions

1) For this question, you need to talk about your extract, then pick out specific examples of prejudice elsewhere in the novel, and explain them in detail. This answer is for 'Anita and Me', but it's worth reading whatever novel you're studying, because it'll give you an idea of the kind of things you should be writing about. Here are some things you could mention:

- The extract highlights the role of education and the media in inadvertently encouraging racism — Meena says that all she learned at school about India was from "tatty textbooks" showing Indians as servants, or from "television clips" showing "machete-wielding thugs". This means that neither she nor her classmates are given a fair picture of the country on which to base their assumptions. It also shows that prejudice can be ingrained in people from an early age, suggesting that it is hard to overcome.
- The novel shows how harmful prejudice can be. In the extract, Meena describes the "shame" that prejudice has caused her to feel about her background, which makes her want "to be someone else". This suggests that prejudice can weaken a person's sense of identity and cause them to try to change who they are. The damage brought about by prejudice is highlighted later in the novel, when Meena breaks her leg directly after hearing Anita's excitement about the racist attack on the bank manager. This could be seen as a physical expression of the emotional pain that Meena feels.
- In 'Anita and Me', racial prejudice is often casual, such as Deirdre calling her dog "Nigger" because it's black, without realising it's offensive. This casual racism shows the ignorance of some of the residents of Tollington, who often don't realise the impact of their racism. This is reinforced later in the novel, when Sam says that he "never meant" Meena when he made racist comments.
- Characters in the novel react differently to racial prejudice. Mama's reaction to racism is to try to disprove racial stereotypes — for example, she purposely speaks English "without an accent". In contrast, Papa tells Meena that she shouldn't accept racist abuse: "first you say something back, and then you come and tell me." The Kumars' mild, non-violent reaction to racism paints them in a much better light than the racist characters in the novel, and emphasises how unfair and illogical racial prejudice is.

2) For this question, you need to talk about your extract and then pick out specific examples of your chosen theme elsewhere in the text, and then explain them in detail. This answer is about social class in 'Pride and Prejudice', referring to an extract from Chapter 29, from "Are any of your younger sisters out, Miss Bennet?" to the end of the chapter, but it's worth reading whatever play you're studying, because it'll give you an idea of the kind of things you should be writing about. Here are some things you could mention:

- 'Pride and Prejudice' was written during the late eighteenth century, when class distinctions based on wealth and family connections were fairly rigid, and people were expected to marry within their own class. This expectation, and the struggle to overcome it, is one of the main themes of the novel.
- In the extract, Austen satirises attitudes to social class using the character of Lady Catherine. Lady Catherine is so convinced that her upper-class status makes her superior that it does not occur to her that the other characters might not act in a subservient way towards her. For example, when Lady Catherine asks about Elizabeth's age, she is "quite astonished" when Elizabeth deliberately avoids giving her a proper answer. The way she takes so much offence over something so trivial exaggerates her self-importance to the reader, which encourages them to laugh at her. Austen therefore mocks Lady Catherine's belief that people should automatically respect her because of her wealth and status. Elizabeth's continuation to deny Lady Catherine a "direct answer" by teasing that she is "not one-and-twenty" adds to this mockery by further undermining Lady Catherine's social authority.
- Austen uses Lady Catherine's rude behaviour in the extract to show the reader that being socially superior to Elizabeth does not make her morally superior. For example, she dominates the conversation by "stating the mistakes of the three others, or relating some anecdote of herself". This description makes Lady Catherine seem tactless and self-centred. Through Lady Catherine, Austen therefore shows that being aristocratic does not make someone a better person.
- Although Elizabeth is aware of the barrier that class creates between herself and upper-class characters like Darcy and Lady Catherine, she is never intimidated by them. For example, in the extract Mr Collins is "employed in agreeing to every thing her Ladyship said", but Elizabeth is not afraid to speak her mind. For example, she disagrees with Lady Catherine about whether her sisters should be "out" in society. Austen uses Elizabeth to challenge the restrictions of the class system, suggesting that some expectations don't need to be as strictly adhered to as some people in Regency society might think.
- The importance of social rules is shown by the awareness most of the characters have about the restrictions of class. For example, Elizabeth recognises that because of her mother's family background, she and Jane are not necessarily 'good enough' to marry Darcy or Bingley, and Darcy himself describes Elizabeth's family as "decidedly beneath" his own.
- Lady Catherine is determined that Darcy will marry her daughter because they are "descended… from the same noble line", despite the fact that Anne is "pale and sickly" and "spoke very little", making it clear that she would not be a good wife for Darcy. This contains an implicit judgement of those who see social class as the most important factor in a happy marriage.

3) For this question, you need to talk about your extract and then pick out specific examples of how the writer creates a sense of fear elsewhere in the text, and explain them in detail. This answer is for 'The Woman in Black', from the start of 'Whistle and I'll Come to You', to "...and then, inexplicably, opened", but it's worth reading whatever text you're studying, because it'll give you an idea of the kind of things you should be writing about. Here are some things you could mention:

- In the extract, Hill uses description of the weather to create a frightening atmosphere. Arthur uses a simile to compare the sound of the wind that is battering the house to the scream of a "banshee". A 'banshee' is a kind of spirit that screams to forewarn death in a household. This comparison suggests that the storm is a bad omen, which gives the reader the impression that something terrible is about to happen and builds an atmosphere of threat. The comparison to a screaming spirit also emphasises the loudness and power of the storm, adding to the overall sense of threat in the extract.
- Hill uses Arthur's perception of a ghostly presence to create a frightening atmosphere in this extract. Arthur has an "absolutely certain sense" that something has passed over the landing just before he arrives there, despite feeling "no disturbance of the air". This creates a chilling atmosphere for the reader, as it suggests that Arthur is sharing the house with a ghost that can move around undetected, and could therefore appear anywhere at any moment. Furthermore, Arthur senses the ghost at the same time as the house is plunged into "pitch blackness" by a gust of wind, which uses the very common fear of the dark to increase the reader's sense of fright.
- Hill also creates a mood of fear in 'The Funeral of Mrs Drablow' through Mr Jerome's reaction to the woman in black. When Arthur mentions seeing the "woman with the wasted face", Mr Jerome falls silent, goes pale and his lips become "tinged with blue". This extreme physical reaction suggests that there is something terrible that Arthur is unaware of associated with the woman, which creates fear of the unknown in the reader. Hill then intensifies the atmosphere of fear that surrounds the woman in black in 'Across the Causeway' when Arthur says that she has a look of "malevolence", indicating that Mr Jerome's extreme reaction to her was justified and that Arthur is in danger.
- Hill structures Arthur's first-person narrative in 'The Sound of a Pony and Trap' to create a fearful atmosphere. When Arthur attempts to cross the causeway in the mist and gets lost, he breaks from his account to tell the reader "What I heard next chilled and horrified me". This tells the reader that something frightening is about to happen without revealing exactly what it is, which creates apprehension. This sense of fear is emphasised by the fact that Keckwick, who Arthur hoped had arrived to bring him to safety, now seems powerless to help him.

4) For this question, you need to talk about your extract and then pick out specific examples of how the writer presents the nature of evil elsewhere in the text, and explain them in detail. This answer is for 'Lord of the Flies', but it's worth reading whatever text you're studying, because it'll give you an idea of the kind of things you should be writing about. Here are some things you could mention:

- Golding uses the idea of the "beast" to explore the idea that evil is within everyone. For much of the novel, the boys don't realise that the evil is inside them, so they make it into a real being — a "beast" — which gives them something to "hunt and kill". In this extract, Simon imagines the Lord of the Flies speaking to him and revealing the truth about the beast, telling him "I'm part of you". This shows that the boys' fear of the beast is actually their fear of the evil that ordinary people seem to be capable of.
- Golding uses imagery of darkness to represent evil. At the end of the extract, Simon looks into the "vast mouth" of the Lord of the Flies, where he sees "blackness within, a blackness that spread". This describes the experience of losing consciousness, but also suggests the growth of evil behaviour among the boys on the island. Golding might be using this image to suggest that once people aren't expected to live by society's moral rules, evil naturally takes over.
- Golding also reminds the reader in this extract that Simon and the other boys are only children. The pig's head repeatedly calls him a "silly little boy", a phrase associated with a parent or "schoolmaster" telling off a child for minor misbehaviour. This highlights the boys' youth, making their acts of evil even more shocking. Their young age could also suggest that evil occurs instinctively, as without adult guidance the boys descend into wicked and destructive behaviour.
- When Simon says of the beast that "maybe it's only us", the others laugh at him — they are unable to accept the idea that there could be evil in each of them. Simon's death therefore symbolises the end of reason and goodness. In the scene in which Simon is killed, the boys are nameless and act as a "single organism" which kills with "teeth and claws". This animal imagery shows how savage the boys have become, and how they are losing the final traces of civilisation. Even Ralph feels "a kind of feverish excitement" when he talks about Simon's murder, which shows how strong evil is and how it is present even in the characters that are usually considered 'good'.
- The novel is set against the backdrop of a nuclear war: Piggy talks about the "atom bomb" and says "They're all dead." This, together with the appearance of the naval officer at the end, reminds the reader that the boys' evil is minor on the wider scale of human evil, and reinforces Golding's message that destructive behaviour is man's natural state.

5) For this question, you need to talk about your extract and then pick out specific examples of how your chosen character is presented elsewhere in the text, and explain them in detail. This answer is about the character of Elsie Norris in 'Oranges Are Not the Only Fruit', using an extract from 'Judges', beginning at "The day after, I did go" and ending after "she disappeared inside", but it's worth reading whatever play you're studying, because it'll give you an idea of the kind of things you should be writing about. Here are some things you could mention:

- Elsie represents the kindness and motherly love which Jeanette is missing from her own mother. In the extract, Jeanette says that Elsie "knew what was happening, but still held me close". As non-sexual physical affection is rare in the novel, this action clearly emphasises the close bond between Elsie and Jeanette, and contrasts strongly with Jeanette's mother's anger immediately before the extract. In this way, Winterson uses Jeanette's relationship with Elsie to highlight what is missing from the relationship between Jeanette and her mother. Winterson's use of the adverb "still" further emphasises the unconditional nature of Elsie's love for Jeanette.
- The extract shows how Elsie demonstrates a different interpretation of Christian morals from the rest of her church. Her acceptance of Jeanette's sexuality is expressed by not talking "about *it*, not the rights or wrongs or anything". Her lack of moral judgement contrasts with the attitude of the rest of the church, especially Jeanette's mother, who demonise and reject Jeanette because of her sexuality, highlighting the lack of compassion in their approach to morality. Elsie's decision not to talk about Jeanette's sexuality could also hint at her concern for Jeanette's welfare by suggesting Elsie doesn't want to discuss things that might be upsetting for Jeanette.

- Through her knowledge of stories, Elsie is presented as more well-rounded than many of her fellow churchgoers. While Jeanette is in hospital, Elsie makes her "feel better" with her non-biblical poems and stories. In contrast to the members of the church, Elsie presents Jeanette with a non-biblical viewpoint, hinting that Elsie believes that it is important to have a balanced view of the world. The impression Elsie's stories have on Jeanette is evident later in the novel when Jeanette uses invented stories to recount parts of her life.
- Elsie's failing health is used to emphasise Jeanette's vulnerability to the reader. When Jeanette's mother tells Jeanette that she has to leave her home, Jeanette says "Where could I go? Not to Elsie's", because Elsie is too sick. The use of the rhetorical question highlights Jeanette's isolation to the reader. Following the question immediately with Elsie as a potential solution emphasises that Elsie is one of the few people Jeanette can rely on, but Elsie's ill health means she is no longer able to protect Jeanette. Jeanette's reliance on Elsie makes Elsie's death more poignant, as the reader is aware of how much Jeanette needs her.

Section Five — Poetry

Page 63 — Warm-Up Questions

1) a) A word that sounds like the noise it's describing, e.g. splash, creak.
   b) A pause or break in a line, often marked by punctuation.
   c) A sentence that runs over from one line to the next.

2) "A messenger's knock cracks smartly"
   E.g. "The onomatopoeic words "knock" and "cracks" sound harsh and violent, shocking the reader."

   "bluebottles / Wove a strong gauze of sound around the smell"
   E.g. "Sibilance creates a buzzing sound, which mimics the sound of flies."

   "Which waves in every raven tress"
   E.g. "The assonance of 'e' and the long 'a' sounds mimic the sounds of waves breaking, causing the line to ebb and flow like the tide and emphasising the woman's natural beauty."

   "The lone and level sands stretch far away."
   E.g. "The alliteration of the soft 'l' and 's' sounds creates an echo effect and emphasises the feeling of emptiness in the surrounding desert."

3) E.g. "The onion is personified through the use of the phrase "Its fierce kiss" The onion being personified as "fierce" creates an aggressive and threatening tone, which contrasts with the traditional idea of Valentine gifts showing affection and love."

4) a) E.g. "The unchanging ABAB rhyme scheme highlights the monotony and relentless suffering the soldiers face."
   b) E.g. "End-stopping slows the poem's rhythm, which mirrors the sensation of the soldiers "fumbling" as they are overwhelmed by fear in the attack."
   c) E.g. "Emotive language such "flound'ring" and "yelling" vividly illustrates the terror of the soldiers and encourages the reader to imagine the emotions that they would feel in that situation."

Section Six — Poetry Anthology

Page 71 — Warm-Up Questions

1) E.g. 'Sonnet 43' by Elizabeth Barrett Browning follows the regular rhyme scheme of a Petrarchan sonnet. This regularity helps to emphasise the constant, reliable nature of the speaker's love.

2) E.g. In 'She Walks in Beauty', the narrator uses the third person to describe a woman. This makes her more difficult to empathise with, because there is no insight into her thoughts or feelings, which creates distance between her and the reader. In contrast, in 'The Manhunt', Armitage uses the first person to explore the experience of the wife of a traumatised soldier returned from war. The first-person perspective allows an intensely personal description of her husband's scarred body and mind, which makes it easier for the reader to empathise with the speaker.

3) a) E.g. "I kill where I please because it is all mine."
   ('Hawk Roosting', Ted Hughes)
   Effect: End-stopping creates a sense of the hawk's power and control.
   b) E.g. "There are just not enough / straight lines. That / is the problem."
   ('Living Space', Imtiaz Dharker)
   Effect: This caesura reflects the chaotic, disjointed nature of the space Dharker is describing.
   c) E.g. "Conspiring with him how to load and bless / With fruit the vines"
   ('To Autumn', John Keats)
   Effect: Enjambment suggests that the vines will be overloaded with fruit.

4) E.g. Hughes uses form to convey a sense of order in 'Hawk Roosting'. For example, end-stopping in "I kill where I please because it is all mine." creates a controlled rhythm that reflects the hawk's power and control over his surroundings. In contrast, in 'Living Space' Dharker uses caesurae to show a lack of order: for example, she says that it "There are just not enough / straight lines. That / is the problem." Here, a caesura is used alongside enjambment to give the reader a sense of the chaotic, disjointed space Dharker is describing.

5) a) E.g. "In every cry of every Man, / In every Infant's cry of fear"
   ('London', William Blake)
   Effect: The repetition of "cry" emphasises the sense of unhappiness, while the repetition of "every" suggests that this despair is widespread.
   b) E.g. "The slap and plop were obscene threats."
   ('Death of a Naturalist', Seamus Heaney)
   Effect: The onomatopoeic words help the reader to vividly imagine the sounds of the frogs.
   c) E.g. "watch the white eyes writhing in his face"
   ('Dulce et Decorum Est', Wilfred Owen)
   Effect: Alliteration draws attention to the injured soldier and the pain that he suffered.
   d) E.g. "At swing and sandpit / Setting free their children."
   ('Afternoons', Philip Larkin)
   Effect: The repeated 's' sounds make the mothers' lives seem repetitive.

6) E.g. 'Death of a Naturalist' uses language to make the frogs seem disgusting. For example, the words "slap" and "plop" are used to describe what the frogs sound like. The use of onomatopoeic words helps the reader to vividly imagine these unpleasant sounds. 'Dulce et Decorum Est' also uses language to convey something unpleasant. Alliteration is used to emphasise the terrible pain the soldier is experiencing. The phrase "watch the white eyes writhing in his face" uses alliteration to draw the reader's attention, encouraging them to focus on the "writhing" soldier. This contributes to Owen's negative description of war overall in the poem.

7) E.g. In 'Cozy Apologia', Rita Dove uses food imagery to characterise her teenage love interests. She compares them to "licorice", which is "Sweet" but also "hollow" — this gives the reader the impression that her crushes were enjoyable but ultimately insubstantial. Licorice sweets are also reminiscent of childhood for many people: by choosing this food, Dove emphasises that these are encounters from the narrator's past.

Page 76 — Exam-Style Questions

1) a) For this question, you have to think about the way the poet uses form, structure and language to present ideas about admiration. Make sure you structure your answer so that it discusses all of these techniques. Here are some points you could make:
   - In 'The Soldier', the narrator seems to worship his country. The poem is a sonnet, which is a form traditionally used in love poetry to express adoration of another person. Brooke's use of it here encourages the reader to consider the similarities between narrator's worship of England and the worship involved in romantic love. The form of the poem therefore emphasises the strength and personal nature of the narrator's admiration. By discussing the narrator's feelings about England in the form of a love poem, the poet also romanticises them. This could reflect the idealistic vision that many had at the beginning of the First World War, as popular opinion initially focused on the soldiers' glory in fighting for their country.
   - The personification of England in the poem suggests that the narrator looks up to his country like a child looks up to their parent. He says that England "bore" and "shaped" him. These verbs refer to key aspects of motherhood, which suggests that the narrator sees England as a mother figure. This is then emphasised by the list in lines five and six, which shows that England has given many pleasant things to the narrator. The reader is left with the impression that the narrator believes England has cared for him throughout his life, as a mother would. This extended metaphor elevates the role of England by comparing it to one of the most significant figures in a person's life, emphasising the depth of the narrator's admiration.
   - The use of religious and natural imagery in 'The Soldier' glorifies England. The narrator feels that he has been "blest" by England, which presents England as a divine figure. Given the importance of religion in early twentieth-century English society, this comparison would have clearly conveyed the narrator's admiration of England to readers of the time. In the octave, Brooke also presents England's beauty, describing natural features such as "rivers" and "suns". His focus on the more picturesque features of England gives an idealistic sense of the country. In combination with the religious language, this portrays England as a paradise, reflecting the narrator's intense admiration and patriotism. This is then reinforced in the sestet, as the narrator describes heaven as "English", implying that heaven will share all the qualities of England that he loves.

1) b) For this question, you have to think carefully about how the poets use form, structure and language in their presentations of admiration. Think carefully about which poem you choose for the comparison, remembering that you need to find similarities and differences between the two poems. This answer is for 'The Soldier' by Rupert Brooke and 'To Autumn' by John Keats, but it gives you an idea of the kind of things you need to write for a comparison question. Here are some points you could make:
   - Both 'The Soldier' and 'To Autumn' use form to convey ideas about the narrators' worship of England and autumn respectively. 'The Soldier' is a sonnet, which is a type of poetry traditionally used to express feelings of love. Using this form presents England as the object of the narrator's admiration. 'To Autumn' is an ode, a form used to praise something or someone. The poem is made up of three equal-length stanzas and is written in iambic pentameter. Its regular form reflects the stability and endurance of the narrator's worship of nature. Additionally, while other odes by Keats typically have ten lines per stanza, 'To Autumn' has eleven. This extra line could suggest that the narrator is overwhelmed by their feelings, to the extent that they cannot express their thoughts about it concisely.
   - In both poems, the poets praise the subjects of their poems using personification. The narrator in 'The Soldier' sees England as a caring, protective mother who "bore" and "shaped" him. This extended metaphor demonstrates how devoted the narrator is to England, as the bond between mother and child is traditionally one of the strongest and most affectionate types of love. 'To Autumn' also features personification, but it is used to establish a different type of relationship. Autumn is personified in a romantic way: images of autumn with "hair soft-lifted" by the wind and "sound asleep" on a furrow make the narrator seem like someone who is fondly recalling images of their beloved. By encouraging the reader to view the narrator and autumn through a romantic lense, Keats emphasises the admiration that the narrator has for autumn.
   - In 'The Soldier', the narrator's love for his country is linked to personal sacrifice. The narrator in 'The Soldier' is prepared to die for the country he admires. This is shown by the structure of the poem, as the narrator references his death in the first and last lines of the poem. This cyclical structure means that the narrator's death dominates the narrative, emphasising to the reader that the narrator remains patriotic even while facing death. His fierce patriotism highlights widespread attitudes at the start of the First World War: many believed that dying for your country was noble and heroic. On the other hand, 'To Autumn' associates autumn with abundance and excess, which contrasts with the self-sacrifice in 'The Soldier'. For example, the narrator describes the season planning to provide fruit and flowers, including to "load" vines with fruit and "bend" trees with "apples". These images of excess suggest that autumn provides so much fruit that the vines and trees can barely cope. This portrays autumn as generous, which emphasises the narrator's positive attitude towards the season.

- In 'The Soldier', the narrator admires England, and Brooke shows the reader that it is not a one-sided relationship. The soldier lists the "thoughts", "sights and sounds", "dreams" and "laughter" that will return to him after his death, which indicates the lasting gifts the country has given the soldier in return. In contrast, 'To Autumn' shows the gifts that autumn gives to the narrator, but it also hints at the fact that both autumn and its gifts will fade away. In the final stanza, the reference to the "stubble-plains" suggests that the harvest is coming to an end and reminds the reader that the abundance of autumn is temporary. This creates a sense of impending loss, which is emphasised by Keats's use of funereal imagery: the "wailful choir" of gnats that "mourn" add a sorrowful tone. The end of the poem therefore hints at the sadness that comes with admiring something that cannot last.

2) a) For this question, you have to think about the way the poet uses form, structure and language to present ideas about war. Make sure you structure your answer sensibly around a discussion of these techniques. Here are some points you could make:
- The poem's regular ABAB rhyme scheme helps to present the harshness of war. In the first stanza, the rhyme scheme emphasises the words "trudge" and "sludge". Owen emphasises the heavy and dull 'udge' sound, which hints at how exhausting and tedious some aspects of war can be. The regularity of the rhyme scheme reinforces this idea, as it echoes the monotony of the soldiers' march. This hammers home Owen's message that the reality of war is very different from the "glory" suggested by those who promote "The old Lie", that it is "Dulce et decorum", or sweet and proper, to die for your country.
- The poem presents war in a realistic and sombre way. This is achieved through Owen's use of first-person narration. This gives the poem a personal tone, highlighting that war has devastating effects on each individual soldier who participates in it.
- In the poem, war is presented as physically damaging through the use of graphic imagery. Imagery of illness, such as "Obscene as cancer" and "vile, incurable sores", gives the reader the impression that the effects of war are like a physical disease. This association of war with disease creates images of pain and suffering in the reader's mind, and suggests that, like disease, war brings misery. Owen served as a soldier on the front line during World War I — this context gives the poem's disturbing images a sense of authenticity, which makes them even more shocking for the reader.
- The poem also shows war to be psychologically damaging. Owen's narrator dreams that the dead soldier "plunges" at him, "guttering, choking, drowning". The use of the present tense suggests that the event is still very real to the narrator, as though he relives the experience each time he dreams. This is reinforced by the way the dreams are described as "smothering", which highlights how they overwhelm the narrator and leads the reader to imagine that the narrator is suffocating in the gas once more. In this way, Owen emphasises that the narrator is haunted by his horrific experiences during the war, which illustrates how soldiers can suffer long-term psychological damage after conflict.

2) b) For this question, you have to think about how the poets use form, structure and language in their presentations of war, so think carefully about which poem to choose from the anthology. Remember, you're comparing the two poems so you need to think about the similarities and differences between the ways in which they discuss war. This answer is for 'Dulce et Decorum Est' by Wilfred Owen and 'Mametz Wood' by Owen Sheers, but it gives you an idea of the kind of things you need to write whichever second poem you choose. Here are some points you could make:
- The poems, which both explore the loss of soldiers in World War I, both use narrative voice to discuss who is affected by war. The first two stanzas of 'Dulce et Decorum Est' are written in a first-person plural viewpoint, for example, in "we cursed through sludge", to represent the soldiers' shared struggle. The viewpoint changes to the first-person singular at the end of the second stanza ("I saw him drowning"), which draws the reader's attention to the soldier's individual suffering. In contrast, 'Mametz Wood' is written in the third person, which creates distance between the narrator and the events. This presents a more reflective tone about the universal experience of the war, as the narrator considers the "wasted young" who fought together and were "buried in one long grave". As a modern writer, Sheers was not personally involved in the war, which could explain why he engages with it in a different way to Owen.
- Owen and Sheers both emphasise how physically damaging war can be. In 'Dulce et Decorum Est', vivid descriptions of the state the soldiers are in, for example "Knock-kneed" and "Drunk with fatigue", show the reader how weak the men have become during the war. The soldiers' physical condition is used by Owen to dismantle the idea that war is noble or glorious. 'Mametz Wood', on the other hand, uses images of physical damage to demonstrate how war can dehumanise those fighting in it. The description of the soldiers' body parts as "A broken mosaic of bone", gives the reader the impression that they are shattered beyond recognition. By making them anonymous, Sheers also distances the reader from the horrors of the soldiers' experiences. This contrasts with 'Dulce et Decorum Est', as Owen presents the reality of the war in order to criticise it.
- 'Dulce et Decorum Est' uses graphic imagery to shock the reader. Disturbing images of the soldier's "white eyes writhing" and his "froth-corrupted lungs" capture the horror that troops had to endure on the front line. Owen's narrator appeals directly to the reader, "My friend", in his attempt to change their mind about "The old Lie". The narrator in 'Mametz Wood' however, contrasts the violence of war with gentle, everyday images, to remind the reader of human fragility. Likening the soldier's shoulder blade to a delicate "china plate" shows how it is easily broken. Like Owen, Sheers demonstrates how unprepared the human body is for the violence of war, but also uses this imagery to stress to the reader how their "unearthing" is an opportunity to honour them. For example, in the second stanza, each image of fragility ends with the name of the body part it discusses, which keeps the focus of the poem on the real-life soldiers who died trying to capture Mametz Wood.

- Both poems discuss the lasting implications of war. The narrator in 'Dulce et Decorum Est' uses present-tense verbs such as "guttering, choking, drowning" to describe the past, indicating how real the event of the dying soldier still is for him. It is clear that he is haunted by the memory of it. In this way, Owen shows how although war ends, it is never over for those who then have to endure the emotional and psychological repercussions. Similarly, 'Mametz Wood' presents the discovery of the soldier's bodies "years afterwards", demonstrating the lasting effects of war. The imagery used by Sheers in the fourth stanza, in which he describes the effects of the war as "like a wound", illustrates to the reader that the earth is also still healing.

3) a) For this question, you have to think about the way the poet uses form, structure and language to present ideas about freedom and constraint. Make sure you structure your answer so that it discusses all of these techniques.
Here are some points you could make:
- In 'London', Blake presents a narrator who has the freedom to comment on the constrained society that they see around them. The verb "wander" creates a sense of leisure, as if the narrator is unrestricted and can go where they like. This sense of freedom is emphasised through the multiple locations across the poem, such as the "Thames", the "Church" and the "Palace", as the reader gets the impression that the narrator has covered a lot of distance.
- Constraint is presented as inescapable in the poem. The emotive language of "the youthful Harlot's curse / Blasts the new born Infant's tear" highlights how the citizens are born into disadvantage. Here, Blake implies that sexually-transmitted diseases, which were widespread in England in the late eighteenth century, have been passed on to babies. This presents many lives as being restricted at birth, as disease disrupts the life babies would normally have. This injustice is emphasised by the use of the plosive 'b' sound in "Blasts", which creates an angry tone and suggests to the reader that the narrator is frustrated that they cannot help those that are born into a disadvantaged life. This reflects the beliefs of the poet — Blake was a believer in social equality who would have disliked the poverty he saw in eighteenth-century London.
- However, Blake suggests that it is partly the citizens' fault that they are constrained. The metaphor of the citizens being fastened in "mind-forg'd manacles" likens the citizens to prisoners. However, the phrase "mind-forg'd" suggests that the narrator believes the restrictions people experience are self-imposed and that they are constrained through their own lack of action — they are partly trapped through their own belief that their misery and suffering is inescapable.
- The theme of constraint is emphasised to the reader using the poem's form. The ABAB rhyme scheme creates a sense of restrictiveness, as its repetitive nature implies that the constraints upon the citizens of the city will never change. This sense of constriction is reinforced through the poem's rhythm. Most lines are written in iambic tetrameter, but some lines, such as line 4, break this by only using seven syllables. The lines with fewer syllables convey a sense of incompleteness to the reader, as if to suggest that, like the lines, the people are missing something. The narrator could be hinting that they believe the citizens are being held back from a better life.

3) b) For this question, you have to write about how the poets use form, structure and language in their presentations of freedom and constraint. Think carefully about which poem you choose for the comparison, remembering that you need to find similarities and differences between the two poems. This answer compares 'London' by William Blake with 'Hawk Roosting' by Ted Hughes, but it gives you an idea of the kind of things you could write for a comparison question. Here are some points you could make:
- 'London' and 'Hawk Roosting' offer two different perspectives on freedom and constraint. Blake depicts the city of London as constricting, and the people who live in it seem trapped in their lives of misery. In 'Hawk Roosting', on the other hand, Hughes emphasises the freedom of the hawk due to its power and ability to hunt.
- Both poets use a first-person narrative to create a sense of the narrators' freedom. 'London' is a first-person dramatic monologue, which allows an insight into the narrator's thoughts and feelings as they walk around the city. The poem shifts through images of other people, which creates the sense that the narrator is the only person free to move around a city full of people who are trapped by their circumstances. Although the narrator also seems constrained by London's "charter'd" streets, their relative freedom emphasises the constraint that has been forced upon the other people they see. 'Hawk Roosting' also uses a first-person narrative, which enables Hughes to personify the hawk. Phrases such as "it is all mine" emphasise the power that the hawk feels over nature, which helps the reader to understand the freedom it has to fly and hunt.
- The form and structure of both poems allows the poets to emphasise a sense of freedom or constraint. Most of the lines of 'Hawk Roosting' are unrhymed, reinforcing the idea that the hawk is free to exist without constraint. However, the rest of the form is more rigid — there are six stanzas of equal length, and most of the lines are end-stopped. This could reflect the constraint that the hawk tries to force on its environment, linking it to human tyrants who want to "keep things like this". Alternatively, the rigid form could hint that the hawk is not as free as it believes, as it is trapped by its own nature. 'London' also has regular four line stanzas, but unlike 'Hawk Roosting' it has a fixed ABAB rhyme scheme. These two elements combine to make the poem seem restrictive and inflexible, which contributes to the overall sense of constraint.
- Both poets use imagery to emphasise the sense of freedom, or lack of freedom, in the poems. In 'Hawk Roosting', imagery is used to emphasise the vastness of the hawk's environment: Hughes refers to "the earth's face", the "high trees" and "the sun's ray"; these images emphasise the huge area that the hawk can see. In contrast, the imagery in 'London' helps to emphasise the sense of constraint in the poem. For example, the image of the "mind-forg'd manacles" likens the Londoners to prisoners and makes their suffering seem permanent. This reinforces how trapped the residents of London are.
- Repetition is used in 'London' to make the reader feel that the city's residents can't escape the constraints of their environment. In the second stanza, the phrase "In every" is repeated at the beginning of the first three lines. This creates a sense of inevitability: regardless of the people's actions, they will continue to be trapped in poverty. In 'Hawk Roosting', on the other hand, repetition is used to emphasise the hawk's power and freedom. In the poem's third stanza, the word "Creation" is repeated twice. This links the hawk's power to that of a god, which emphasises its freedom to act as it wishes.

4) a) For this question, you have to think about the way the poet uses form, structure and language to present relationships. Make sure you structure your answer so that it discusses all of these techniques. Here are some points you could make:

- Barrett Browning uses the sonnet form of 'Sonnet 43' to show the narrator's love for somebody. The poem takes the form of a Petrarchan sonnet: it has fourteen lines that consist of an octave followed by a sestet. Sonnets are traditionally used when writing love poetry. This links the narrator's love to an established literary tradition, which emphasises how important she perceives her relationship with the subject of the poem to be.
- The poem's rhyme scheme reinforces the constancy of the relationship the narrator has with the other person. The poem has a regular, unbroken rhyme scheme, which gives it an unfaltering rhythm that reinforces the steadfastness of the narrator's feelings. This is emphasised by the poet's use of repetition: the phrase "I love thee" is repeated at the beginning of several lines throughout the poem; the phrase becomes a simple refrain that sticks in the reader's mind and emphasises the sincerity of the narrator's feelings.
- The poem links the couple's relationship to religion. The narrator says that her love for the subject of the poem has replaced her "lost Saints". This highlights the positive impact that the relationship has had: for the narrator, it is equivalent in importance to religion. By comparing her relationship with religion, the narrator also hints at the strength of the relationship, as it suggests the narrator has complete faith in it. Nineteenth-century society was very religious, and so making this comparison would have been a very strong sentiment when the poem was written.
- The narrator emphasises that her relationship with the other person has taken over almost all aspects of her life: she uses a list to explain that she loves the person in the poem with "the breath, / Smiles, tears, of all my life!" This list makes it seem as though her love for the subject of the poem is all-encompassing. This is strengthened by the description of how she loves him "by sun and candlelight". These mundane aspects of life suggest that the relationship is a part of their everyday life. The use of mundane imagery might also give the reader the impression that their relationship is down-to-earth and isn't superficial.

4) b) For this question, you have to think carefully about how the poets use form, structure and language in their presentations of relationships. Think carefully about which poem you choose for the comparison, remembering that you need to find similarities and differences between the two poems. This answer compares 'Sonnet 43' by Elizabeth Barrett Browning with 'The Manhunt' by Simon Armitage, but it gives you an idea of the kind of things you need to write for a comparison question. Here are some points you could make:

- Both 'The Manhunt' and 'Sonnet 43' present different relationships, with each written from the perspective of a woman. Both poems are about real-life relationships. 'The Manhunt' tells the story of soldier Eddie Beddoes and his wife, Laura, as they struggle to readjust after Eddie returns from war. On the other hand, 'Sonnet 43' is written from Elizabeth Barrett Browning's perspective, and it describes her seemingly effortless relationship with her husband, Robert Browning, which lasted their entire lives.
- The poets both use form to emphasise the narrators' feelings of affection in their relationships, although they approach this in different ways. 'The Manhunt' is structured in couplets, some of which rhyme, and some of which do not. The regularity of the two-line stanzas reflects the dedication with which the narrator attempted to heal and understand her husband, while the irregularity of the rhyme scheme mirrors how difficult this was. This contrasts with the regular rhyme scheme and sonnet form of 'Sonnet 43', which create an overall feeling of constancy to hint at the couple's enduring affection for each other.
- The different way each narrator expresses their love for another person reveals something about the nature of their relationship. In 'The Manhunt', the couple's relationship is illustrated through physicality and action: this is suggested by the poet's use of verbs such as "handle and hold", which emphasise the physical, tangible nature of their relationship. In contrast, the love of the narrator in 'Sonnet 43' is less physical and more idealistic; the poem uses hyperbole such as describing how she loves him to the "depth and breadth and height" her "soul can reach". Her hyperbolic language could suggest that she is exaggerating when trying to express love for him. This could make her relationship seem less rooted in the realities of life than the portrayal of the relationship in 'The Manhunt'.
- The narrator in 'Sonnet 43' describes the stability of their relationship, whereas in 'The Manhunt' the relationship is presented as more of journey. In 'Sonnet 43', this is shown through the repeated "I love thee" refrain. This refrain appears across the poem which reflects how permanent the couple's love is. Ending the poem with the phrase "after death" reflects Barrett Browning's strong religious background and emphasises how she hopes their love is eternal. On the other hand, most of the couplet-length stanzas that make up 'The Manhunt' have an enjambed first line followed by an end-stopped second line. This creates a hesitant rhythm that reflects how their relationship slowly progresses forward as the couple begin to feel comfortable with one another again. However, the sense of movement created through the enjambment between the final three stanzas of the poem hints that this distance between the couple may not be permanent, and could symbolise the barriers between the couple breaking down.

Section Seven — Unseen Poetry

Page 85 — Warm-Up Questions

1) E.g. It's about the narrator's sense of loss after someone they love dies.

2) E.g. The narrator means that they never got the chance to live with their lover and make a home, because the lover died.

3) E.g. The descriptions of spring are vivid and life-like, which contrasts with the narrator's dead lover. Phrases like "the violets peer" and "Every bird has heart to sing" describe the beauty and joy of spring and rebirth. At the same time, the final line of each stanza describes the narrator's feelings — they are unable to appreciate the beauty of spring, and feel only loss and regret, rather than joy.

4) E.g. The rhyme scheme is ABAB. This gives the poem a simple rhythm, which emphasises the sadness of what the narrator is saying.

5) The final line is missing four syllables compared to the other lines. This emphasises the last line and makes it feel like it finishes too soon, which reflects the relationship between the narrator and their lover — it ended too soon, and now something is missing.

Pages 86-87 — Exam-Style Questions

1 a) For this question, you have to think about what the poet is saying, how they're saying it and your personal response to the poem. Make sure you comment on how form, structure and language are used to present feelings and ideas in the poem. Here are some points you could make:
- The poem has a nightmarish quality. It is about a woman who is alone at home, waiting nervously for her husband's safe return. The atmosphere is tense, as if something bad may be about to happen. The second stanza deals with the woman's actual nightmare, and the alliterative words "coming", "climbing" and "creeping" encourage the reader to view the sea as very menacing and hostile. It's like someone creeping in and stealing her lover. She wakes up, but with the "screaming gulls" and the sea's "chill in her arms" the reader gets the impression that she's still in a nightmare.
- The main feeling of the first stanza is boredom. The woman has "nothing to do now he's gone". She needs to keep busy, so she cleans the house. But the cleaning is futile; the broom "leaves a trail of grit". This could show that the act of cleaning can't cleanse her mind of her fear and anxiety.
- The second stanza describes the woman going to bed. She "sleeps downstairs", perhaps because she can't bear to be alone in their shared bed. This shows how even small things can be a painful reminder of the person you're missing. She also uses a "coat for a pillow" — the coat could well be her partner's, and by sleeping with it she may feel closer to him. These actions show that the narrator misses her partner, which makes the reader feel sympathy for her situation.
- In the third stanza, the onomatopoeic "screaming gulls" creates a vivid image that stands out to the reader because it contrasts with the silence of the rest of the poem, where the only sounds are the sweeping of the broom and the sibilance of the sea creeping closer. The screaming gulls might also be reminiscent of the screams of drowning sailors, highlighting the woman's fear that her partner will die at sea.
- His shirts are hanging on the washing line, which is a reminder that he's coming back, and feels homely and hopeful for a moment. But the final two lines, "and the high tide's breakers' / chill in her arms", immediately recall the sea and the woman's constant fear that her partner will never return. The "chill" of the waves in the woman's arms seems like a forewarning of death, as though she's holding her partner's cold, drowned body in her arms. The reader is left with a sense of the danger that the narrator's partner may well be facing.
- The structure of the poem, broken into three stanzas, mimics the structure of the woman's life whilst her partner is away — it's divided into day, night, day. There's no rhyme, which gives the reader a sense of her anxious state of mind. The final stanza is heavily enjambed, which creates a feeling of time moving faster, of disorder and confusion. The final stanza is also a line shorter, possibly reflecting her partner's early death.

1 b) For this question, you have to think about similarities and differences between the two poems. Make sure you comment on how form, structure and language are used to present feelings and ideas each poem. You should also think about the effects that each poem creates and your personal response to the poem. Here are some points you could make:
- Both poems present the sea as something dangerous. The subject of 'At Sea' fears that her partner will die at sea, while 'The Sands of Dee' describes the death of a girl who is drowned by "The western tide". The way the two poets personify the sea gives the reader a sense of its threatening nature. Kingsley describes it as "cruel, crawling" and "hungry", while Copley depicts it "coming", "climbing" and "creeping". In both cases, the imagery the poets use and the harsh alliterative 'c' sounds give the reader the impression that the sea is menacing. The action of "climbing" and "creeping" also gives the reader the impression that the sea is a predator, which adds to its menace.
- The poets both create a tense, frightening atmosphere through the imagery they use. For example, the onomatopoeic image of "screaming gulls" in 'At Sea' creates tension and anxiety by suddenly breaking the silence of the poem with a sound that suggests fear and suffering. In 'The Sands of Dee', the imagery of the "rolling mist" and the alliterative description of the "wild" "western wind" make the reader worry for Mary's safety. However, while 'At Sea' remains tense throughout, in 'The Sands of Dee', Kingsley breaks the tension in the final stanza. The last two lines of the poem show that time has passed since Mary's death, creating a more reflective mood which is less tense for the reader.
- The form of the two poems is very different, and is used to create different effects. 'At Sea' is written in free verse, with variable line lengths and no rhyme, which makes it seem unstructured and chaotic. This reflects the lack of structure in the woman's life when her partner is away at sea. In contrast, the form of 'The Sands of Dee' reflects the movement of the sea. Unlike 'At Sea', Kingsley's poem has a regular rhyme scheme, AAABAB, which creates a strong rhythm, mirroring the relentless movement of the waves and helping the reader to understand the sea's power.
- The poems each approach nature in a different way. 'The Sands of Dee' is dominated by natural imagery: for example, the discovery of the woman's body is presented alongside images of "weed" and "salmon". This gives the reader a sense of the close relationship between the people in the poem and the landscape they work in. However, 'At Sea' combines natural imagery with images of domestic life. The woman sweeps "sand" from "the bleached verandah" and dreams of the sea "creeping in through the door". These images make the sea seem like an unfriendly intruder in her home, and suggest she is trying to shut it out. The two poems' attitudes towards nature reflect the different situations in the poems, as Copley's narrator is afraid that nature will cause death to intrude on her life, whereas the narrator in 'The Sands of Dee' has already had time to process the woman's death at the hands of the sea.

Pages 89-94 — Paper 1: Section A (Shakespeare)

1.1) For this question, you need to write about how an audience might react to the extract. You need to analyse the extract and pick out the techniques and language used which have an effect on the audience. Keep in mind how the extract relates to the rest of the play. Remember to use quotes to support your points. Here are some points you could make:

- The extract leads the audience to question Friar Lawrence's motives for agreeing to marry the couple. When he likens Romeo and Juliet's situation to "fire and powder", he highlights the inevitability of the couple's downfall, as he implies their relationship is destined to burn brightly and powerfully, but it will ultimately "consume" them. The Friar's decision to marry Romeo and Juliet, despite his concerns, shows that the couple's well-being isn't his main motivation. It encourages the audience to think back to Act 2, Scene 3 when the Friar tells Romeo the "alliance" may turn their families' "rancour to pure love". He might therefore agree to marry them out of a desire to bring their two families together and end the feud.
- Romeo's speech reminds the audience of his youth and naivety. He taunts "love-devouring death" and claims that no sorrow can "countervail" his passion for Juliet. This bravado, which the Friar scolds him for, stems from Romeo's belief that their love is invincible. An audience may find Romeo's view of his and Juliet's love childlike and idealistic, especially as getting married places them in danger from their feuding families. By presenting Romeo as naive, Shakespeare reminds the audience that the couple are young and rash, which builds a sense of foreboding in the audience, who already know that the marriage ends in tragedy.
- The extract builds a sense of tragedy through the use of dramatic irony. Romeo poses a challenge to "death" to "do what he dare". The audience learns from the Prologue that the couple will die, so Romeo's defiance of death here seems to be in vain, highlighting to the audience how powerless he is to prevent his fate. This powerlessness is something that is referenced throughout the play, frequently reminding the audience of Romeo and Juliet's future demise.
- The Friar's words at the start of the extract would make an audience feel uneasy. The Friar appeals to the heavens, hoping that sorrow won't "chide" (make them regret) the marriage. This foreshadows the sadness to come, contrasting with the happiness that should precede a marriage, and creates an ominous atmosphere. The Friar's appeal to the heavens also creates sympathy for Romeo and Juliet by associating their marriage with goodness and divine approval.

1.2) For this question, you have to write about romantic love, so you need to pick out important bits of the play where Shakespeare addresses this theme, and explain how each bit you write about relates to the question. Here are some points you could make:

- Romantic love isn't always presented as true love in the play. At the start of the play, Romeo's romantic feelings for Rosaline appear juvenile. Mercutio mocks him for crying "Ay me!" and Friar Lawrence criticises him for "doting" on her rather than "loving" her. This shows that the other characters think Romeo is being silly about his romantic feelings for Rosaline. By portraying Romeo's romantic feelings for Rosaline as childish and unrealistic, Shakespeare makes the audience doubt whether his love for Juliet is any more authentic.
- In the play, romantic love is linked to sexual love. Throughout the play, there is a strong sense of Romeo's physical attraction for Juliet, as he enjoys looking at her and imagining being with her: "See how she leans her cheek upon her hand. / O that I were a glove upon that hand". Shakespeare shows that Romeo physically desires Juliet and their desire to spend their wedding night together shows that their connection goes beyond the words and promises they exchange.
- Romantic love is presented as passionate and impulsive. Romeo quickly forsakes his family name and allegiances for Juliet, "Henceforth I never will be Romeo", while Juliet swears for Romeo she'll "no longer be a Capulet". Their passion is dramatic, given that the two have not known each other for long, and suggests that the depth of Romeo and Juliet's love is great as it easily triumphs over lifelong connections. Their romantic feelings for each other help them to see the futility of their families' feud, suggesting that romantic love has the potential to overcome powerful obstacles.
- Juliet's reaction to the news that Romeo killed her cousin Tybalt presents romantic love as more powerful than familial love. After the Nurse curses Romeo for killing Tybalt, Juliet says "Blistered be thy tongue". The graphic verb "Blistered" emphasises Juliet's anger at Nurse by wishing pain and discomfort on her, which shows how strongly Juliet comes to Romeo's defence. Despite Romeo killing her cousin, Juliet remains loyal to Romeo, which suggests that romantic love can overcome the love someone has for their family. This idea is reinforced later in their exchange, when Juliet claims that Romeo's banishment is worse news than if all of her family had died.

2.1) For this question, you need to write about how an audience might respond to the extract. You need to analyse the extract and pick out the techniques and language used which have an effect on the audience. Keep in mind how the extract relates to the rest of the play. Remember to talk about the characters and use quotes to support your points. Here are some points you could make:

- An audience would be fearful for Macbeth in this extract. The Witches create uncertainty using riddles. For example, the Witches tell Banquo that he will "get kings, though thou be none" having just told Macbeth he will become king. These paradoxes create apprehension by making it seem like the Witches are toying with Macbeth. They establish their power over him by giving him enough information that he demands to be told "more", but without revealing specific details about how events will unfold. The fear for Macbeth is heightened in the extract as just before it, the Witches say "the charm's wound up". This means that the audience is aware that the Witches' have cast a mysterious spell, but Macbeth is not.

- The language used by the Witches encourages the audience to see Macbeth and Banquo's fates as linked. The prophecies by the Witches conclude with "all hail Macbeth and Banquo", followed by "Banquo and Macbeth, all hail!" The way the Witches reverse the order of Macbeth and Banquo's names emphasises to the audience that the prophecies are equally important for them both. The fact that the Witches predict Banquo's future by comparing him to Macbeth, such as saying he will be "Lesser than Macbeth, and greater", also hints to the audience that the pair may become rivals later in the play.
- Macbeth and Banquo's questioning of the Witches shows the similarities between the characters to the audience. Banquo inquires whether the Witches are "fantastical", and Macbeth asks the Witches "what are you?" These questions show both characters desire to know more about the Witches, highlighting that they have a shared natural curiosity. The pair also use imperatives such as "Speak" and "Tell me" which emphasises the strength of their desire to know more from the Witches, implying to the audience they are similarly entranced by the prophecies. The ease with which the pair are enticed by the prophecies could make the audience uneasy, as it suggests that they are both falling under the Witches' influence and want to believe what they say.
- The way the Witches refer to Macbeth as "Thane of Cawdor" reinforces the supernatural atmosphere of the extract. When told by the Witches he is Thane of Cawdor, Macbeth responds "But how of Cawdor? The Thane of Cawdor lives". Macbeth's question highlights the Witches' supernatural knowledge, and his confusion reminds the audience that Macbeth himself doesn't know about his new title yet. This could make the audience feel unsettled by the Witches' apparent power. The Witches' power in the extract is reinforced by dramatic irony, as the audience knows that what they're saying about the Thane of Cawdor is true.

2.2) For this question, you have to write about masculinity, so you need to pick out important bits of the play where Shakespeare addresses this theme, and explain how each bit you write about relates to the question. Here are some points you could make:
- Through Lady Macbeth, Shakespeare links the idea of masculinity to bravery and violence. In Act 1, Scene 7, Lady Macbeth bullies her husband into killing Duncan by saying "When you durst do it, then you were a man". This shows Lady Macbeth's view that being brave and committing violent acts is a key element of masculinity. Lady Macbeth's ability to successfully manipulate Macbeth here suggests that masculinity is an important source of pride for Macbeth, as he is scared of being seen as a coward.
- Shakespeare associates masculinity with loyalty and honour through Macbeth's initial reluctance to kill Duncan. He explains that to kill his king would not "become" a man, and that if he commits the murder he is "none" (not a man at all). Macbeth incorporates concepts of honour and loyalty into his ideas about masculinity, which shows that he is morally more principled than Lady Macbeth. However, Macbeth is soon persuaded to 'prove' his masculinity through treachery and his ambitious desires to become king overrule his principles. This presents Macbeth as a man who is weak and cowardly, which is ironic as Shakespeare links masculinity to strength throughout the play.
- Shakespeare challenges the view that unfounded violence is an acceptable version of masculinity. When Lady Macbeth and Macbeth kill Duncan in his sleep in Act 2, they decide to "smear the sleepy grooms with blood" so the servants will be blamed for the murder. The verb "smear" means to mark or stain something, but it can also mean to tarnish someone's reputation. This verb therefore highlights the dishonourable nature of Macbeth's deed to the audience, rather than the strength or courage behind the murder. By stressing his immorality at this point, Shakespeare might be suggesting that Lady Macbeth and Macbeth's interpretation of masculinity is corrupted.
- As the play progresses, Macbeth becomes less willing to commit 'masculine' acts of violence and instead he manipulates others to achieve his own ends. In Act 3, Scene 1, he goads others into murdering Banquo, rather than facing him himself. This suggests that he is moving away from the masculine ideal of the "brave" warrior he was in Act 1. This idea is emphasised through the contrast he forms with Macduff in Act 4, Scene 3, who vows to face Macbeth "Front on front" after Macbeth murders his family.

3.1) For this question, you need to write about what the extract reveals about Othello's state of mind. You'll need to look carefully at the techniques used in the extract, but keep in mind where the extract fits into the play too. Remember to back your points up with quotes. Here are some things you could mention:
- The extract begins with a monologue from Othello which presents his conflicted state of mind to the audience. This monologue shows Othello's complicated feelings regarding Desdemona — he admires her "whiter" than "snow" skin, but believes that it is necessary "she must die". These contrasting sentiments emphasise Othello's conflicted state of mind. Structuring the scene so that this monologue comes first allows the audience to see Othello's conflicted thoughts about killing Desdemona before he confronts her later in the extract. This creates tension for the audience because they are aware that Othello is seriously considering killing Desdemona while they are speaking.
- The extract shows that Othello is reluctant to kill Desdemona because of his lingering love for her. Othello's repetition of the mantra "it is the cause" indicates that he needs to remind himself that killing Desdemona is the 'right' course of action, suggesting that he is upset by the idea of killing her. Othello then goes on to delay killing Desdemona when he twice steals just "One more" kiss. His desire to kiss Desdemona repeatedly emphasises to the audience that he still loves her and is upset about having to kill her. An audience may get the impression that Othello is not setting out to kill Desdemona because he wants to, but because he feels he must do it so she can't "betray more men" like himself.
- Othello's conversation with Desdemona later in the extract indicates to the audience that his resolve to kill her has strengthened. When Desdemona asks if Othello is coming to bed, he deflects the question by asking "Have you pray'd tonight, Desdemona?" By ignoring Desdemona's question and asking his own, Othello takes control of the conversation, which suggests he is feeling more resolute. His question also begins to lead the conversation towards Desdemona's eventual death, which could emphasise that his mind is made up about killing her. However, Othello ignoring Desdemona's question could also indicate that he is worried he will be led astray from his task if he answers her question — Desdemona's "balmy breath" has already almost persuaded Othello not to kill her and so Othello may still be wary of being swayed.

- It is made clear to the audience in this extract that Othello believes he is being merciful in his actions towards Desdemona. He allows Desdemona the chance to pray for her sins before he kills her because he doesn't want to "kill" her "soul". This affords her the opportunity to make peace with God, which would allow her to be sent to heaven despite her adultery — Othello believes he is being merciful by saving her soul. This contrasts with the audience's perspective: they know that Desdemona is innocent, so they know that Othello's actions, despite his sense of mercy, are unjust.

3.2) This question requires you to think carefully about the importance of a single character across the whole play, so all your points need to be clearly about that character. Here are some points you could make:
- Cassio is presented as a source of jealousy for the other male characters in the play, including Iago. Before Roderigo ambushes Cassio, Iago reveals he'll benefit if Cassio dies because Cassio has a "daily beauty" which makes Iago "ugly". This shows that Iago resents Cassio's beauty because it highlights his own "ugly" nature. The use of "daily" emphasises that Cassio's "beauty" is a constant problem for Iago by pointing out that there isn't a day where Cassio's beauty isn't clear to see. Cassio's attractive appearance may also be a source of jealousy for Othello, which makes him more likely to see Cassio as a genuine threat to Othello's marriage.
- Cassio is a charming character, particularly towards Desdemona when seeking favour with Othello. For example, he claims himself to be her "true servant". This shows that he is trying to show devotion towards Desdemona by elevating her to a higher level than himself. Iago uses Cassio's interaction with Desdemona to make Othello jealous of Cassio, telling Othello to "observe her well with Cassio". While Cassio's behaviour towards Desdemona is intended to repair his reputation with Othello, Iago's interference means that Cassio's charming nature plays a part in driving the two men further apart.
- Cassio is presented as an honest and trusting man. For example, he is happy to divulge his ability to get drunk easily to Iago, stating "I have very poor and unhappy brains for drinking." The use of two adjectives ("poor" and "unhappy") strengthens this statement, showing that Cassio isn't trying to hide his weakness and trusts those around him not to take advantage of his honesty. However, his trust in Iago makes him seem naive: he doesn't recognise Iago's ulterior motives when Iago insists he drinks despite his admission, and as a result Cassio gets drunk and causes Othello offence just as Iago hoped.
- After the drunken fight in which Montano is wounded, Cassio bemoans the loss of his post as lieutenant and his subsequent loss of reputation. Cassio says the word "reputation" six times in four lines, beginning and ending the passage with this word. This repetition emphasises how important reputation is to Cassio and gives the audience the impression that he feels ashamed of his failure to uphold the values expected of him as a high-ranking member of society. Cassio is so distraught by the loss of his reputation that he feels he has "lost the immortal part" of himself, which could hint that the sorrow he feels is due to him believing he has lost his soul as a result of his immoral behaviour.
- Cassio's treatment of Bianca reveals a crueller side to his personality. When pressed by Iago about whether he would marry her, Cassio laughs about her behaviour and claims that Bianca is someone who "haunts" him in "every place". Cassio uses the verb "haunts" to characterise Bianca as a ghost or pest who won't leave him alone, possibly because he wants to distance himself from Bianca in order to protect his social status. This mocking of Bianca shows the audience the unkind side of his personality. Cassio's treatment of Bianca also presents him as two-faced because he treats Bianca with affection in private, calling her "sweet love", contrasting his attitudes towards her in public. This shows that he is only happy to display kindness towards his lover in private where his reputation isn't at risk.

4.1) For this question, you need to write about how an audience might respond to the extract. You need to analyse the extract and pick out the techniques and language used which have an effect on the audience. Keep in mind how the extract relates to the rest of the play. Remember to talk about Benedick and Beatrice and use quotes to support your points. Here are some points you could make:
- An audience may be surprised by Beatrice's attitude at the beginning of this extract. She acts submissively towards Benedick, saying she has come to Benedick because he called for her and will depart when "bid" to do so. Her comment makes her seem willing to be at Benedick's beck and call, which contrasts with her attitude in the first half of the play when she says that she is disgusted by the idea of being "overmastered" by a man. However, by saying she'll do as she is "bid", Beatrice creates a chance to outwit Benedick, pretending to leave when he asks her to remain until he says "then". This could suggest that Beatrice's obedient attitude here is actually an act to outsmart Benedick.
- In the extract, Benedick acts openly on his love for Beatrice, telling her "I will kiss thee". He presents his desire for her in plain, uncomplicated language, using a short, monosyllabic statement which expresses his feelings in a simple and direct way. This would give an audience the impression that he is confident about his love for her. Benedick's continued affectionate behaviour towards Beatrice in this scene would be satisfying for an audience, who would be expecting a happy ending for the couple given that the play is a comedy.
- Beatrice and Benedick's playful behaviour in this extract gives the audience the impression that their love is genuine. For instance, Benedick asks Beatrice which of his "bad parts" she first fell in love with; Beatrice replies by claiming that he has no space for "any good part" to fit. These teasing insults show that their witty and playful relationship will continue even though they are now in love. This encourages the audience to view their love as authentic, as it hasn't caused them to change. This may also hint to an audience that because the way they speak to each other hasn't changed, Benedick and Beatrice always had strong feelings for one another from the beginning of the play, even if they didn't properly recognise them.
- Despite the argumentative nature of their relationship, the extract presents Beatrice and Benedick's love as being very grounded in reality. Benedick claims that he and Beatrice are "too wise to woo peaceably". This shows they understand that the reality of love doesn't match the idealistic view put forwards by conventional courtly lovers. Benedick's statement also encourages an audience to compare the two couples in the play. Claudio and Hero follow courtly traditions and their relationship nearly falls apart, whereas Benedick and Beatrice enjoy their more humorous, less traditional relationship. As a result of this comparison, Benedick and Beatrice's unconventional courting methods make their love seem stronger than that of Claudio and Hero.

4.2) This question requires you to think carefully about the importance of a single character, so all your points need to be clearly about that character. Here are some points you could make:
- Shakespeare uses Dogberry's language to present him as a comic character throughout the play. Dogberry frequently uses malapropisms, for example, he refers to one of the watchmen as "senseless" when he means to call him sensible. This creates humour, as Dogberry unintentionally insults the watchman when he means to compliment him. Many of the malapropisms in Dogberry's speech occur when he attempts to imitate the graceful speech of high-status characters. The fact that he misuses words in these instances adds to his presentation as a comic character, as it makes him sound particularly foolish.
- Dogberry's incompetence also creates tension. When trying to explain to Leonato in Act 3, Scene 5 that he has arrested Conrade and Borachio, Dogberry speech is rambling as he talks about irrelevant topics such as Verges's incompetence. Dogberry's lack of focus creates suspense, as the audience grows worried that Leonato won't find out about the plot against Hero before the wedding. Dogberry's incompetence leads the audience to feel frustrated with him, which makes him a less likeable character in spite of his comic role.
- Dogberry isn't shown to be completely incapable. In Act 5, Scene 1 he and the Watch are credited by Borachio when he tells Don Pedro "What your wisdoms could not discover, these shallow fools have brought to light". The opposition in this sentence creates a contrast between Don Pedro's failure to find out about Don John's plan and Dogberry's success, emphasising Dogberry's achievement. However, Borachio's comment isn't wholly flattering to Dogberry, as he refers to Dogberry as one of the "shallow fools". Borachio's statement isn't necessarily intended to elevate Dogberry's status, but more to insult Don Pedro by implying he was outsmarted by the foolish Dogberry.
- Dogberry is clearly easily impressed by high-status characters in the play. When Leonato thanks him for uncovering Don John's plot in Act 5, Scene 1, Dogberry address him as "your worship" numerous times. The repetition of this admiring term emphasises Dogberry's respect for Leonato, showing that pleasing those of high status is important to him. However, Dogberry is generally not respected in return by the high status characters in the play, such as when Don Pedro sarcastically calls him "cunning" (clever) in the same scene. This might create sympathy for Dogberry among the audience, as despite his good intentions, he is widely viewed as an object of ridicule.

5.1) For this question, you need to write about how an audience might respond to the extract. You need to analyse the extract and pick out the techniques and language used which have an effect on the audience. Keep in mind how the extract relates to the rest of the play. Remember to talk about Henry and use quotes to support your points. Here are some points you could make:
- In this extract, Henry attracts sympathy from the audience by stating the responsibilities put on him by his people. In the first three lines, he lists the burdens that are laid "on the king". The long list emphasises the responsibilities weighing on Henry's mind and makes the audience sympathise with his challenging role. Having Henry be open about the burden of his responsibilities provides a contrast to his ruthless behaviour earlier in the play, such as his threats to the Governor of Harfleur in Act 3, Scene 3. This extract therefore encourages the audience to reassess their opinion of Henry as an emotionless leader and see him instead as a king who is trying his best to be an effective ruler.

- Henry's speech also presents him as a lonely, unhappy figure. He talks about how the "ceremony" of kings creates "fear" in other men, and states he is "less happy, being fear'd" than his subjects are in fearing him. This passage presents Henry and his men as opposing entities who are each unhappy with their relationship to the other and emphasises his separation from other men in society. Henry's isolation may encourage an audience to reflect on the role of monarchy in society and consider the difficulties of being king.
- Henry's discussion of "ceremony" emphasises that he doesn't believe it's of any practical benefit to a monarch. He points out that when someone of "great greatness" is "sick", ceremony cannot "cure" them, which emphasises his belief that the trappings of royalty are of little use. Henry's repetition of "great" creates a mocking tone that implies he is bitter about the way "ceremony" is useless at making him feel better. Henry's assessment of ceremony as worthless makes him more likeable to the audience by showing him not to be motivated by the supposed benefits of royalty, but by other things such as responsibility to his country and men.
- Henry thinks life as someone not in the public eye would be preferable to his position as king. He says that "private men" enjoy "infinite heart's-ease" which kings do not. Henry's jealousy of ordinary men shows that he pines for the simple experience of being at ease, which could make him seem more relatable to an audience. However, this comparison could also present Henry as naive and insensitive because he doesn't seem to appreciate the luxuries that come with being king, or acknowledge that "private men" also face difficulties.

5.2) This question requires you to think carefully about the importance of a single character, so all your points need to be clearly about that character. Here are some points you could make:
- Pistol is first discussed in Act 2, Scene 1. He is presented in a negative way, as Nym and Bardolph discuss how he married Nym's bride-to-be. Nym says he will "hold out" his "iron" to Pistol — this allusion to violence emphasises the severity of Pistol's actions and how upset Nym is. Before he even arrives on stage, Pistol is therefore presented as lacking in morals and happy to act dishonestly. This structure gives a general idea of Pistol's character before he appears on stage, but it could also make the audience think he is more villainous than he actually is. This then has the effect of emphasising the more comic aspects of his character when he appears later in the scene.
- Despite his negative presentation, Pistol also shows moments of loyalty to his friends, such as when he tries to convince Fluellen not to execute Bardolph. He describes Bardolph as "firm and sound of heart" and tries to suggest that Bardolph is a victim of "cruel fate" — although Bardolph has committed a crime, Pistol makes him seem unlucky rather than malicious. While his efforts are not successful, Pistol's positive descriptions of Bardolph and attempt to save him show that he does place some value on his friends. However, his inability to change Fluellen's mind suggests Pistol is not respected enough by the higher ranked soldiers to be granted such a large favour.
- This lack of respect is echoed in the Boy's monologue in Act 3, Scene 2. The Boy describes Pistol as having "a killing tongue and a quiet sword". This suggests that Pistol is very boastful about his exploits in battle but doesn't do a lot of fighting, implying that he's a coward and showing the Boy's lack of respect for him. Pistol's boasting is also spoken of by other characters throughout the play, such as Gower, who says Pistol goes to war not to fight but so he can "grace himself" in London as a soldier. This hints that Pistol's negative reputation is widespread throughout the army.

- Although Pistol is mostly presented as an amoral, cowardly caricature, his wife's death at the end of the play portrays him in a more sympathetic light. He says that his "rendezvous is quite cut off", meaning that he has no home to return to, and that his honour is "cudgelled". Pistol's use of violent language compares the brutality of war to the pain Pistol feels at losing his wife. However, Pistol quickly moves on to speak of his new plans for the future, saying he will become a "cutpurse" when he returns to England. This is his final speech in the play, and these words leave the audience with a sense of satisfaction as it seems Pistol will continue to be the same comic rogue figure as he is in the rest of the play.

6.1) For this question, you need to write about how an audience might respond to the extract. You need to analyse the extract and pick out the techniques and language used which have an effect on the audience. Keep in mind how the extract relates to the rest of the play. Remember to talk about Portia and use quotes to support your points. Here are some points you could make:
- Portia's speech portrays mercy as holy. She says that mercy is an "attribute to God" and implies that it comes from "heaven". These religious images present mercy as a divine attribute, which encourages an audience to perceive mercy as a positive quality. An audience is therefore more likely to support the Christian characters in their desire to achieve mercy for Antonio.
- In contrast to her presentation of mercy, Portia presents justice negatively. She states that if decisions were based on the idea of justice alone, then no one "Should see salvation". The sibilance draws the audience's attention to the fact that no one will reach heaven by only following justice. This implication suggests to the audience that Shylock's desire to pursue the legal terms of his bond, while refusing to show Antonio mercy, is a sinful one.
- An audience could view Portia as a compassionate character. She spends this extract encouraging Shylock to have pity on Antonio by speaking in the second person plural, using "we" and "us" in an attempt to encourage a sense of unity. Portia's use of this persuasive language gives the audience the impression that she wants them to put their differences aside in the hope of saving Antonio. However, a modern audience may interpret Portia's character slightly differently here, as she is trying to impose her Christian ideals on him in a way that shows a lack of respect for his religious beliefs, which would be unacceptable to an audience today.
- The way Portia refers to Shylock in this extract may make a modern-day audience uneasy. She addresses him as "Jew" rather than using his name, which defines him by his religion. This shows that she is prejudiced because she is judging him by a stereotype rather than seeing him as an individual. Although this might make a modern audience uncomfortable, anti-Semitism was widespread in England when Shakespeare wrote the play. It is therefore likely Shakespeare did not mean to present Portia negatively, especially as this contrasts with her presentation as merciful in the rest of this extract.

6.2) This question requires you to think carefully about when an audience might feel sympathy towards Antonio, so you need to pick out bits of the play where this might happen. Remember to refer to the plot and characters in your answer, and to back up your points with quotes. Here are some points you could make:
- Antonio is portrayed as a sympathetic character at the beginning of the play. Antonio opens the play by explaining that his sadness gives him "much ado to know myself", and that it "wearies" both him and his companions. The fact that he barely recognises himself suggests that he used to be cheerful and happy, which emphasises the depth of his current sorrow by showing the audience how much he has changed. This would produce sympathy from the audience. Even at the end of the play when Antonio's ships have returned, the audience may still feel sorry for him because he ends up alone and unmarried, unlike the other main Christian characters.
- The audience would feel particularly sorry for Antonio in Act 3, Scene 3. The fact that he has been arrested would encourage them to feel sympathetic towards him, particularly as Shylock repeatedly refuses to "hear" his pleas. The power that Shylock has over Antonio in this scene contrasts with their previous interaction in Act 1, Scene 3, when they were equally confident and scornful of one another. This change highlights Antonio's vulnerability at this point in the play, which encourages the audience to feel sympathy for him.
- Shakespeare uses the other characters' descriptions of Antonio to create sympathy for him. Salerio claims that a "kinder gentleman treads not the earth" in Act 2, Scene 8, and Solanio calls him "the good Antonio, the honest Antonio" in Act 3, Scene 1. This focus on his virtues encourages the audience to feel he doesn't deserve to suffer because he is a good person. His goodness also makes his resignation to his fate seem more tragic, as his death at Shylock's hands seems inevitable.
- Antonio's powerlessness makes him a sympathetic character. The fact that his "griefs and losses" are caused by things he is unable to control, such as a shipwreck, makes him seem like a victim of fate and circumstance. The unfair nature of his misfortunes is emphasised by the fact that he is only in trouble because he was trying to help Bassanio, which makes the audience feel like his punishment is unwarranted.

Page 95 — Paper 1: Section B (Poetry)

7.1) For this question, you have to think about the way the poet uses form, structure and language to present ideas about childhood. Make sure you structure your answer so that it discusses all of these techniques. Here are some points you could make:
- In the excerpt from 'The Prelude', the narrator fondly remembers ice skating as a child. This is reflected through language associated with happiness such as "rapture" and "exulting". The positive tone gives the reader the impression that the narrator is rejoicing in how happy his childhood was. These carefree descriptions makes the narrator's childhood seem idyllic to the reader and suggests that they are being nostalgic about their childhood. This sense of nostalgia reflects the poet's own feelings about growing up, as 'The Prelude' is an autobiographical poem.

- The narrator's childhood is presented as carefree and fun. He describes how he "heeded not the summons" from his home and instead "flew" and "wheel'd" on the ice. This monosyllabic language adds pace to the excerpt, which creates an energetic tone to recreate the excitement that the narrator felt that day. Because the narrator "heeded not the summons" to return home, the reader senses that the narrator mainly cared about having fun as a child and didn't worry about the consequences of his actions. Through this, Wordsworth could be suggesting that having fun is an important part of childhood.
- As a child, the narrator doesn't fully appreciate nature. This is shown when he describes how the sounds of "distant hills" were "not unnoticed", which uses a double negative to suggest that, while he noticed nature, he didn't fully understand its power. Wordsworth was a Romantic poet — the Romantics believed that humans had a very close connection with the natural world, so here Wordsworth may be hinting that nature contributed to the narrator's childhood joy, but it is only now the narrator has matured that he can fully appreciate this connection.
- The narrator becomes more reflective about his childhood towards the end of the excerpt. This is shown through a shift in perspective, as the narrator moves his focus away from childhood "games" and "woodland pleasures" and shifts it onto the immensity and power of nature, as shown through describing the "distant hills" and "stars". This change in perspective suggests that the narrator has become more observant and thoughtful since his childhood. This maturity is emphasised through the more negative language at the end of the excerpt, such as "melancholy" and "died", which could hint how the narrator's carefree outlook has been lost over time.

7.2) For this question, you have to think about the way the poets use form, structure and language in their presentations of childhood. Think carefully about which poem you choose for the comparison, remembering that you need to find similarities and differences between the two poems. This answer compares the excerpt from 'The Prelude' by William Wordsworth with 'Death of a Naturalist' by Seamus Heaney, but it gives you an idea of the kind of things you need to write for a comparison question. Here are some points you could make:

- The excerpt from 'The Prelude' and 'Death of a Naturalist' both present vivid childhood memories. In the excerpt from 'The Prelude', the narrator remembers how he and his friends "hiss'd along the polish'd ice". This use of sibilance recreates the sounds of the ice skates carving into the ice, highlighting how detailed his memory of childhood is. Similarly, in 'Death of a Naturalist', the narrator remembers how the "bluebottles / Wove a strong gauze of sound around the smell" of the flax-dam. This sensory image reflects how rich the memories are in the narrator's mind. Both poems are first-person narratives that are considered autobiographical: Wordsworth wrote 'The Prelude' about his childhood growing up in the Lake District and much of Heaney's poetry focuses on his experiences growing up in Ireland. This autobiographical, first-person style gives the reader the impression that these vivid childhood memories are personal and important to each poet.
- The poets use different registers to present their memories of childhood. The excerpt from 'The Prelude' uses more advanced language, such as "in games / Confederate, imitative of the chace", which gives the poem a more formal tone. This suggests that while the narrator looks back on his childhood fondly, it is from a more mature perspective — the reader senses that the narrator now feels distanced from his childhood. The narrator in 'Death of a Naturalist', however, uses more childlike language, such as "and how the mammy frog / Laid hundreds of little eggs". This informal language emphasises the narrator's simple outlook as a child, reminding the reader that childhood is a time of innocence.
- Both poets link childhood with nature. In the excerpt from 'The Prelude', the narrator describes himself as being part of a "Pack", an "untir'd horse", as well as describing how the group "flew" through the darkness. These words evoke images of wildlife, such as a pack of hunting dogs, a horse and a bird, which suggests the narrator feels he shared characteristics with animals as a child. This relates to Wordworth's position as a Romantic poet, as he placed great emphasis on the link between humans and nature. Similarly, the narrator in 'Death of a Naturalist' also links his childhood with nature. The narrator describes how they would "wait and watch" the frogspawn until it changed into tadpoles. This suggests the narrator had a strong interest in nature as a child, as the alliteration of the 'w' in "wait and watch" uses a repeated sound to highlight how the narrator was interested in little else. This is reinforced by the overall focus of the poem — the narrator focuses solely on memories that are linked to nature, which indicates that it played a prominent role in their childhood.
- Both poems initially focus on the joy of childhood but move towards a more negative perspective by the end. In the excerpt from 'The Prelude', the narrator shifts from a joyful tone to a more solemn one. Describing how the "orange sky of evening died away" has connotations of the theme of loss, perhaps reflecting that the narrator realises he will never truly be able to relive the freedom and carefree feelings of childhood. On the other hand, in 'Death of a Naturalist', the narrator's perspective changes from an enthusiastic tone to one of disgust at the end of the poem, as shown when the narrator says "I sickened, turned, and ran". This short sentence is made up of three verbs, which quickens the pace and highlights the narrator's urgent need to escape the nature which now disgusts and scares him. Because both poems change to a negative perspective as the narrator ages, the poets could each be encouraging younger readers to cherish their childhood while they still enjoy it.

Pages 97-100 — Paper 2: Section A (Post-1914 Prose/Drama)

1) For this question, you're asked to write about fear, so all your points need to be about that theme. You need to write about how Golding presents fear, so make sure you mention the techniques that he uses. These points give you some ideas of the kind of things you could include:
- In the novel, the boys' fear is expressed through the beast. This is demonstrated in the extract when Jack describes how there has been talk of a "dark thing, a beast, some sort of animal." His description suggests that the boys have tried to justify their fear by convincing themselves that there is something physical to be afraid of on the island. However, the use of vague language such as "thing" and "some sort of" suggests that they have no clear identity of the beast in mind, which hints to the reader that it only exists in the boys' imaginations.
- Golding presents fear as dangerous. In the extract, Jack is adamant that "there is no beast in the forest." He uses logic to back up his point, claiming he would have seen it when he was hunting, and that "You don't get big animals on small islands." His attitude here contrasts with his behaviour later in the novel. In Chapter 9 he encourages boys to seek protection from the beast by joining his tribe. The difference in his perspective shows how dangerous fear can be: it either shows that Jack becomes so afraid that he loses his ability to reason, or that he is able to use fear to manipulate others.

- Fear of the unknown on the island is shown earlier in the novel by the littluns' nightmares. In Chapter 4, they experience "untold terrors in the dark"— the reference to darkness indicates that their fear is rooted in being unable to see or understand things. Jack and Ralph agree that building shelters is important so that the littluns feel they have some sort of 'home'. This suggests that Jack and Ralph are trying to fight fear of the unknown by recreating something familiar — the comforts of civilised society. The boys' feeling that creating a society can fend off fear continues throughout the novel.
- The events of the novel take place against a backdrop of fear in the form of nuclear war. Piggy suggests in the first chapter that they will never be rescued because of "the atom bomb" which means their potential rescuers are "all dead". We are reminded again about this war at the end of the novel when the naval officer arrives and behind him "another rating held a sub-machine gun." This backdrop of fear serves to remind us that fear and evil are not confined to life on the island, but exist all over the world.

2) For this question, you have to write about Meena and Anita's relationship, so you need to pick out important bits of the novel where the writer addresses this, and explain how each bit you write about relates to the question. Don't forget to write about the extract in detail as well as the rest of the novel. These points give you some ideas of the kind of things you could include:

- It is clear to the reader that Anita doesn't value Meena's friendship. In the extract, Meena explains that "Anita talked and I listened". This suggests that, instead of trying to engage with Meena's life and form a meaningful relationship with her, Anita simply enjoys Meena's "admiration". This lack of real care causes her to behave callously towards Meena, driving many of the novel's events, such as Meena's fall from the horse in Chapter 11 and her subsequent stay in hospital.
- Anita is the dominant figure in her relationship with Meena. In Chapter 3, for example, she approaches Meena and gets her to follow her. This shows how Anita takes control and leads their friendship from the beginning. By highlighting the unequal nature of their relationship early on in the novel, Syal is able to explore Meena's insecurities about her identity and her physical "ache" to be accepted by popular girls.
- Meena values and is heavily influenced by her relationship with Anita. She says that it makes her "shed inhibitions" and try to emulate Anita's behaviour. This leads Meena to act against her conscience, for example when she steals the charity collection tin in Chapter 6. The fact that she selfishly blames it on Baby hints that she could become hardened as a result of the friendship, creating a sense of anxiety that Meena will become progressively more like Anita.
- The friendship plays a significant role in Meena's development, ultimately helping her to understand herself better. The relationship causes Meena physical and emotional damage, and these experiences help her to understand that Anita is not a true friend. This realisation helps her to learn the value of real friendship, her family and her Indian heritage; through this understanding, she comes to accept her own identity instead of trying to become someone she is not.

3) For this question, you're asked to write about the author's ideas about memory, so all your points need to be about that theme. You need to write about how Ishiguro presents memory in the extract and the rest of the novel, so make sure you mention the techniques that he uses. These points give you some ideas of the kind of things you could include:

- The extract shows how valuable memories — especially those of Hailsham and her friends — are to Kathy. She can still remember what it looked like approaching "the South Playing Field from the other side" and a girl called Susanna "a couple of years above" her who was a Sales monitor. The detail in her memories shows how well she remembers Hailsham, which hints at how strongly she values those memories. The significance she places on them may reflect how limited her future is as a clone, meaning her happy memories of the past are more significant to her.
- The extract also suggests that memory can be unreliable. The donor Kathy talked to commented that even "precious" memories "fade surprisingly quickly". By including this, Ishiguro makes Kathy's confidence that her memories will stay with her seem optimistic. This encourages the reader to view her memories as a coping mechanism, as her determination not to "lose" them highlights her over-reliance on memories of her past.
- The idea that memories can be lost or become unreliable undermines Kathy's status as a trustworthy narrator. Kathy states that she is going over her past to "order" her memories "carefully"; the adverb "carefully" emphasises that she wants to take a thought-out approach. Yet she acknowledges that her early memories could "blur into each other", and that different people can remember an event differently, such as her and Ruth's differing memories of how long the "'secret guard' business" lasted. This makes it clear to the reader that Kathy is an unreliable narrator, and emphasises that memories can be false, even if, as in Kathy's narrative, care is taken over how they are recalled and arranged.
- Elsewhere in the novel, characters often use memory as a way of avoiding their fears about the present or future. Kathy's patient in the first chapter of the novel tries to create false memories of Hailsham to cope with the trauma of his situation. He asks her for more detail about the school so that the memories will "really sink in", reflecting his desire to remember it as if it had been his own school. This suggests that memories, including those of other people, can be a form of escapism in response to a frightening present or future.

4) This question requires you to think carefully about how a single character is presented, so all your points need to be clearly about that character. Don't forget to write about the extract in detail as well as the rest of the play. Here are some points you could make:

- Arthur is presented as determined in the extract. After Arthur decides to continue his bike ride, he describes how he "turned" his bike, "remounted" it and "pedalled" off, "putting" his back to the marshes. This series of active verbs emphasises that Arthur is choosing to resist the strange draw of the marshes and stick to his original plan of going for a bike ride. Arthur's determination is reinforced in the next chapter when he tells Mr Daily that he "won't run away" from his responsibilities at Eel Marsh House, despite the bad things that have happened to him there.

- In the extract, Arthur is presented as a man who has undergone a mental transformation. He examines his emotions and notes that they have become "so volatile and so extreme" as a result of his experiences at Eel Marsh House that he is now "living in another dimension". The word 'dimension' is used to describe an invisible aspect of something, such as time or physical space. This suggests that Arthur's mental state has changed so drastically that it is as if he isn't even in the same world as he was before. Immediately after this, Arthur wonders whether he also "looked different", which shows that Arthur feels transformed in his body as well as his mind.
- In the narrative of the events in Crythin Gifford, Hill presents Arthur as a man who hasn't fully left his childhood behind. In 'Spider', when Arthur has decided to return to Eel Marsh House, he says that he feels the same way that a man would feel if he was going "into battle" or to "fight with giants". Arthur compares his situation to occurrences that might be seen in a children's story. This childish comparison reminds the reader of Arthur's relative youth, which might make them feel more concerned about the danger that he's in. This link with childhood is also seen elsewhere in the novel. For example, in 'The Funeral of Mrs Drablow', Arthur likens himself to a "small child" who is safe in their "nursery". These references make Arthur seem particularly young and innocent before his experiences at Eel Marsh House.
- Hill uses a frame narrative to show that Arthur has been deeply affected by the experiences of his youth. In 'Christmas Eve', Arthur is sent into a "frenzy of agitation" by the ghost stories his family are telling. The novel then moves backwards in time to a younger Arthur who has yet to encounter the woman in black. Younger Arthur quickly dismisses the rumours about Mrs Drablow and her house as "superstition and tittle-tattle". Structuring the novel in this non-chronological way allows Hill to emphasise how Arthur's character changes thanks to the events in the novel — he is no longer able to respond to fear and mystery in the rational way that he did as a young man. Hill reinforces the idea that Arthur has been significantly affected by his experiences through Arthur's first-person narrative, which allows the reader an insight into his thoughts and feelings, and the extent to which they have changed.

5) This question requires you to think carefully about the importance of a single character, so all your points need to be clearly about that character. Don't forget to write about the extract in detail as well as the rest of the novel. Here are some points you could make:
- In the extract, Melanie is presented as being less certain of her love for Jeanette than Jeanette is of her love for Melanie. After Jeanette says she loves Melanie almost as much as she loves God, Melanie's "eyes clouded" and she responds with "I don't know". The use of the verb "clouded" emphasises Melanie's uncertainty, as clouds are often associated with an inability to see or think clearly. Melanie's response could also suggest that she is uncomfortable with Jeanette comparing her love to the love that she has for God, reflecting Melanie's strong faith and religious nature.
- Later in the extract, when Melanie and Jeanette's relationship is revealed to the church, Melanie is frightened and gives in to the church's demands. Jeanette describes Melanie as "pale" and "trembling" as the pastor condemns her, and she instantly says "Yes." when asked to "give up" Jeanette. Melanie's physical reactions emphasise her extreme fear, which is reinforced by her response in the form of a simple sentence. In this way, Winterson emphasises that Melanie is scared to challenge the church's judgement of her relationship with Jeanette. Jeanette's reaction, in which she "yelled" at the pastor, contrasts with Melanie's obedience and emphasises Melanie's loyalty to the church, as well as her betrayal of Jeanette.
- Melanie is presented as a calm character when she returns later in the novel for the nativity at Christmas. She is twice described as "serene", once at the nativity and once the day after it. This repetition emphasises how little Melanie is affected by re-encountering Jeanette, and indicates that Melanie has been able to recover from her traumatic experience at the church. This behaviour might shock the reader, as they would expect Melanie to be more affected by seeing Jeanette, given that their relationship ended in a distressing way.
- After Melanie gets married and bumps into Jeanette towards the end of the novel, she is presented as unwilling to acknowledge the impact their relationship had on Jeanette. Jeanette says Melanie "laughed" and "laughed again" about what had happened. The repetition of "laughed" suggests Melanie doesn't appreciate or realise how difficult things were for Jeanette as a result of their relationship coming to the church's attention, and that she sees it more as a funny incident than anything serious. However, Melanie's light-heartedness could also suggest that she's worried that the truth of their affair could come to light again, and so she is determined to laugh it off as unimportant.

6) In this question, you're asked to write about honesty and dishonesty, so all your points need to be about these ideas. You need to write about how Stephens presents ideas about honesty and dishonesty, so make sure you mention the techniques that he uses. These points give you some ideas of the kind of things you could include:
- In this extract, Stephens explores the reasons why people might not be honest. For example, Ed explains that he lied about Judy dying because he was "in such a mess" and "didn't know how to explain" what had happened. This suggests that people can be dishonest because they are upset or confused, rather than to deliberately hurt someone else. Stephens therefore shows how families do sometimes lie to each other, but that this is not always done with malicious intent.
- The extract also show how lying and dishonesty in families can undermine trust. Ed's admission here that he "killed Wellington" is the main turning point of the play, as it pushes Christopher away and causes Christopher to make the journey to London. This example of the negative repercussions of dishonesty suggests that it is important for families to be truthful with each other, underlining Ed's realisation that "if you don't tell the truth now, then later on it hurts even more". Ed's insistence that Christopher "can trust" him is therefore shown to be misguided, as Christopher loses faith in his father because of his dishonesty.
- Judy, in contrast to Ed, is very honest in her letters that Christopher reads in Part One, including about her own failings, such as confessing that she "was not a very good mother". Although this openness is painful for Christopher, causing him to throw up, Judy's perspective on her experiences gains the audience's respect, and Christopher's decision to stay with her in London shows that she has his trust even though the truth has upset him. Judy's honesty therefore reflects positively on her character, reinforcing the view that being honest is the better approach for people to take.
- Towards the start of Part One, it is revealed that Christopher views some forms of speech as dishonesty. For example, he believes that a metaphor "should be called a lie". His objection to the phrase "a real pig of a day" on the grounds that "a pig is not like a day" makes it seem absurd by applying logic to it. This perspective highlights how complicated language can be, because it can seem untruthful even though the person speaking means to be honest. Christopher's strong dislike of this sort of speech shows that honesty and dishonesty are not always as straightforward as they seem, particularly from Christopher's point of view.

Answers

7) This question requires you to think carefully about how a single character is presented, so all your points need to be clearly about that character. Don't forget to write about the extract in detail as well as the rest of the play. Here are some points you could make:
- Delaney uses the analogy of Jo's artwork in the extract to reveal aspects of her personality. Geof describes her as having "no design, rhythm or purpose" like her drawings. This comparison to artwork helps the reader to understand Jo's personality as a whole, as well as hinting that she is unafraid to be different, both artistically and in life. Geof's dislike of the paintings therefore reflects the disdain she faces from wider society due to her independence and status as a future single mother.
- The extract shows how Jo wants to be independent in life. When when Geof asks if she wants "taking in hand" by a man, she insists "No, thanks." The short, blunt reply suggests that she feels strongly that she wants to rely on herself rather than a man. This indicates that having independence is important to her, as well as reflecting her negative experiences with a man in the past.
- In other parts of the play, Jo is also shown to want to be self-reliant. For example, in Act 1, Scene 1, she looks forward to being an "independent working woman", and in Act 2, Scene 1, she declares "it's mine. All mine." when discussing her flat; the repetition of "mine" shows how proud she is to have her own accommodation. These statements indicate that Jo wants to be financially self-sufficient, perhaps because she has been let down by others in her life, such as her mother.
- However, there is evidence in the play that Jo may not achieve very much in life. As a teenager in Act 1, Scene 1, she says that she has "had enough of school", even though her mother thinks she's "not stupid" and is "wasting" herself. In the extract, Geof also asks Jo why she won't go to a "decent school". Her disinterest in education suggests that she does not always make practical choices for her future, at least in other people's eyes. This adds to the feeling of uncertainty at the end of the play, as Jo is left in a precarious situation. The reader is unsure whether she is mature or practical enough to make her way in life now that she is a single parent and has nobody to support her.

8) For this question, you have to write about social class, so you need to pick out important bits of the novel where the writer addresses this theme, and explain how each bit you write about relates to the question. Don't forget to write about the extract in detail as well as the rest of the novel. Here are some points you could make:
- The Birling family believe the working classes to be inferior, which is reflected in the way Sybil refers to Eva/Daisy dismissively in the extract as a "girl of that sort". However, Eva/Daisy is shown to be morally superior to some of the middle-class characters, turning down Eric's stolen money even though she needs it. This suggests that Priestley thought that social class didn't define a person's character or moral values.
- Priestley uses Mrs Birling's behaviour in the extract to criticise class prejudice. Mrs Birling dismisses Eva/Daisy's explanation about the father as "silly nonsense", partly due to Eva/Daisy's lower social status. Shortly after the extract, the audience learns that Eva/Daisy was telling the truth. This shows how unfounded Mrs Birling's assumptions in the extract are. In dismissing Eva/Daisy as a liar, Mrs Birling also contributed to her eventual death: Priestley uses her character to show the dangers of class prejudice.
- The play emphasises the power that social class can give — earlier in the play, Sheila uses her "power" as the daughter of the well-known, well-off Mr Birling to have Eva/Daisy fired, and it's heavily implied that as a result Eva/Daisy is forced to turn to a life of prostitution. Although this event had a huge effect on Eva/Daisy's life, Sheila says that, to her, it "didn't seem to be anything very terrible at the time". Priestley shows that a relatively unimportant decision by a middle-class woman like Sheila can prove catastrophic for a working-class woman such as Eva/Daisy.
- The Inspector, who reflects Priestley's own socialist views and acts as his 'mouthpiece', presents an alternative to the Birlings' snobbish, class-obsessed perspective. He disagrees with Arthur Birling's selfish, characteristically middle-class beliefs — the Inspector says that all people "are members of one body" who shouldn't ignore each other's needs, regardless of social class. The lack of importance the Inspector places on class helps Priestley to suggest that people should be judged by their actions, rather than by their social status.

9) In this question, you're asked to write about education, so all your points need to be about this idea. You need to write about how Bennett presents ideas about education, so make sure you mention the techniques that he uses. These points give you some ideas of the kind of things you could include:
- The character of Hector represents the belief that education should be well-rounded and not constrained by examinations, which he describes in the extract as "the enemy of education". By personifying examinations as an "enemy", Hector makes them seem like an active and dangerous threat to his view of education. This is reinforced elsewhere in the play — for example, in Act 1, Scene 1 he says that all learning is "precious" even if it doesn't have "the slightest human use", which reflects his belief that education and knowledge is valuable in its own right, rather than being merely a means to an end.
- In the extract, Hector characterises education as mysterious. He does this using mystical language, for example "spells" and "runes". These make education seem grand and unknowable, suggesting Hector is trying to elevate his version of education to more than just memorising or understanding facts. This contrasts to Irwin's description of them as something to "tip the balance" in an examination — here, Irwin likens knowledge to an object on a scale, which suggests it is something more concrete and knowable than Hector's language suggests.
- The Headteacher's views on education contrast with Hector's. Like Hector, he thinks that wider education is important, but for different reasons: he tells Mrs Lintott that "something more" than good grades is required, but only in order for the boys to get places at a good university. His motivations are shallow: he is interested in how the boys' achievements will affect "league tables", which shows that he is primarily motivated by his desire to improve the reputation of the school. This makes his perspective on education seem short-sighted, in contrast to Hector, who is trying to prepare the boys for "Grief. Happiness." and even "dying": he wants their education to equip them for life outside of formal education.
- After Hector's death at the end of the play, the Headteacher speaks positively about Hector's teaching: he uses a metaphor to describe the "bank of literature" in which Hector's pupils have become "shareholders". This suggests that the events of the play have caused him to re-evaluate his stance on Hector's value as a teacher. However, his choice of words indicates that he still doesn't understand Hector's perspective: the language he chooses is linked to money and profit, which shows that he still sees education as a tool that should be used to achieve wealth and success.

Answers

- Irwin's teaching style involves disregarding the truth in order to achieve an academic objective. He explains to the boys that an interesting opinion is more important than the facts: he says that truth in an exam is as unimportant as "thirst at a wine-tasting or fashion at a striptease". These activities are frivolous and unimportant, which highlights Irwin's dismissive attitude towards the truth. At some points during the play, there are hints that Bennett disagrees with Irwin's views. For example, when Dakin suggests that Nazi "death camps" have to be "seen in context", Irwin's view is that this is "inexpedient", as opposed to Hector's more humane, compassionate view that they were an "unprecedented horror". This gives the audience more perspective on Irwin's claims, making them lose sympathy for his particular views, and thereby strengthening their support for Hector's approach.

10) This question requires you to think about a central character and how they change throughout the play, so all your points need to be about that character. You're asked to write about how Mickey is presented, so make sure you write about the techniques Russell uses. These points give you some ideas of the kind of things you could include:
- Mickey becomes withdrawn in Act 2 after he is released from prison. In this extract, he tells Linda that he takes medication because he wants to be "invisible". This suggests that he doesn't want to be part of society and reflects the way he has started to push away the people he loves. Mickey's desire for isolation contrasts with his behaviour in Act 1, where he is outgoing and easily bonds with Edward immediately after meeting him. His desire to hide himself away reflects the fact that he feels isolated by his circumstances and emphasises that he has been let down by society.
- Mickey's language in this extract shows that he is less willing to confide in Linda after he returns from prison. He speaks in short, abrupt sentences and gives Linda blunt commands, such as "Now give". This shows that he is trying to shut down Linda's attempts to help him. This contrasts with his willingness to confide in her when he tells her "I don't wanna die" after being bullied in Act 1, which suggests that he has lost confidence in her advice. This change in his relationship with Linda shows how adult responsibilities have pulled them apart.
- Over the course of the play, Mickey's attitude towards adulthood becomes more negative. In Act 1, he longs to be older because he can "go to bed dead late", but in Act 2 he bitterly tells Eddie that he "grew up" because he had to, and he can't be a child any more. This shows that he has come to believe that adulthood doesn't bring excitement and freedom from rules, but rather pain and loss. The contrast between Eddie and Mickey at the point in the play demonstrates the role misfortune plays in Mickey's change in attitude.
- Mickey becomes more willing to break the law during Act 2. In the first half of Act 2 when Sammy tries to rob the bus conductor, Mickey tries to stop him and uses an imperative tone when he sees Sammy's knife, telling him "put that away". However, later in the act after Mickey loses his job, he is persuaded to rob the petrol station with Sammy. Mickey's silent acceptance of Sammy's plan contrasts with his determination to stop Sammy from committing a crime earlier in the act, which shows that he has been driven to compromise his morals. However, the fact that Mickey only agrees to the job after Sammy has promised him "Fifty notes" suggests that he takes part because he is desperate for money, not because his sense of right and wrong has changed.

Pages 101-106 — Paper 2: Section B (The 19th-Century Novel)

2.1) For this question, you have to write about poverty, so you need to pick out important bits of the novel where the writer addresses this theme, and explain how each bit you write about relates to the question. Don't forget to write about the extract in detail as well as the rest of the novel. Here are some points you could make:
- Scrooge's encounter with Ignorance and Want in this extract represents a turning point for his character, as he has a strong reaction to the way they look and begins to understand the effects of his attitude towards the poor. Ignorance and Want look like starving children: they are "ragged" and "wretched", which causes Scrooge to feel "appalled". By presenting Ignorance and Want as children, Dickens reinforces the message that the poor are not to blame for their situation, and that they should be helped rather than punished.
- Scrooge's emotional reaction to Ignorance and Want in the extract contrasts with the portrayal of him as unfeeling at the beginning of the novel, where he asks "Are there no prisons?" for the poor to go to. This suggests that he regards poverty as a crime, which is in keeping with the attitudes of many people in Victorian society: people in debt could be thrown into 'debtor's jail', and they were not released until their debts were repaid.
- Dickens also uses the characters of Ignorance and Want in the extract to convey a wider message to his audience. The Ghost of Christmas Present explains that the children are a result of "Man's" neglect, which reflects Dickens's belief that Victorian society was to blame for the lack of education (Ignorance) and basic amenities such as food (Want) among poor children. The spirit explains that ignoring the problems of poverty will lead to "Doom", which suggests that Dickens thought upper- and middle-class attitudes to poverty would have negative repercussions for the whole of society.
- Dickens uses Scrooge's character to attack the mentality that Victorian society had towards the poor. Scrooge initially represents selfish members of the middle and upper classes in Victorian society. He refuses to give to charity, and he calls poor people "surplus population", saying it would be better if they died. The description of Scrooge as a "sinner" shows that his attitude to the poor is ungodly and morally wrong.
- As the book continues, Scrooge learns to reject his selfish views: in the final chapter, he buys the Cratchits a "prize Turkey", and he makes a large donation to a charity that helps the poor. Helping those less fortunate makes him happy: he greets everyone with a "delighted smile" and repeatedly acts with a "chuckle". Scrooge's happiness at the end of the novel shows that it can be satisfying and enjoyable to help the poor. His actions also have a dramatic effect on the Cratchit family, as Tiny Tim survives thanks to Scrooge's financial help. Dickens highlights the ability of the middle and upper classes to have a huge effect on the lives of those in poverty.

2.2) This question requires you to think carefully about the importance of a single character, so all your points need to be clearly about that character. Don't forget to write about the extract in detail as well as the rest of the novel. Here are some points you could make:
- In this extract, Eliot presents Dolly as a kind person. In this scene, hearing about the theft of Silas's money, Dolly has brought him a gift of lard-cakes. Even in his state of grief, Silas can see Dolly's "desire to give comfort" through this gift, emphasising to the reader the kind motives behind Dolly's actions. Eliot reinforces this impression of Dolly's kindness by using adverbs like "gently" and "mildly" to describe Dolly's actions and speech, which suggest that she is aware of Silas's grief and is treating him with care.

- In the extract, Eliot also shows the reader that Dolly has a simple but strong religious faith. Although she is unable to read the letters on the cakes, Dolly reasons that the letters must have a "good meaning", since she has seen them in church. This illustrates that, despite not understanding everything, Dolly believes trustingly that everything connected with the church is good. It also shows Dolly's lack of education, which would have been usual for a working-class woman in the early 19th century.
- Dolly's religious beliefs are important to Silas's reconciliation with his past and return to faith. For example, later in the novel, Dolly tells Silas she believes that for all the bad that happened to him, it is "clear as daylight" to her there is a greater plan at work. Dolly's use of simile highlights the conviction and clarity of her belief, which she is able to use to help Silas overcome his bitterness about the past, and recognise that although his past was difficult, it ultimately brought him to his present happiness with Eppie. This exchange also shows Dolly's modesty, as she repeats that there are things she "don't know on", which downplays her own intelligence and usefulness.
- Eliot presents Dolly as a mother figure to Eppie. She takes an active role in bringing up Eppie both practically, for example teaching Silas how to dress Eppie, and spiritually — she insists that Eppie is christened. By the time Eppie is grown up, her interactions with Dolly have "made her feel that a mother must be very precious". The fact that it is Dolly who has given Eppie this impression suggests that Dolly has been a positive figure in Eppie's life. Dolly's character emphasises Eliot's message that support from a warm and loving family is key to happiness and full participation in community life.

2.3) For this question, you have to write about humans, so all your points need to be clearly about humans and how they are presented. Don't forget to write about the extract in detail as well as the rest of the novel. Here are some points you could make:

- Humans as a group are frequently presented as a frightened mob in the novel. In Chapter 12, the Narrator likens the fleeing refugees to a "confusion of ants in a nest" as they try to hide underwater from the Heat-Ray. Comparing humans to a "confusion of ants" in this image makes humans seem small and frightened by creating a sense of their chaos and panic. The image of "ants in a nest" also gives the reader the impression that they're looking at the humans from a distance, as though from under a microscope. This idea echoes the way Wells uses the novel to examine the breakdown of civilisation under attack.
- Wells's presentation of people in the novel allows him to comment on human nature. In this extract, humans are shown to be capable of acts of kindness, but these are presented as the exception rather than the norm. For example, the injured man "wrapped about with bloody rags" is considered "a lucky man to have friends", suggesting that this is a rare occurrence, and the lost girl "became quite still, as if frightened" when the Narrator's brother tries to help her, rather than being relieved. These responses suggest that people are likely to be selfish and cruel towards others in times of fear and crisis. This is echoed in the selfishness of the Curate whilst he and the Narrator are trapped in the ruined house at Sheen.
- In the extract, Wells's presentation of humans disputes the idea that some humans are naturally superior to others. The Narrator's brother explains that people's "skins were dry, their lips black and cracked" from hunger and thirst, describing women with "dainty clothes smothered in dust" and "weary faces smeared with tears". By focusing on the dishevelled state of these "well dressed" women, Wells suggests that class becomes insignificant in times of disaster because all humans are equally weak compared to the strength of the Martians. This contrasts greatly with general opinion in late Victorian society when Wells was writing, when many upper-class people believed they were naturally more respectable and dignified than the lower classes.
- The powerlessness of the humans in the novel highlights the immense power of nature. At the end of the novel, "all man's devices" have "failed" to defeat the Martians, who are defeated instead by bacteria. Mankind has been saved by the natural world. Despite man's powerlessness against the Martians from early on in the novel, the reader suspects humans will eventually succeed. This is hinted at by the Narrator's retrospective narration, as he is able to inform the reader of his brother's experience as well as his own; it is unlikely they would have been able to communicate if the Martians had remained in charge. However, it's unlikely that Wells ends the novel in this way to demonstrate the power of humanity. By providing society with a chance to learn from the Martians' attack, he encourages the reader to view mankind's position in the natural world with more humility.

2.4) For this question, you have to write about Mr and Mrs Bennet's relationship, so you need to pick out important bits of the novel where the writer addresses this, and explain how each bit you write about relates to the question. Don't forget to write about the extract in detail as well as the rest of the novel. Here are some points you could make:

- The extract shows how Mr and Mrs Bennet have an unequal and often difficult relationship. When they discuss Mr Bingley's arrival at Netherfield, Mr Bennet mocks Mrs Bennet's vanity by suggesting that "Mr Bingley may like you the best of the party." This shows that Mr Bennet is more intelligent and witty than Mrs Bennet, and does not regard her as an equal, but rather makes fun of her, realising that she won't understand the joke. His behaviour is quite cruel, which also reveals his lack of affection for her. The fact that she does not appear to be offended by his teasing and lack of respect for her may be due in part to the fact that society in the early nineteenth century would not have allowed a woman like Mrs Bennet to earn a living, so she would have been entirely dependent on Mr Bennet, and could not afford to drive him away.
- Mrs Bennet switches between berating her husband for not doing as she asks, and treating him affectionately when he does what she wants. For example, in the extract she is angry and resentful when he refuses to visit Bingley, and says "You take delight in vexing me", but when she later learns that he has visited Bingley, she is delighted and immediately forgives him: "What an excellent father you have, girls". The speed with which her attitude to Mr Bennet changes shows how shallow her feelings towards him are. This highlights that their marriage isn't based on deep feelings of love, respect or equality, which reinforces the idea that they are not particularly happy together in their relationship.

- Mr and Mrs Bennet are both largely comic characters, Mr Bennet because of his quick, dry wit, and Mrs Bennet because of her ignorance and lack of decorum. However, their relationship has more serious undertones; it is clear that the marriage was a mistake and they are fundamentally unsuited to one another. For example, Mr Bennet is described as "a mixture of quick parts", whereas Mrs Bennet is "a woman of mean understanding", which illustrates the difference in their intellect. We are told that Mr Bennet was initially "captivated by youth and beauty", showing that his feelings were superficial, and all "Respect, esteem, and confidence" for his wife were quickly lost. This illustrates one of Austen's messages: that it is important to select a partner on the basis of intellect, compatibility and love, rather than on the basis of wealth or sexual attraction.
- The Bennet's unhappy marriage is echoed in other marriages in the novel that are motivated by financial or superficial reasons, namely Charlotte and Mr Collins, and Lydia and Mr Wickham. In this way, Austen uses Mr and Mrs Bennet as a way of foreshadowing what will become of these couples, and as a way of emphasising that the cycle of unhappy marriages will never be broken until people realise that the only good reason to marry is for love.

2.5) This question requires you to think carefully about the importance of a single central character and how they change throughout the novel, so all your points need to be clearly about that character. Don't forget to write about the extract in detail as well as the rest of the novel. Here are some points you could make:
- Mr Rochester undergoes a series of dramatic changes over the course of the novel. In the extract, he describes his younger self as "stiff-necked" and "proud", a judgement that is supported by Jane's early encounters with him. The extract takes place after Jane has been absent from his life for some time; when she returns, he is presented as a changed man. The hardships he has gone through have made him understand and overcome the flaws in his character, and he has learned "humility".
- The most obvious change in his character that the extract reveals is his newfound respect for and worship of God: he admits that he initially "almost cursed" the fate that had taken Jane away, but believes that the hardships he went through were "chastisements" from God, which re-establish his faith in a "beneficent" God who "sees... far clearer" and "judges... far more wisely" than man. For the novel's 19th-century audience, Rochester's newfound piety would have been a sign of his virtue and goodness. Later, he regains his sight in one eye, which Jane describes as a sign of God's "mercy". This indicates that Rochester has earned forgiveness for his past sins, and has become a virtuous man.
- This newfound virtue manifests itself in Rochester's actions. Earlier in the novel, Rochester calls his younger self a "trite, commonplace sinner" for his relationship with Céline Varens. His treatment of his wife, Bertha Mason, could also be seen as sinful: he locks her in an attic and denies her existence. However, by attempting to rescue her from the Thornfield fire, Rochester demonstrates that he has already begun to change for the better. This hints that Jane's departure is a necessary step that allows him to re-evaluate his past behaviour and atone for his mistakes.
- Rochester is "humbled" by his experiences, and this is also reflected in his attitude towards wealth and material possessions: when he and Jane first become engaged, he is excited to "pour" jewels into her lap and dress her in "satin and lace". However, when Jane finds Rochester at Ferndean he is no longer interested in "fine clothes and jewels"; instead Jane is described as "the most precious thing he had". This progression of character shows that he has come to understand what is truly valuable in life, and to reject the shallow obsession with wealth and status that characterises the upper classes in the novel.
- By the end of the novel, Rochester has overcome his flaws, and the reader sees that he is now worthy of marrying Jane. This makes the novel's resolution satisfying for the reader, who sees that the characters have received the outcome they deserve.

2.6) For this question, you have to write about morality, so you need to pick out important bits of the novel where the writer addresses this theme, and explain how each bit you write about relates to the question. Don't forget to write about the extract in detail as well as the rest of the novel. Here are some points you could make:
- The novel emphasises the internal conflict that can be caused by immoral desires. This can be seen in the extract, as Jekyll says that he has "called" Hyde from his "own soul". This highlights the link between them, and reinforces the idea that Hyde's "depravity" represents the dark side of Jekyll's personality. Elsewhere in the novel, Stevenson uses the language of battle to show how Jekyll struggles to suppress this dark side: there is a "war" within Jekyll, and the "two natures that contended in the field" of his mind sound like two forces meeting on a battlefield. Jekyll claims that this struggle applies to all of mankind: he says that "man is not truly one, but truly two". This reflects Stevenson's message that all humans have an immoral side.
- Jekyll's language in the extract hints at his ambiguous morality: he describes Hyde's behaviour using some positive language, suggesting that he cannot bring himself to entirely condemn Hyde's actions. Whilst he claims to be "aghast" at Hyde's behaviour, he also describes the "sea of liberty" that Hyde brings him, and he reacts to Hyde's "depravity" with "a kind of wonder". This hints at the conflict between how Victorian ideas of morality dictate that Jekyll should feel and how he actually feels: whilst he feels forced to condemn Hyde's actions in writing, there is a sense that underneath he envies and almost admires him.
- Stevenson also uses other characters in the novel to illustrate the flaws in Victorian views of morality. Victorian society had a rigid set of moral values, so to maintain a good reputation, people had to repress many of their true feelings and desires in public. For the characters in the novel, preserving a good reputation appears to be more important than actually acting morally. For example, Utterson is more concerned about preserving Jekyll's reputation than bringing Hyde to trial: after Carew's murder, he says to Jekyll, "If it came to a trial, your name might appear." This shows his concern for Jekyll's reputation, and emphasises that he prioritises it over the pursuit of justice.
- The novel suggests that evil is ultimately more powerful than moral behaviour. Hyde grows stronger as the novel progresses, and eventually he overpowers Jekyll, and causes his death. This highlights Stevenson's message that trying to hide immoral desires beneath a civilised, moral exterior is very dangerous.

Pages 107-108 — Paper 2: Section C (Unseen Poetry)

3.1) For this question, you have to think about what the poet is saying and how she says it. Make sure you comment on how form, structure and language are used to present feelings and ideas in the poem, and how the poem makes you feel. Here are some points you could make:

- 'For a Five-Year-Old' is about the relationship between a mother and a child, and the responsibility that the mother feels for her child's upbringing. This responsibility is emphasised using the form of the poem. It is mostly written in iambic pentameter, which creates a steady rhythm that gives the reader a sense of the narrator's dedication and commitment to her child.
- The narrator's close connection with her child is evident in the poem. She addresses the narrative directly to the child, repeating the pronouns "you" and "your" throughout. This reflects her constant awareness of how her actions affect her child, and gives the reader the impression that the child is at the forefront of her mind. The repetition of the refrain "from me" in the second stanza also reinforces the idea that the narrator and her child are closely connected and reminds the reader of the narrator's influence in the child's life.
- The child's innocence is stressed to the reader using changes in tone. The violent verbs in the second stanza such as "trapped", "shot", "drowned" and "betrayed" create a harsh tone that contrasts with the parental verbs "carry" and "explain" in the first stanza. This creates a divide between the harsh external world and the sheltered environment of the child's bedroom. The reader feels as if the child has been protected from the harsh realities of life. At the end of the poem, the narrator moves away from the external world and returns to the motif of the snail. This structure shows that the mother is not yet ready to let the child confront reality.
- The snail could be seen to symbolise the child in the poem. The care and delicacy with which the narrator teaches her child to handle the snail reflects her belief that the responsibilities of parenthood must be carried out with similar care and delicacy. In the first stanza, the snail is presented as fragile using the alliterative phrase "carry it outside, with careful hand". This makes the word "careful" stand out to the reader, which shows the care and attention that the child pays to the snail, and hints at the snail's fragility. In the second stanza, the narrator refers to the child's "gentleness" and her own ability to 'mould' the child. This gives the reader the impression that, like the snail, the child is fragile, and highlights the responsibility that the narrator feels to make sure that the child is treated with the same kindness and care that they show to the snail.

3.2) For this question, you have to compare the way that both poets use form, structure and language to convey their viewpoint to the reader. Comparing them means writing about the similarities and differences, so make some links between the poems in your answer. Here are some points you could make:

- Adcock and Pugh both write about the process of a child learning about the world around them. Both poems are written in the first person, which allows the reader an insight into the narrators' thoughts and feelings and makes their descriptions of their relationship and experience feel more personal. However, the fact that Pugh's narrator is speaking in the past tense and without directly addressing the child creates a sense of distance compared to Adcock's narrator, who addresses the child directly in the present tense. This could reflect the ambiguous relationship Pugh's narrator has with the child, as the reader never learns the exact nature of their connection, unlike in 'For a Five-Year-Old', where the narrator states clearly "I am your mother".
- Both poems contain characters who feel responsible for a child's moral education. In 'For a Five-Year-Old', the narrator understands that her child's "gentleness" is "moulded" by her own words. The verb "moulded" emphasises the patience and care that goes into such teaching. In 'The Beautiful Lie', the child's grandmother asks the boy, "Did you do that?", in order to teach him that his actions are wrong. The hard 'd' and 't' sounds in this phrase make the grandmother sound harsh and angry. This increases the reader's pleasure in the unexpected side-effect of her words: they "showed him" he had the "choice" of lying.
- Although both poems are about the joy of watching a child learn, the poets present different messages about what it is important for a child to learn. Adcock focuses on the innocence of the child, and the mother's pleasure in preserving this innocence. In contrast, Pugh's narrator takes pleasure in seeing a small loss of innocence, as the child learns how to lie.
- The poets reinforce these messages using their rhyme schemes. The middle six lines of each stanza of 'For a Five-Year-Old' use rhyming couplets. This careful use of form highlights the care and attention with which the narrator tries to preserve the child's "gentleness". In contrast, 'The Beautiful Lie' has no rhyme scheme and an irregular rhythm. This reflects the freedom that the narrator believes the boy gains by learning how to "*tell a story*": the realisation that he is able to lie opens up a world of imagination. The poem presents this as a "moving" and "momentous" occasion for the narrator, showing how an adult can experience the world afresh through a child, and hinting at how, for an adult, the achievements of a child they love can be more important than their own accomplishments.
- Both poems explore the theme of lying. In 'The Beautiful Lie', Pugh uses a series of images to indicate that a child's first lie is a fundamental and positive part of growing: she compares it to "the first time a baby's fist clenches" a finger, and "the first / taste of fruit". These images appeal to the reader's senses of touch and taste respectively, which helps the reader to understand how vivid and important an experience a child's first lie is. In 'For a Five-Year-Old', on the other hand, it is not the child who lies: it is the mother, who teaches the child to be "kind" to animals without mentioning that she has previously killed "mice", "birds" and "kittens". The poem suggests that it is necessary for parents to lie to their children: in the narrator's case, lying about her past actions helps her to bring her child up to be "kind" and to protect them from the harsh truths of adulthood.

Glossary

allegory	When the characters, settings and events of a story are used to represent something else, e.g. the alien invasion in 'War of the Worlds' is an allegory for 19th-century European empires.
alliteration	When words that are close together start with the same sound. E.g. "lone and level".
aside	When a character in a play makes a short comment that reveals their thoughts to the audience, and no other character can hear it.
assonance	When words share the same vowel sound but their consonants are different, e.g. "I love thee freely".
audience	The person or group of people that read or listen to a text.
autobiographical	Describing something that happened in the writer's life.
blank verse	Lines from a play or poem that are written in iambic pentameter and don't rhyme.
caesura (plural caesurae)	A pause in a line of poetry. E.g. the semicolon in "All went lame; all blind" in 'Dulce et Decorum Est'.
chronological	When events are arranged in the order in which they happened.
cliffhanger	A break or ending to a text that leaves the reader in suspense about what will happen next.
colloquial language	Informal language that sounds like ordinary speech.
comedy (Shakespeare)	A type of Shakespeare play that tries to make the audience laugh, often by using exaggerated events and characters.
consonance	Repetition of a consonant sound in nearby words, e.g. "full-grown lambs loud bleat".
context	The background to something, or the situation surrounding it, which affects the way it's understood. E.g. the context of a text from 1915 would include the First World War.
couplet	A pair of lines in a poem, which usually have the same metre and often rhyme.
cyclical structure	Where key elements at the start of the text repeat themselves at the end.
dialect	A variation of a language spoken by people from a particular place or background. Dialects might include different words or sentence constructions.
dialogue	When two or more characters talk to each other in a text.
direct address	When a narrator or writer speaks directly to another character or to the reader, e.g. "you might recall..."
double negative	A sentence construction that incorrectly expresses a negative idea by using two negative words or phrases, e.g. "I don't want no trouble."
dramatic irony	When the reader or audience knows something that a character does not know.
dramatic monologue	A form of poetry that uses the assumed voice of a single speaker who is not the poet to address an implied audience.
ellipsis	A set of three dots which can give the impression of an unfinished thought or of missing details, e.g. "in the far South Land..."
embedded narrative	A story within the main story, e.g. the letters in 'Dr Jekyll and Mr Hyde'.

Glossary

emotive	Something that makes you feel a particular emotion.
empathy	The ability to imagine and understand someone else's feelings or experiences.
end-stopping	Finishing a line of poetry with the end of a phrase or sentence, usually marked by punctuation.
enjambment	When a sentence or phrase runs over from one line or stanza to the next.
first person	A narrative viewpoint where the narrator is one of the characters, written using words like 'I', 'me', 'we' and 'our'.
flashback	A writing technique where the scene shifts from the present to an event in the past.
foreshadowing	A literary device where a writer hints or gives clues about a future event.
form	The type of text (e.g. a novel, a novella) or poem (e.g. a sonnet or a ballad).
frame narrative	An overarching story that contains other stories within it.
free verse	Poetry that doesn't rhyme and has no regular rhythm or line length.
Gothic	A genre of text that was popular in the 19th century, which usually involved mysterious locations, supernatural elements, troubling secrets and elements of madness. E.g. 'The Strange Case of Dr Jekyll and Mr Hyde'.
half-rhymes	Words that have a similar, but not identical, end sound. E.g. "hurt" and "heart".
history (Shakespeare)	A type of Shakespeare play based on real historical events.
iambic pentameter	Verse with a metre of ten syllables — five of them stressed, and five unstressed. The stress falls on every second syllable, e.g. "Two households, both alike in dignity".
imagery	Language that creates a picture in your mind, e.g. metaphors, similes and personification.
imperative	An order or direction, e.g. "run away" or "stop that".
inference	A conclusion reached about something, based on evidence. E.g. If you read the phrase "They tiptoed from room to room", you could infer that the characters don't want to be heard.
internal rhyme	When two or more words rhyme, and at least one of the words isn't at the end of a line. The rhyming words can be in the same line or nearby lines.
irony	When words are used to imply the opposite of what they normally mean. It can also mean when there is a difference between what people expect and what actually happens.
limited narrator	A narrator who only has partial knowledge about the events or characters in a story.
metaphor	A way of describing something by saying that it is something else, e.g. "his feet were blocks of ice".
metre	The arrangement of stressed and unstressed syllables to create rhythm in a line of poetry.
monologue	One person speaking alone for a long period of time.
monosyllabic	When a word only has one syllable, e.g. "had", "thought", "play".

Glossary

montage	A series of short scenes that are put together, often to show how something changes over time.
mood	The feel or atmosphere of a text, e.g. humorous, peaceful, fearful.
narrative	Writing that tells a story or describes an experience.
narrative viewpoint	The perspective that a text is written from, e.g. first-person point of view.
narrator	The voice or character speaking the words of the narrative.
ode	A poem written in praise of a person or thing.
novella	A prose text that is longer than a short story, but shorter than a novel, e.g. 'A Christmas Carol'.
omniscient narrator	A narrator who knows the thoughts and feelings of all the characters in a narrative.
onomatopoeia	A word that imitates the sound it describes as you say it, e.g. 'whisper'.
pace	The speed at which the writer takes the reader through the events in a text or poem.
paradox	A statement that contradicts itself or cancels itself out.
paraphrase	Describing or rephrasing something in a text without including a direct quote.
personification	Describing a non-living thing as if it's a person. E.g. "The sea growled hungrily."
phonetic spellings	When words are spelt as they sound rather than with their usual spelling, e.g. "yow" instead of "you". It's often used to show that someone is speaking with a certain accent or dialect.
prose	Any kind of writing that isn't poetry, and doesn't have a set metre or rhyme scheme.
pun	A word or phrase that's deliberately used because it has more than one meaning, often for humorous effect.
quatrain	A type of stanza which has four lines.
Realism	A type of writing where the author aims to give an accurate picture of everyday life.
rhetorical question	A question that doesn't need an answer but is asked to make or emphasise a point, e.g. "Do you think the planet is worth saving?"
rhyme scheme	A pattern of rhyming words in a poem, e.g. if a poem has an ABAB rhyme scheme, this means that the first and third lines in each stanza rhyme, and so do the second and fourth lines.
rhyming couplet	A pair of rhyming lines that are next to each other.
rhyming triplet	Three rhyming lines that are next to each other.
rhythm	A pattern of sounds created by the arrangement of stressed and unstressed syllables.
romance (Shakespeare)	A type of Shakespeare play that is similar to a comedy but with darker elements.
Romantic	A genre of text that was popular in the late 18th and early 19th centuries, which tried to capture intense emotions and experiences, and presented nature as a powerful force, e.g. Wordsworth's 'The Prelude'.

Glossary

sarcasm	Language that has a scornful or mocking tone, often using irony.
sensory language	Language that appeals to the five senses.
sibilance	Repetition of 's' and 'sh' sounds, e.g. "shaped so shortly".
simile	A way of describing something by comparing it to something else, usually by using the words 'like' or 'as'. E.g. "The apple was as red as a rose".
slang	Words or phrases that are informal, and often specific to one age group or social group.
soliloquy	When a single character in a play speaks their thoughts out loud, but no other characters can hear them.
sonnet	A form of poem with fourteen lines, that usually follows a clear rhyme scheme.
stage directions	Written instructions in a play that describe how the play should be staged or performed.
staging	How a play appears on the stage, including the set, costumes and where the actors stand.
Standard English	English that is considered to be correct because it uses formal, standardised features of spelling and grammar.
stanza	A group of lines in a poem.
structure	The order and arrangement of ideas in a text. E.g. how it begins, develops and ends.
syllable	A single unit of sound within a word. E.g. "all" has one syllable, "always" has two.
symbolism	When an object stands for something else. E.g. a cross symbolises Christianity.
syntax	The arrangement of words in a sentence or phrase so that they make sense.
tense	Writing about the past, present or future. E.g. "I walked" is the past tense, "I walk" is the present tense and "I will walk" is the future tense.
tercet	A type of stanza which has three lines.
third person	A narrative viewpoint where the narrator remains outside the events of the story, written using words like 'he' and 'she'.
tone	The feeling of a piece of writing, e.g. happy, sad, serious, light-hearted.
tragedy (Shakespeare)	A type of Shakespeare play that has a serious tone. It is usually about the downfall of the main character and often has a moral message.
unreliable narrator	A narrator who isn't necessarily trustworthy, and who might present things from their own point of view, e.g. Kathy from 'Never Let Me Go'.
viewpoint	The attitude and beliefs that a writer is trying to convey.
voice	The characteristics of the person narrating a poem or text.
volta	A turning point in a poem, when the argument or tone changes dramatically.

Index

19th-century texts 43, 46-48, 50, 51

A
alliteration 61
apostrophes 9
asides 27
assessment objectives 1
assonance 61
audience 17, 28, 29

B
blank verse 35

C
caesurae 59
characters 12-15, 30, 32, 35, 44
checking your work 7
chronological order 43
cliffhangers 43
colloquial language 18, 57
colons 9
comedies (Shakespeare) 32
commas 9
comparisons 62, 65, 66, 81-84
conclusions 66
context 1, 30, 31, 33, 46-48, 68, 70
couplets 56
cyclical structure 36

D
dialogue 27-28
direct address 57
double negatives 10
drama 12-36
dramatic irony 29
dramatic monologues 56

E
education 30, 47
embedded narratives 44
end-stopping 59
enjambment 59
evidence 1, 4, 67, 70
exaggeration 32, 60
exam structure 1
explaining words and phrases 5
extract questions 2, 8, 12, 17, 21

F
first-person narrators 45, 57
flashbacks 20, 44
foreshadowing 20, 44
form 1, 12, 55, 56, 62, 66, 67
frame narratives 44
free verse 56

G
gender 16, 31, 46, 47
Gothic genre 48
grammar 1, 7-10

H
histories (Shakespeare) 32
humour 32, 34

I
iambic pentameter 35, 59
imagery 18, 28, 34, 44, 61
inference 6
informal language 5
introductions 66

K
key scenes 36
key words 2, 65, 81

L
language 1, 12, 18, 28, 34, 35, 44, 55, 57-62, 67, 69
linking words and phrases 5, 81

M
metaphors 18, 28, 34, 44, 60
metre 59
minor scenes 36
modern plays 30, 31, 40, 41
monologues 27
montages 28
mood 26, 29, 56, 58, 60, 61, 77

Index

N
narrators 45, 57
non-standard grammar 18, 44

O
omniscient narrators 45
onomatopoeia 61

P
pace 29, 36, 56, 58, 59, 61
paradox 34
paragraphs 5, 7, 19, 62, 66, 81
paraphrasing 4
P.E.E.D. 3-5, 66
personal response 17
personification 18, 28, 34, 44, 60
phonetic spellings 57
planning 2, 62, 65
plots 15, 36, 43
poetic techniques 57-61
poetry anthology 1, 55, 65-76
prose 12-21, 35, 43-48
punctuation 1, 7, 9, 59
puns 33, 34
purpose 14, 77

Q
quatrains 56
quotations 4, 13, 21, 35, 65, 67, 77

R
Realism 30, 48
religion 48
Renaissance 33
repetition 18, 36, 44
rhyme 56, 58
rhythm 56, 58, 59
romances (Shakespeare) 32

S
semi-colons 9
sensory imagery 61
sentence structure 1, 19
settings 19, 30, 46
sexuality 31
Shakespeare 32-36, 38, 39
sibilance 61
similes 18, 28, 34, 44, 60
slang 5, 30, 44
social class 16, 30, 47
soliloquies 27
sonnets 56
speech 14, 18, 27, 35
spelling 1, 7, 8
spoken language 57
stage directions 26, 29, 31
stagecraft 29
Standard English 5
stanzas 56
structure 1, 12, 20, 28, 36, 43, 44, 55, 56, 62, 67
  of exam answers 5, 66
syllables 59
symbolism 20

T
tercets 56
themes 12, 16, 21, 32, 65, 77
third-person narrators 45, 57
tone 6, 61
tragedies (Shakespeare) 32, 36

U
unreliable narrators 45
unseen poetry 1, 55, 77-87

V
verbs 10
verse 35
vocabulary 1, 18, 69
voice 45, 57

W
writer's message 12, 16, 77